Newslore

RUSSELL FRANK

Newslore

CONTEMPORARY FOLKLORE ON THE INTERNET

UNIVERSITY PRESS OF MISSISSIPPI / JACKSON

www.upress.state.ms.us

The University Press of Mississippi is a member
of the Association of American University Presses.

Copyright © 2011 by University Press of Mississippi
All rights reserved
Manufactured in the United States of America

First printing 2011
∞
Library of Congress Cataloging-in-Publication Data

Frank, Russell, 1954–
  Newslore : contemporary folklore on the Internet /
Russell Frank.
     p. cm.
  Includes bibliographical references and index.
  ISBN 978-1-60473-928-2 (cloth : alk. paper) — ISBN
978-1-60473-929-9 (ebook) 1. American wit and humor—
History and criticism. 2. Folklore—United States. 3. Folk-
lore and the Internet. 4. Social psychology—United States.
I. Title.
  PS439.F73 2011
  818'.607—dc22   2010038815

British Library Cataloging-in-Publication Data available

CONTENTS

vii   PREFACE
Greetings from a Desk Chair Traveler

3   INTRODUCTION
Tiny Revolutions

31   1. Where Is the Humor?
ANTI-HILLARY JOKES IN THE NEWS

45   2. I Could Throw All of You out the Window
THE DEMOCRATS

63   3. When the Going Gets Tough
NEWSLORE OF SEPTEMBER 11

96   4. Got Fish?
NEWSLORE OF HURRICANE KATRINA

107   5. It Takes a Village Idiot
BUSHLORE

128   6. You Can't Raffle Off a Dead Donkey
NEWSLORE OF COMMERCE

151   7. Not-So-Heavenly Gates
NEWSLORE OF THE DIGITAL AGE

166   8. Diana's Halo
NEWSLORE AS FOLK MEDIA CRITICISM

189   CONCLUSION
Attention Must Be Paid, but for How Much Longer?

197   APPENDIX A
           A Week in the Life of My In-Box: A Newslore Miscellany

209   APPENDIX B
           Collecting and Analyzing Newslore

231   NOTES

245   REFERENCES

255   INDEX

PREFACE
Greetings from a Desk Chair Traveler

In some ways, this book is the culmination of my entire work history to date; in other ways it is a departure. For sophomoric reasons having to do with what I thought would best prepare me for a career as a professional poet (I considered just living in the world, but that seemed too scary), I joined the tiny band of scholars who pursue advanced degrees in the study of folklore. My idea was to study ancient myths and texts so that I could lace my poems with learned allusions, the way my heroes, Pound and Eliot, did. To my dismay, the graduate program in folklore and mythology at UCLA had little to do with mythology and much to do with folklore—folktales and ballads, principally, but also folk art and craft and belief and custom. Folklorists, we learned, were collectors, primarily: they tromped through the countryside asking folks if they knew any old stories or songs. And if they could coax an affirmative reply to that question, they set up their tape recorders, took the lens caps off their cameras, and got down to business. If we graduate students wanted to be folklorists, we would have to do the same, though for reasons I'll get to later, we no longer had to journey to the southern mountains to find folklore. We could do fieldwork right in Los Angeles.

I was not at all sure I wanted to be a folklorist, but I was at least committed to finishing my degree, so I embarked on a field research project not in Los Angeles but three hundred miles north, in California's Mother Lode country, where I hoped to record the folklore of late-twentieth-century gold miners. This was a far cry from learning Sumerian and producing a close reading of the Epic of Gilgamesh, but once I found the informants I was looking for, I so enjoyed interviewing live human beings that after finishing my master's thesis and working for a couple of years, I went back to school to get the Ph.D.

After two years of coursework at the University of Pennsylvania, I returned to California to renew my acquaintance with and write my dissertation about my gold miner friends. I was down to my last $100 when I applied for a job at the *Union Democrat*, "Leading Newspaper of the Mother Lode." I had no experience and no training, but the owner took a chance on me because I aced his editing test. (I even knew how to spell "ukulele.") I loved being a reporter for the same reason I loved being a folklorist: I got to ask people to tell me stories.

I worked at newspapers for thirteen years. I thought I had found my life's work. But just when I had given up on an academic career, an opportunity arose to finally put my Ph.D. to use. As a tenure-track professor of journalism, I was expected to do research, and since my only research experience was as a folklorist, I began looking for ways to bridge the gap between seemingly disparate areas of inquiry. Topical folklore, or newslore, is quite literally the perfect marriage of news and folklore.

My only misgiving about doing this book stemmed from my low tolerance for Web surfing and my reluctance to commit to a project that would rely so much on staring at a computer screen and so little on field research.[1] After years of trotting around with a reporter's notebook in my back pocket or a portable tape recorder dangling from my shoulder, I worried about turning into one of those academics whose idea of an adventure is leaving the office to hunt for a book in the library stacks. A critic of my column in the local newspaper once wrote a letter to the editor that began, "Russell Frank needs to get out more often." I agreed. I taped the letter to my office door as a reminder.

To spend so many hours in cyberspace, though, is to visit many strange lands and to return bearing wondrous tales. I hereby invite armchair travelers to relive my desk chair travels.

But first the thank-yous, which, though pro forma, are heartfelt. First there's my editor, Craig Gill, who was beyond patient with me. Two years into this project, I told him that as a former newspaperman, I was never going to get it done if I didn't have a deadline. "Fine," said he. "When would you like it to be?" I thought Labor Day was realistic. "Okay," he said. "Get it to me by Labor Day." So I did.

Help in the form of forwarded e-mail came from many quarters: from my mother, Nettie Frank, my sister, Meryl Harari, and my brothers-in-law, Andy Franklin and Marty Harari; from old friends Michael Yonchenko, Rich Appel, and Witt Monts; from Penn State friends, colleagues, and students past and present Ken Yednock, Bill Mahon, Kate Delano, Ron Bettig, Wayne Hilinski, Tim Molnar, Michael Horning, Michael Hecht, Lee Ahern, Dan Walden, Steve Herb, Jeremy Wright, Kevin Hagopian, Dave Swanson, Bill Nickerson, Jes Gregoire, Alison Kepner, and Zach Ludescher; and from faithful readers Betty Grudin and Judith Frankel.

Then there were those whose company, on walks, at meals, as hosts and guests, kept me feeling stimulated and cared about: Dorn Hetzel, Gabeba Baderoun, Heidi Evans, Josh Getlin, Lea Bergen, Michael Yonchenko.

Thanks also to the dean of my college, Doug Anderson, associate deans John Nichols and Anne Hoag, and my department head, Ford Risley, for their support.

Above all, thanks to Sylvie, Rosa, and Ethan for fifty-plus wonderful parent-years, and to Han, for the past four years and for all the years to come.

Newslore

INTRODUCTION
Tiny Revolutions

It was the first day of school and a new student named Suzuki, the son of a Japanese businessman, entered the fourth grade. The teacher said, "Let's begin by reviewing some American history. Who said, 'Give me liberty, or give me death'?"

She saw a sea of blank faces, except for Suzuki's. He answered, "Patrick Henry, 1775."

"Very good! Who said, 'Government of the people, by the people, for the people, shall not perish from the earth'?"

Again, no response except from Suzuki, "Abraham Lincoln, 1863."

The teacher snapped at the class, "You should be ashamed of yourselves. Suzuki, who is new to our country, knows more about its history than you do."

She heard a loud whisper, "Screw the Japs."

The teacher screamed, "Who said that?"

Suzuki put his hand up. "Lee Iacocca, 1982."

At that point, a student in the back said, "I'm gonna puke."

The teacher glared and demanded, "All right! Now, who said that?"

Again, Suzuki's voice was heard, "George Bush to the Japanese Prime Minister, 1991."

Now furious, another student yelled, "Oh yeah? Suck this!"

Suzuki jumped out of his chair, waving his hand and shouting to the teacher, "Bill Clinton to Monica Lewinsky, 1997!"

Now, with almost a mob hysteria, someone said, "You little shit. If you say anything else, I'll kill you."

Suzuki frantically yelled at the top of his voice, "Gary Condit to Chandra Levy, 2001."

The teacher fainted. And, as the class gathered around the teacher on the floor, someone said, "Oh shit, now we're in BIG trouble!"

Suzuki said, "Arthur Andersen, 2001."

Get it? Not if you don't read the papers, you don't. To "get" a joke isn't to laugh at it, or to think it's funny, necessarily, but to understand why it's a joke, which is to understand why somebody thinks it's funny even if you don't. To get that, you first have to get the references.[1] Here is what one needs to know to understand this version of "Suzuki" (there are many, including one that ends with "the Taliban, 2001," that's in BIG trouble and another with "Americans in Iraq, 2004"):[2]

LEE IACOCCA: Iacocca ran the Chrysler Corporation from 1978 to 1992. At the time referred to in the joke, the so-called Big Three American automakers—Chrysler, Ford, and General Motors—were losing customers to Toyota and Nissan, Japanese car makers whose products were perceived to be more reliable and more fuel efficient than America's gas-guzzling behemoths. Iacocca became the most public face of the American automakers' aggressive response to Japanese encroachment.

BUSH–JAPANESE PRIME MINISTER: The president we now refer to as George H. W. Bush became ill and vomited during a dinner in his honor in Japan in 1991.

CLINTON–LEWINSKY: In 1998, news that President Clinton had had a sexual affair with a White House intern nearly toppled his presidency. Clinton apparently was able to truthfully deny that he had sexual relations with Lewinsky—if by relations we mean sexual intercourse. It later came out that Lewinsky had performed oral sex on the president.

CONDIT–LEVY: Chandra Levy was an aide to California congressman Gary Condit. When Levy disappeared in 2001, it was rumored that she and Condit had been having an affair and that Condit had murdered her. In 2009 a twenty-seven-year-old undocumented immigrant from El Salvador was charged with Levy's murder.

ARTHUR ANDERSEN: Arthur Andersen is the name of the auditing firm that aided and abetted the Enron Corporation in defrauding stockholders in 2001.

Knowing who these players are, one can understand how Suzuki would connect them to his classmates' comments. What makes the joke funny is that Suzuki's identifications of Iacocca, et al., as the speakers of the quotes are apt: his identifications encapsulate what the joke's dramatis personae are best known for. What makes the joke funnier is that though Suzuki's answers are apt, they're wrong. In fact, they're doubly wrong. They're wrong because the joke's dramatis personae did not actually say the words that Suzuki is attributing to them, and they're wrong because he has failed to notice that the quiz frame with which the class began no longer applies: his classmates are not contributing additional quotations but commenting on his know-it-all responses. The teacher is no longer asking for the names of the sources of the quotations; she's asking for the names of the sources of the inappropriate remarks.

The disconnect between Suzuki's knowledge of American history and current affairs and his lack of knowledge of the social situation in which he finds himself in the classroom would be enough to make the joke funny. But as is so often the case with jokes, there's also a latent element that maybe isn't so funny. Just as the Japanese automakers are making the Big Three look bad, so Suzuki is making his classmates look bad. Is America falling behind educationally? Does the performance of Asian companies in the American marketplace and Asian students in the American classroom foreshadow a changing of the guard in the arena of world dominance? Perhaps so, but the joke alleviates that anxiety by giving young Suzuki his comeuppance. He's smart, but he's also maladroit.

Another joke from my collection asks, "Why did the chicken cross the road?" In the traditional version, the answer, which any child raised in America knows, is "To get to the other side." This is a classic example of a riddle joke. The question sets up the expectation of some clever or trick answer. The joke resides in subverting that expectation by making the answer entirely obvious and logical. The version I received by e-mail from a friend in February 2006, which she apparently received in May 2003, offers a list of answers from twenty-eight well-known personages. Here are a few of the highlights:

George W. Bush
We don't really care why the chicken crossed the road. We just want to know if the chicken is on our side of the road or not. The chicken is either with us or it is against us. There is no middle ground here.

Colin Powell
Now at the left of the screen, you clearly see the satellite image of the chicken crossing the road.

Rush Limbaugh
I don't know why the chicken crossed the road, but I'll bet it was getting a government grant to cross the road, and I'll bet someone out there is already forming a support group to help chickens with crossing-the-road syndrome. Can you believe this? How much more of this can real Americans take? Chickens crossing the road paid for by tax dollars, and when I say tax dollars, I'm talking about your money, money the government took from you to build roads for chickens to cross.

Jerry Falwell
Because the chicken was gay! Isn't it obvious? Can't you people see the plain truth in front of your face? The chicken was going to the other side. That's what they call it: the other side. Yes, my friends, that chicken is gay. And, if you eat that chicken, you will become gay too. I say we boycott all chickens until we sort out this abomination that the liberal media whitewashes with seemingly harmless phrases like the other side.

Ralph Nader
The chicken's habitat on the original side of the road had been polluted by unchecked industrialist greed. The chicken did not reach the unspoiled habitat on the other side of the road because it was crushed by the wheels of a gas-guzzling SUV.

Barbara Walters
Isn't that interesting? In a few moments we will be listening to the chicken tell, for the first time, the heart-warming story of how it experienced a serious case of molting and went on to accomplish its life-long dream of crossing the road.

Bill Clinton
I did not cross the road with THAT chicken. What do you mean by chicken? Could you define chicken, please?

To understand this joke, you have to have paid enough attention to the news to know the following:

- President Bush made similar statements in response to hesitation on the part of some of America's allies about joining what Bush referred to as the Coalition of the Willing in the invasion of Iraq in 2003.
- Former secretary of state Colin Powell used satellite images to make his now-discredited case for invading Iraq when he appeared at the United Nations in January 2003.
- The conservative radio commentator Rush Limbaugh routinely delivers tirades against liberalism.
- Ralph Nader is a consumer advocate and political maverick who speaks against corporate malfeasance.
- Jerry Falwell was a gay-bashing televangelist.
- Barbara Walters is known for her sob-sister television interviews.
- President Clinton issued similar denials about his sexual liaison with Monica Lewinsky.

The Suzuki joke and the chicken joke are examples of what I call news-lore—folklore that comments on, and is therefore indecipherable without knowledge of, current events. Newslore takes multiple forms: jokes; urban legends; digitally altered photographs; mock news stories, press releases, or interoffice memoranda; parodies of songs, poems, political and commercial advertisements, and movie previews and posters; still or animated cartoons and short live-action films.[3] Before I discuss where and how I obtained this material or why I think it is worthy of our consideration, I would like to situate newslore in the world of folklore scholarship.

Without recapitulating the entire history of the study of folklore (though it's a short history; the word "folklore" itself has only been around for 160 years), I think it is fair to say that in the earliest conceptualizations of folklore, the "folk" were rural people whose lore was passed down from generation to generation and circulated via face-to-face interaction. Verbal genres were synonymous with oral tradition. Crafts were learned through informal apprenticeships rather than from schools and books. Newslore possesses none of these attributes: its longevity can be measured in presidencies rather than generations, and it circulates remotely rather than face-to-face, among people who are likelier to live in an urban apartment or a suburban house than on a family farmstead.

To understand how newslore comports with the way the definition of folklore has evolved, we need to break the compound word into its constituent (and originally hyphenated) parts: Who are the folk? What is lore? (Folklorists, who, according to the profession's own folklore, used to be able to hold their conferences in phone booths back in the days of phone booths, can skip this part, but they won't, because they'll want to see if I know what I'm talking about, and if I do, whether I express any of these familiar ideas in felicitous ways.)

The old equation of folk and peasants held up only as long as people mostly stayed put. Nineteenth-century folklorists were interested in the survival of ancient beliefs and customs into the modern world. They believed that such vestiges were likely to persist among people whose lifeways changed little from one generation to the next. Literacy and in- and out-migration would muddy the pure stream of tradition with external cultural influences.

Inevitably, though, folklorists had to reckon with the mass migration of workers from the farm to the factory, and mass immigration from the Old World to the New. Did country people immediately slough off their old ways when they came to the city? Did immigrants abandon Old World beliefs and customs when they came to the New World? The answer to both questions was, of course not. The first shift, then, might be thought of as a reconceptualization of the folk from peasants to proletarians.

This was a particularly welcome change in the United States, which lacked a peasant population who had worked the land for generations. Accordingly, American folklorists were drawn to the traditions of cowboys, miners, loggers, and merchant sailors—isolated occupational groups that were thought to be the best laboratories for the study of tradition in its unadulterated state.[4] In the 1960s and 1970s, even as researchers continued delving into the folklore of fishermen,[5] firefighters,[6] and Pullman porters,[7] folklore and anthropology began coming to grips with the lingering classist-colonialist implications of "studying down,"[8] as well as the blurring of status and wage distinctions between blue- and white-collar jobs.[9] The folklore of all occupational groups—medical doctors, rocket scientists, even folklorists[10]—began to be viewed as a fertile field of inquiry. The expansion of the concept of folk was complete when Alan Dundes redefined the term to mean "any group of people whatsoever who share at least one common factor" and offered examples of the folklore of families, localities, religious and ethnic groups, hobbyists, and occupational groups.[11] Another way to think about folk is that it refers less to a kind of group than to a kind of informal or spontaneous or homemade communication in which members of all groups engage at least some of the time.

Dundes, for his part, began paying attention to the volume of hand-drawn cartoons, parody memos, and written jokes circulated by office workers. He decided that this material, though printed rather than orally communicated, bore enough of the hallmarks of folklore to warrant collection and analysis: it exhibited variation, and it expressed the same anxieties and frustrations with modern life as orally transmitted jokes and narratives. "If old-fashioned rural folklore reflected rural American values and worldview," Dundes wrote, "then it is equally likely that common urban folklore will reflect themes of importance in contemporary urban American life."[12] Removing longevity and orality as defining parameters of folk tradition leaves us with a definition of folklore as the forms of artistic behavior that express a group's values and worldview, regardless of how they are circulated or how long they are circulated.

Dundes and Pagter's first collection of "folklore from the paperwork empire" acknowledges the role of the photocopier in the dissemination of this kind of folklore but refers to the data as "folklore by facsimile," "white-collar folklore," and "folklore of bureaucracy."[13] The second collection, published in 1987, introduces the term "office copier folklore."[14] The third, published in 1991, mentions that fax machines, too, may be contributing to the worldwide proliferation of office copier folklore.[15] The fourth volume, published in 1996, favors the term "photo-copier folklore" while noting the role that personal computers, the Internet, and e-mail have begun to play in the "creation and dissemination" of the material.[16] A fifth volume, published in 2000, observes that the Internet, "which connects myriads of individual Personal Computers, further accelerated the exchange . . . of many items of folklore."[17] Now, with so much folklore being created and transmitted on computers without ever being printed at all, the folklore of the paperwork empire has become the folklore of the paperless empire. Faxlore has given way to netlore—which brings us to yet another once-essential element of folklore that has become less salient: variation.

The existence of multiple versions of the same joke or cartoon helped Dundes make the case for the inclusion of office folklore in the folklore canon by so neatly paralleling the variation folklorists were accustomed to finding in the texts of ballads and folktales. Variation, however, is the hallmark of the handmade object and the performance, whether the differences are by design, because tradition allows for creativity, or inadvertent, because perfect reproduction is impossible. In the world of computer-mediated communication, variation, too, ceases to be essential. One could create one's own version of a joke, legend, or composite image one has received via e-mail, but nothing could be simpler than to pass it on as is. It is therefore not uncommon to find identical versions of a joke in multiple locations on the Web.

Netlore, then, is not oral, is not communicated face-to-face, is not passed from generation to generation, and does not exhibit much variation. It is nevertheless folklore because as expressive behavior it is a form of subversive play, circulating in an underground communicative universe that runs parallel to and often parodies, mocks, or comments mordantly on "official" channels of communication such as the mass media.[18]

The newslore I will present and analyze in this book was all obtained electronically, either via e-mail or from Web sites.[19] Since topical folklore may be communicated face-to-face or passed from hand to hand, not all newslore is netlore. Since netlore may include material that does not respond in any obvious way to what's going on in the news, not all netlore is newslore. In fact, only a fraction of netlore is. An e-mailed priest-minister-and-rabbi joke without any topical references would be an example of netlore that isn't newslore.

Why devote a book to newslore? Three reasons: (1) the phenomenon is widespread, (2) the phenomenon is revealing of widely held attitudes and widely shared preoccupations, and (3) the phenomenon is largely ignored and shouldn't be, given the first two reasons.

1. The phenomenon is widespread. It is easy to assume, if everyone you know uses a computer at home and at work, that everybody everywhere is similarly plugged in. It's worth keeping in mind, in terms of ongoing inequalities of access to technology and information, and therefore to money and power, that this is not so. Writing in 1993, Nancy Baym noted that the people who dominate the Internet are an "overwhelmingly American, generally well-educated, predominantly white, economically comfortable substrata of the population."[20] I don't think much has changed in the new millennium. The latest Pew Internet and American Life Project survey (updated in 2009) found that 74 percent of American adults use the Internet, but a breakdown of that number by age, education, and race/ethnicity showed that only 39 percent of people with less than high school educations and 38 percent of people over sixty-five described themselves as Internet users.[21]

That said, I am going to assume that anyone who picks up this book uses a computer at home and at work and uses e-mail much as I do: to exchange information, to make plans, and to chat with friends. And part of that chatting, for many of us, is the exchange of netlore.

There are, broadly speaking, three types of netlore users: the forwarders, who read whatever flows into their in-box, then pass it along to members of their own network of e-mail buddies; the spikers, who have decided they're too busy for such foolishness and delete all forwarded material along with the commercial spam; and the readers, who are willing to look at the forwards but are reluctant to add to anyone else's online waste stream. I belong in the reader category, and if I am at all representative—a daily computer user with friends and relatives all over the country, if not the world, who are also daily computer users—I can attest, from personal experience, that there is a lot of netlore circulating in cyberspace.[22]

In most of the newslore that is forwarded to me by friends or family, my name is one of many on a list of addressees who are linked only by our relationship with the sender. In some cases, the body of the e-mail includes lists of the addresses of one or more previous rounds of recipients. From these glimpses at the history of any given item, I inferred that any folklore text that lands in my in-box must land in a lot of other people's in-boxes as well. There are also countless Web sites devoted to netlore of one kind or another (mostly jokes), and for reasons I will explain in appendix B, I augmented the in-box material with newslore I found in my wanderings around cyberspace.

2. *The phenomenon reveals widely held attitudes and widely shared preoc-cupations.* The basic premise of this book is the basic premise of all folklore studies: as Alan Dundes put it, "No piece of folklore continues to be trans-mitted unless it means something—even if neither the speaker nor the audi-ence can articulate what that meaning might be."[23] The task I have assigned myself here is to trace the individual items of newslore back to the news that precipitated them and then to ask Elliott Oring's open-ended question of each: "What does this joke [or legend] communicate?"[24] Such a question does not bind me to a single, invariably reductive theory, but the idea I will return to again and again is that newslore is subversive. It violates the rules of deference and discretion when it comes to authority figures, bodily func-tions, and social conflict in a way that may appear anarchic, even nihilistic, but is, at bottom, quite moralistic: its target is hypocrisy. Its mood is grimly amused exasperation with false piety, with speaking respectfully of those who deserve no respect, with euphemism, with all attempts to ignore the eight-hundred-pound gorillas in the room. In Mary Douglas's words, the joke "is an image of the leveling of hierarchy, the triumph of intimacy over formality, of unofficial values over official ones."[25] Orwell wrote that "every joke is a tiny revolution."[26]

Of course, it is easy to defy the conventional pieties when the room is virtual. As a newspaper columnist, I have been flamed by readers who I am quite sure would not have spoken so harshly to me face-to-face or even on the telephone. Electronic communication is like strong drink: it gives cour-age to timid souls. Or, to switch similes, it's like paintball, a harmless way to vent aggressive impulses. Those who take offense at nasty Web content assume the rules of ordinary social interaction apply. They may not. If cor-nered, posters of the nastiest comments would probably say they mean no harm; it's all in fun.

Functionally, the material in this book does all the things that philoso-phers, psychologists, sociologists, anthropologists, and folklorists say humor and urban legend are supposed to do. It's cathartic, it's expressive, it engen-ders feelings of solidarity, of superiority, and ultimately, perhaps, of sanity: if people can recognize and agree on the absurdities of modern life, it might be the world that's mad, not them.

The real question is, does the exchange of newslore do any good beyond offering, like an over-the-counter medication, some small and temporary relief from anger and frustration? Some scholars say no: lacking the power to effect real change, newslore forwarders are doing little more than grumbling about the state of the world.[27] Newslore, like a sneer, is "the weapon of the weak."[28] The urban-legend Web site Snopes.com likes the term "slacktivism" as a descriptor of those whose social or political engagement is limited to the forwarding of e-mails.[29] Gregor Benton writes:

> But the political joke will change nothing. It is the relentless enemy of greed, injustice, cruelty and oppression—but it could never do without them. It is not a form of active resistance. It reflects no political programme. It will mobilize no one. Like the Jewish joke in its time, it is important for keeping society sane and stable. It cushions the blows of cruel governments and creates sweet illusions of revenge. It has the virtue of momentarily freeing the lives of millions from tensions and frustrations to which even the best-organised political opposition can promise only long-term solutions; but its impact is as fleeting as the laughter it produces.[30]

Others say that newslore highlights social and political problems. "It is absolutely imperative to note," writes Steve Jones, "that these same users are not simply 'consuming' news but are engaging in its critical analysis as well as passing it along."[31] Critically examining problems is obviously not the same as solving them, but it is a crucial first step. I side with those who take the view that newslore is a form of empowerment rather than an expression of powerlessness. I think back to when Aleksandr Solzhenitsyn, after he had lived in the United States for a while, admitted that he missed his native land. Aware that Solzhenitsyn had been persecuted in the Soviet Union, I didn't understand him at the time, but I think I do now. He wasn't just homesick for people and places. He missed his fellow citizens' passion for talking about politics. American life was so comfortable and stable, he said, that Americans can afford to ignore politics. The lack of civic engagement, of everyday political discourse, drove him crazy, just as my students' ignorance of politics and world affairs drives me crazy. These are journalism students, whom one could reasonably expect to take a greater interest in the news than their peers do. So when I examine newslore, what strikes me again and again is how much background knowledge is necessary to make sense of it. The people who forward these e-mails are paying close attention to the news.[32] And their "oppositional reading" of the news suggests, as Joshua Gamson puts it, that "commercial culture is not nearly as powerful, and those consuming it not nearly as powerless, as the critics propose."[33]

3. The phenomenon has largely been ignored and shouldn't be. More than twenty-five years after Dundes and Pagter made their case against orality as a defining feature of verbal folklore,[34] and more than ten years after personal computers became widespread, despite Jan Brunvand's acknowledgment that the Internet is "the latest great conduit for the transmission of folklore,"[35] studies of netlore remain scarce.[36] The problem, as John Dorst noted, is that folklorists remain wedded to Robert Redfield's "little community," both as a concept and as a fieldwork site.[37]

In fact, the advent of netlore came at an awkward time in the history of folklore studies. Beginning in the 1960s and culminating in a special issue of the *Journal of American Folklore* in 1972, the dominant paradigm for folklore research shifted from collecting and comparing folkloric texts to observing and describing when, how, and why those texts emerged in specific social situations. Text was inextricable from context; to study folklore was to watch it being performed and thereby to gain insight into folklore's function in everyday life.

The shift in research methods was wholly consistent with long-standing conceptualizations of the folk as members of small communities whose interactions with each other are mostly face-to-face. But what do you do if you're a student of netlore? Writing in 1990, Dorst insisted that those who communicate electronically constitute "communities that, though dispersed, display attributes of the direct, unconstrained, unofficial exchanges folklorists typically concern themselves with."[38] At the same time, he conceded that these exchanges "are not readily susceptible to the conventional methods of performance analysis and ethnography of speaking."[39] Similarly, Bill Ellis wrote that the existence of virtual communities "challenges our assumption that folklore is the property of small, localized groups," while acknowledging "the difficulty of gathering contextual information."[40]

Yet Ellis,[41] Nancy Baym,[42] and Jan Fernback[43] have gone a long way toward showing the possibilities of "virtual ethnography"[44] by focusing on online discussion groups. Whether they are members of a discussion group devoted to daytime television soap operas, as are Baym's informants, or contributors to an assortment of message boards, as are Ellis's and Fernback's sources, these people are doing more than exchanging items of folklore; they are conversing, and their conversations include their reactions to the folklore.[45]

Still, just as virtual relationships are no substitute for the real thing (for most of us), so virtual ethnography cannot possibly have the texture of an account of actors, scene, and setting.[46] Doubtless many people in this great land have the freedom to play at being political cartoonists. For each item I examine in this book, it would be lovely to know who created it, when, under what circumstances, and for what purpose, but such information is almost as hard to track down as the authorship of a centuries-old ballad.[47]

The other half of the folklore-as-performance equation is the audience. We can, as Ellis has done, identify start dates and winding-down dates for each of the items, and we can ask receivers and forwarders what they thought of the item, but we cannot reconstruct their facial expressions, body language, and verbal responses, if any, at the moment they opened the e-mail. Even if it were feasible to do an ethnographic study of this shadowy community, I confess I am less interested in the behavior and pronouncements of the people who create and actively seek and know where to find this material than I am in what might reasonably be inferred from the material itself about how people feel about the news.

Beyond the academic study of folklore, biases against folklore, especially humorous folklore, run deep. It is considered inane, offensive, and unimportant. In fact, the whole teeming mess that is the Internet, writes David Weinberger, "is the elite's nightmare of the hoi polloi, the rabble, the mob."[48] Certainly some newslore is inane, just as some movies, books of verse, and newspaper stories are inane. But some of the folklore we are going to look at is wickedly clever. Some of our material is certainly offensive, but what of it? Hate speech is offensive, but as Alan Dundes wrote when he defended the study of Auschwitz jokes, we need to know as much as we can about it if we are to combat it.[49] Where I make my stand on newslore is that it is important: more than any other instrument for sampling public opinion we have, it tells us about what people think about what is going on in the world.[50]

Yet the Pew Internet and American Life Project almost totally ignored netlore in its 2002 study of Internet use. The study, "Getting Serious Online," measured the "usefulness" of e-mail for communicating with family and friends, and its use in communicating with family members about problems or to solicit advice. The possibility that people might use e-mail playfully seems not to have occurred to the authors. In a section on "online amusements," the report measured use of the Internet for hobby information, game playing, downloading or listening to music, video or audio, and unspecified browsing "just for fun." And in a section on spam, the study limited its discussion of unwanted e-mail messages to sales solicitations and "adult content," overlooking chain letters, virus warnings, jokes, and legends.[51]

The mainstream news media, as they have come to be called in this age of news-and-comment hybrids, which both take themselves more seriously than other communications media and are more loath to risk giving offense, also pay little attention to newslore.[52] In this I think they do their audiences a disservice, though the anonymous producers, consumers, and distributors of newslore may prefer operating under the mainstream media's radar and are averse to co-optation. Though I define newslore as the news in folklore, I also intend to look closely at folklore in the news.

The few remaining defenders of the objective tradition in journalism say that the purpose of journalism is not to tell citizens what to think but simply to tell them what's going on so they can decide what, if anything, they want to do about any of it. But then what? Critics of the objective tradition complain that telling people what's going on is not enough; news organizations should help the communities they serve *respond* to what's going on. The logical next step after telling people what's going on is finding out how they react to what they have been told. Newslore may be a poor sort of activism in itself, but reporting on newslore is one of the ways journalists can bring those anonymous reactions to the attention of the people who are most often the targets of newslore.[53]

Would President Bush's handlers have continued to dress the set with slogans (see chapter 5) if they knew how much ridicule was heaped on them in cyberspace? Probably: the handlers weren't worried about persuading the cynical few, only the gullible many. But reporting on the parody versions of the slogans might have reached not just Bush's handlers but members of the public who hadn't seen the e-mails, which might then have increased the number of cynical respondents to the point where the slogans were no longer viewed as an effective marketing tool. It's impossible to predict just how such reporting would play out. The results are not really the point, which is simply that if newspapers are truly going to show us "the way we live now," to quote both the Trollope novel and, more to the point, the grab-bag section of the *New York Times Magazine*, they are going to have to get over their squeamishness and plunge more deeply into the world of newslore. So why don't they?

For all the lip service paid to the role of advocacy in journalism, to the project of "afflicting the comfortable and comforting the afflicted," study after study has shown that the news is dominated by official sources. The journalistic defense of the prevailing sourcing practices is that the primary determinant of newsworthiness is impact: decisions that affect many people are more newsworthy than decisions that affect few people. People in positions of power in the worlds of government and business are more likely than the proverbial man in the street to make decisions that affect large numbers of people.

Journalists might also point out, correctly, that the news is less dominat-ed by movers and shakers than it used to be. If, before the 1970s, folklorists and anthropologists mostly "studied down," journalists mostly "studied up." Human-interest stories tended to consist of man-bites-dog oddities, society news at one end of the socioeconomic spectrum, and the criminal behaviors of the lower classes at the other end.[54] Incremental but significant changes in the ways ordinary Americans lived and worked were largely ignored. A story the former newspaper publisher Michael Gartner likes to tell is instructive. An old-time newspaperman is showing a cub reporter the ropes. "I want you to remember that there's 2 million people in this town, and every single one of 'em has a story tell," the old-timer says. "The thing for you to remember is that most of those stories are really shit!"[55]

Anthropology and folklore studies have contributed to a democratizing trend in journalism. The stance of cultural relativism, arising from profes-sional ethnographic research and reinforced by the crises of confidence in the prevailing ideologies and power structures brought on by the horrors of two world wars, the dislocation of the Great Depression, and the racial and social upheavals of the 1960s, eventually made its way into American newsrooms. Part of the problem with keeping the focus on "the centers of power,"[56] as reporters learned again and again in covering the Cold War, the civil rights movement, and the Vietnam War, was that official sources were not always trustworthy.[57] While the press scurried to "pseudo-events"[58] such as the press conference, the speech, and the photo opportunity, the voices of people most affected by the pronouncements and policies of those in power went unheard.

Just as the study of folklore "invites researchers to listen on the margins and to give voices to muted groups in our society,"[59] so the 1995 iteration of the Code of Ethics of the Society of Professional Journalists renewed the call to journalists to "give voice to the voiceless."[60] Editors urged their beat reporters to assess the impact of the news on ordinary citizens:[61] If you're writing a budget story, don't just bombard your readers with percentage increases. Tell them what the proposed budget will mean in people's lives. Ask citizens which municipal services they would be willing to pay more for. The weak news story is general and abstract. The strong story is specific and concrete—and it gets its specificity and its concreteness from the stories it tells about the people behind the statistics and the legislation.

An increased focus on the lives of "unknowns" also boosted the status of feature writers. Once a backwater of rewritten press releases touting com-munity and arts events, and puff pieces extolling local heroes and volunteers, the feature pages now brimmed with trend and slice-of-life stories—stories that had long been staples of magazines but were seldom the stuff of daily journalism.

Literary journalism—a term that has come to seem less problematic than "new journalism"—took the slice-of-life story a step further. Given a little extra time and space by an indulgent editor, the reporter melded the narrative techniques of the fiction writer with the meticulous observation and information gathering of the investigative reporter in crafting stories "on the lives of people at work, in love, going about the normal rounds of everyday life."[62] "Without doing violence to the connotation of the term," write Myerhoff and Ruby, "it is possible to see new journalists as 'folk' or naive ethnographers."[63]

In writing these kinds of stories, reporters rely on a combination of observation of what is going on in their sources' lives in the ethnographic present and interviews that elicit personal-experience narratives of events that preceded the reporter's arrival on the scene. The story follows an individual or set of individuals over time. Something happens. Change occurs. We learn enough about the characters to care about them as individuals.

The advent of the twenty-four-hour electronic news cycle has lent new urgency to the storytelling turn in journalism. The front page of the morning paper offers little news that one does not already know from having watched television or browsed the Internet the night before. One thing the newspaper can provide that the electronic media cannot, however, is a satisfying reading experience. And so, like folklorists who entered the field hoping to increase their own repertoires of stories or songs, reporters are becoming more zealous story collectors in their zeal to become better storytellers.[64]

Yet one journalistic sourcing bias remains: the quintessential American bias toward the individual over the group. When big news happens, the media have no time to execute any sort of scientific or comprehensive survey of public reaction. So reporters hit the streets and obtain a small but what they hope is a representative sample of the range of reactions "out there." Ultimately, though, representativeness is less important than particularity. The assumption is that hearing or reading the words of a named individual, who works at a particular job and lives in a particular place, is more compelling than a summary of what masses of people are thinking.

Eventually a news organization may conduct its own survey or avail itself of a polling service to complement the anecdotal snapshot with a statistical one. Newslore is neither fish nor fowl: it's anonymous, like survey data, but qualitative, like the person-in-the-street interview. A search for newslore yields texts rather than quantifiable opinions, and in the world of journalism, texts that cannot be attributed to a named source are less valuable than texts that can be attributed to a named source.

This is not to say that journalists ignore newslore altogether. Sometime in the 1970s, well before I became a folklore student, I saw a short wire story in a Denver newspaper about a woman who put her shivering dog in the microwave for a quick warm-up—with explosive results.[65] Since then, journalists have gotten more savvy about urban legends: one is less likely to see such a story reported as straight news than to see an urban legend debunked or to see a true story, like the finger in the Wendy's chili, compared to an urban legend. (The story turned out to be half-true: yes, there was a finger in a bowl of Wendy's chili; the customer who found it put it there.)[66] Even folklorists not named Jan Brunvand will get an occasional call from a reporter seeking confirmation that warnings about Blue Star acid[67] or gas pump handles booby-trapped with AIDS-infected needles[68] or, as we will see in chapter 3, terrorists targeting shopping malls on Halloween[69] are groundless.

In January and February 2006, I did a number of searches for feature stories and columns about jokes and urban legends. For each search, I selected the fifty largest-circulation English-language newspapers in the LexisNexis database and went back five years. The total number of "newspaper days" when there could have been a story about any of these topics was 91,750 (50 papers x 5 years x 365 days). Here is what the searches yielded:

- Stories mentioning David Emery, keeper of the About.com urban legends site: 34
- Stories mentioning About.com and urban legends: 81
- Stories mentioning Barbara or David Mikkelson, keepers of the Snopes.com urban legends site: 81
- Stories mentioning Snopes.com: 435
- Stories mentioning online humor: 37
- Stories mentioning e-mailed jokes: 20

The numbers tell us two things: journalists do not pay much attention to online folklore, and they are more interested in urban legends than they are in jokes. Why?

LEGENDS IN THE NEWS

Journalists are ambivalent debunkers. On the one hand, they seem to love learning that some juicy morsel of information that everyone believes to be true, isn't. After all, part of the function of journalists is to do the leg-work that their readers don't have time to do. Just as it's a public service to report on the borough council meeting so that citizens do not have to go themselves, it's a public service to disabuse people of their misapprehensions. Indeed, one of the columns I found was written by the newspaper's consumer affairs reporter.

On the other hand, journalists seem to get exasperated with how gullible their readers are. Part of what is at stake is the franchise: to the extent that readers suspect that the mainstream news media are withholding explosive information or spinning the news for propagandistic purposes, readers begin to believe information of unknown provenance that they get by e-mail or read on a Web site of unproven reliability. Thus we often see columnists exhorting readers to be skeptical and do a little homework. "It doesn't matter if you got the e-mail from your boss, your best friend or your mother-in-law," writes Margie Boule of the *Oregonian*. "Before you pass along the rumor, the warning, the political dirt—just check the facts." And Boule lists several Web sites—About.com, Snopes.com, and Scambusters.org—to get people started.[70]

Another columnist, Winda Benedetti of the *Seattle Post-Intelligencer*, wants readers to back up a step. The best course of action when you receive a forward, she writes, is to assume it's false and spike it rather than clutter up your friends' in-boxes. "They have become a plague," Benedetti writes, "a loathsome cyber-scourge spreading misinformation, fear and panic across a country already more jittery than a caffeine junkie hepped up on a qua-druple latte."[71]

Benedetti does a nice job of identifying the telltale signs that we have entered the realm of netlore. Beware, she says, of forwards that are attribut-ed to friends of friends, of capital letters and exclamation points and vouch-ers such as "I don't normally forward these kinds of e-mails, but . . ." or "I don't want to scare you, but . . ." or "This is NOT a hoax."[72] To that list, Shan-non Beatty of the *Columbus Dispatch* adds spelling and grammar errors and anecdotes or news stories that lack details and dates.[73]

If all of that is not enough to persuade you not to hit that forward but-ton, Benedetti provides the names of the debunking Web sites, including the Urban Legend Combat Kit, which comes with a stock response one can copy and paste: "Thank you for forwarding me the most recent 'send this e-mail to all of your friends and something great will happen' story. Unfor-tunately, the story you sent me is yet another in a long string of Internet hoaxes.'"[74]

PHOTOSHOPS IN THE NEWS

The Society of Professional Journalists Code of Ethics makes clear that the profession frowns on deception.[75] During the early days of the war in Iraq, Brian Walski, a photographer for the *Los Angeles Times*, transmitted a photo of an armed British soldier, standing and gesturing toward a group of Iraqi civilians, all but one of whom, a man holding a child, were seated on the ground. Somebody at one of the *Times'* sister papers, the *Hartford Courant*, took a close look at the image and noticed that some of the civilians appeared twice. Inquiries were made, and Walski confessed that the photo was actually a composite of two photos.[76] A day after the composite appeared in the *Times*, the paper reprinted it along with the two original images and a note explaining what Walski had done and announcing that he had been fired.[77]

The Walski incident was the latest in a series of embarrassing episodes involving digitally altered photos in newspapers. The Society of Professional Journalists Code of Ethics calls for doctored images to be labeled as such, but even disclosure is not enough. Consider the case of a front-page image published in *Newsday* on the eve of the 1998 Winter Olympics that showed Nancy Kerrigan and Tonya Harding skating side by side. The text made it clear that the photo was a phony. "Tonya, Nancy to Skate," said the headline at the bottom of the page. The future tense suggested it hadn't happened yet. In smaller type, the caption explained that the rivals "appear to skate together in this *Newsday* composite illustration." Doubtless whoever was in the newsroom when they put the paper to bed that night thought they had done an adequate job of disclosing that the scene had not taken place. But according to Steve Knowlton, the author of a journalism ethics textbook, when *Newsday* editor Anthony Marro picked up his paper the next morning, he looked at the front page and thought, "Uh oh."[78]

Marro was concerned because he knew that image can overpower text. Many people would glance at the front page, not bother to read the words, and, knowing the history (Tonya hired thugs to bust Nancy's kneecaps), say to themselves, "These women hate each other's guts. What must be going through their heads?" In other words, despite the newspaper's best efforts, it probably misled at least some of its readers into believing that a tableau created on a computer screen had in fact occurred. And when readers learn that they were duped into thinking a fake image was real, editors fear that readers will start thinking that real ones are fake; thus the credibility of all news photos is undermined.[79]

Knowing that printing a fake photograph may lend credence to it—
"Hey, I saw it in the paper"—even in the context of debunking it, we should
not be surprised at the rarity of photoshops in the news. A notable exception appeared in the *New York Times* along with a story aptly headlined
"Another Big Fish Story Comes Unraveled." "Seeing is not believing," wrote
the reporter Dylan Loeb McClain. "Again." The story described the image of
a great white shark going after a diver on a helicopter ladder, then quoted
the accompanying e-mail text: "Although this looks like a picture taken from
a Hollywood movie, it is in fact a real photo, taken near the South African
coast during a military exercise by the British Navy. It has been nominated
by the National Geographic as 'the photo of the year.'"[80] The story about
the shark-diver encounter ended by citing another example of a doctored
photograph: the shot of President Bush holding a book upside down at an
elementary school (discussed in chapter 5).

While newspapers are reluctant to print fake photographs, they have
been quick to defend the integrity of authentic news photos against the
fraudulent claims of pranksters or propagandists. A notorious example of
real images that were rumored to be fakes were the photographs of Palestinians celebrating the September 11 attacks that appeared in many newspapers
around the world. An e-mail immediately began to make the rounds challenging the authenticity of the photos. One claimed that the photos were
"recycled" images taken in 1991. Another claimed that a woman shown celebrating in Jerusalem had been bribed by the photographer. Some quoted
a BBC executive: "It's simply unacceptable that a superpower of communications as CNN uses images that do not correspond to reality in talking
about so serious of an issue."[81] The story took hold because it reinforced
widespread suspicions that the news media are not independent sources of
accurate information but organs of government propaganda. Images of celebrating Palestinians put a face on a faceless enemy and suggested an obvious target for retaliation.

Then the debunking of the debunkers began—in the news media. The
cameraman denied bribing anybody. CNN and Reuters denied recycling
old material. As the reporter Felicity Barringer pointed out in the *New York
Times*, the diction in the accompanying message was rather poor for a BBC
higher-up. The author of the original e-mail confessed to perpetrating a
hoax.[82] The 9/11 celebration photos echoed the persistent rumors that images of the 1969 moon landing were faked to further the U.S. government's
propaganda goals of appearing to have beaten the Soviets in the space race.[83]

As the (London) *Guardian* columnist Owen Gibson wrote of the 9/11 hoax-that-wasn't, "Everyone loves a vaguely plausible conspiracy theory."[84]

Another September 11 hoax legend concerned an Associated Press photo of the smoke billowing from the World Trade Center. While some viewers saw the face of Satan in the smoke, more skeptical types concluded that the face of Satan appeared in the smoke because the photographer put it there. Not so, AP executive photo editor Vin Alabiso told Kenny Irby of the Poynter Institute, a journalism think tank: "Readers were reacting to natural indentations in the smoke clouds. AP has a very strict written policy which prohibits the alteration of the content of a photo in any way. . . . The smoke in this photo combined with light and shadow has created an image which readers have seen in different ways."[85]

While to those with an apocalyptic turn of mind, the devil in the smoke may have conformed to and confirmed their view of the world, the skeptics thought the photo could be neither Satan nor a trick of "light and shadow." It had to be a photographer's trick. As with the photo of the celebrating Palestinians, this legend gives voice to the view that the news media are no longer to be trusted to tell the truth—which is exactly why the news media try to nip such stories in the bud.

JOKES IN THE NEWS

To the extent that the press mirrors the society it serves, we can learn a great deal about American mores from what is and is not considered fit to print in American newspapers. Three anecdotes from my own newspaper experience:

I once wrote a profile of the owner of a small-town diner. I tried to include a bit of xerographic lore I noticed tacked to a wall of the kitchen. "Our boss," it said, "51% sweetheart, 49% bitch. Don't push it." An editor cut the "49% bitch" part: some of our readers would be offended.

In 2006 I wrote a column about some preachers who came to the Penn State campus wearing T-shirts that said "Homos Go to Hell." That passed muster—both at the university and in the newspaper. But I wondered, in the column, whether the university would have been as tolerant if the T-shirts said "Niggers Go to Hell." A university spokesman assured me that free-speech considerations would trump university conduct codes calling for civility and discouraging harassment and intolerance. But an editor changed "nigger" to "N-word" (a coinage I find offensive with its implication that we adults are no better able than schoolchildren to distinguish between use of a slur and discussion of use of a slur).

In another column, I described what the streets looked like after a thaw had exposed all the refuse hidden under the snow. The town, I wrote, "looked like hell." That comment was printed as written. But the next day I got a call from a woman who found the word "hell" offensive. It particularly bothered her that her son was of an age when she had begun to encourage him to read the paper, and she did not want him to be exposed to that kind of language or to have to screen the paper for inappropriate content before allowing him to look at it.[86] When it comes to the use of the word "hell," which is surely among the milder oaths in common use in our society, hers was clearly a minority view, but the encounter sheds light on attitudes about the unique status of the newspaper in people's lives.

However crass the culture, it is "out there," in the theaters and the bookstores and the newsstands. One may partake of it, out there, while maintaining the home as a world apart, a place where one should be able to prevent or at least limit one's exposure—and, more important, one's family's exposure—to unsavory influences. Newspapers and television are different. They are guests in the home. They bring news from the world out there, but they are expected to wipe their feet before they come in. John Soloski's 1989 study of newsroom policies showed how seriously reporters took the idea that they were working for "a family newspaper." A junior editor told him, "Nothing of bad taste—sex, immoral, bodies—gets in unless it is really necessary."[87]

The obscenity-profanity-vulgarity entry in *The New York Times Manual of Style and Usage* sheds further light on mainstream newspaper standards in this area. The entry helps us understand how people at the *Times* interpret their unsettling motto, "All the News That's Fit to Print." Adolph S. Ochs's rather quaint promise that the news would be presented "in language that is parliamentary in good society,"[88] the authors of the style manual declare, remains the standard more than 150 years later.

Except when it doesn't: "Profanity in its milder forms can on some occasions be justified." By way of example, the manual cites some of the expressions that appeared in transcripts of taped White House conversations about the Watergate scandal, published in the *Times* "because of the light they shed on news matters of utmost importance."[89] The entry goes on to explain, in effect, that when the president or some similarly august personage curses, it's news; when anybody else curses, it isn't. On the subject of describing sexual activities and sexual organs, the 1976 manual is mum. But here is what the *Los Angeles Times* stylebook says on the subject:

It can be roughly said that phrases with a sexual connotation are considered obscene, those with a religious connotation are considered profane, and those with an excremental connotation are considered vulgar.... No words or phrases in these categories are to be used casually, gratuitously or merely for shock effect.[90]

In his introduction to the 1989 edition of the *Washington Post Deskbook on Style*, editor Ben Bradlee quoted Eugene Meyer, who, shortly after he bought the paper in 1935, declared: "As a disseminator of the news, the paper shall observe the decencies that are obligatory upon a private gentleman. What it prints shall be fit reading for the young as well as for the old." To which Bradlee added: "These principles are re-endorsed herein."[91] But there are exceptions: "We shall avoid profanities and obscenities unless their use is so essential to a story of significance that its meaning is lost without them."[92]

Bit by bit, obscenity, vulgarity, and profanity that do not necessarily have anything to do with august personages have gotten into the paper, mostly via increased coverage of health issues. Describing how one could and could not be exposed to the AIDS virus in particular seemed like no place for euphemisms. Then came the Lewinsky scandal. Special prosecutor Kenneth Starr's report on his investigation contained stunningly graphic descriptions of who did what to whom in the Oval Office—which put editors in a bind. On the one hand were the traditional "family newspaper" constraints. On the other, members of Congress were going to decide whether to impeach the president based on the information contained in this document; shouldn't the American people also be able to see it so they could let their representatives in Congress know what they thought?

A secondary rationale for printing the report was that it revealed more about Ken Starr than it did about President Clinton. To some readers, including this one, I must confess, Starr's interest in the details of the assignations seemed more prurient than legalistic. Ready as some of us were to believe the worst about the special prosecutor, we were tickled to learn, via forwarded e-mail, that Starr said the following during a *60 Minutes* interview in 1987:

Public media should not contain explicit or implied descriptions of sex acts. Our society should be purged of the perverts who provide the media with pornographic material while pretending it has some redeeming social value under the public's "right to know."

All of which proves that even folklorists get taken in sometimes: the quote was a fake.[93] In any case, many papers printed excerpts from the Starr report that read like passages from a pornographic novel, accompanied, to be sure, by an editor's warning and explanation so that parents could, if they chose, shield their children from the salacious material. If editors were also motivated by the distinct possibility that people would buy the paper to be titillated rather than merely well-informed, they weren't saying.

In each instance where the prohibitions against vulgarity or profanity were set aside, it was, arguably, "really necessary." It is much harder to make that case where humor is involved. Naughty words aside, newspapers make little room for humor, apart from the funnies. When a humor columnist I know was trying to self-syndicate, editors told him again and again that they didn't need another humor column because they had Dave Barry. Did newspapers have a humor quota? he asked. Clearly, humor is dangerous. Even the gentlest satire is sure to offend people who take themselves or their preoccupations seriously. As my correspondence over a newspaper column I wrote about Hillary Clinton jokes will make clear in chapter 1, when people are offended by jokes, they don't consider them to be jokes at all. They were "attacks," according to one writer, "hateful comments parading as 'jokes,'" according to another. (I consider it a minor moral victory that in the course of my exchange of views with the latter writer, he stopped putting quotation marks around the word "jokes.") The outpouring of Muslim rage over cartoonists' depictions of the prophet Mohammed in the winter of 2006 is perhaps the most extreme case of how much trouble the news media can get into when they traffic in humor.

The uproar began with a Danish newspaper editor challenging cartoonists to take on the Prophet without censoring themselves. The results were offensive on two levels. First, any representation of the Prophet is anathema to devout Muslims. Second, some of the depictions were insulting, particularly one where the Prophet's turban is a bomb. After a slow start, the controversy spread, first to other European newspapers, then to Islamic countries, where protests against the cartoons turned destructive and violent. Few American editors, I believe, would dare provoke such a response. They learn to pick their battles. If they're going to take guff from readers, they want it to be over a serious story, not a silly one.

But once the protests started, the cartoons became newsworthy. So now what were editors to do? The *Philadelphia Inquirer* justified printing the turban-bomb cartoon thus: "But when a use of religious imagery that many find offensive becomes a major news story, we believe it is important for readers to be able to judge the content for themselves."[94] The *Inquirer* claimed to be running the cartoon "discreetly" on an inside page, an odd characterization given that the inside page was the continuation from the front page, where the cartoon story was the lead item. The inside page also included a box directing readers to the paper's Web site to see the rest of the controversial cartoons. But most papers took a middle path of describing the content of the cartoons, but not reprinting them—which suggests a strategy for dealing with newslore. If photoshops are deemed unfit to print, why not just describe them?

The attitudes and sentiments expressed toward current events in folklore are clearly news themselves, but much of the material, apparently, is not considered fit to print. Despite the omnipresence of profanity and vulgarity in the movies and on cable television and a loosening of entrance requirements at mainstream newspapers, it is hard to imagine newspaper gatekeepers abandoning their posts altogether and allowing any and all scatological and sexual humor onto their pages. And yet it seems a dereliction of duty for newspapers to ignore this material.

As I began to write this book, I started noticing a few encouraging signs of a thaw at the *New York Times*. The Sunday Week in Review section now routinely runs a sampling of "news jokes" by television's late-night comedians. The *Times* also took note in separate stories of an explosion of parodies and parody posters for the movie *Brokeback Mountain*.[95] In February 2006, coverage of Vice President Cheney's accidental shooting of a quail-hunting partner in Texas included sidebars about the jokes that immediately sprang up on both broadcast television and the Internet.[96] Elsewhere in the paper, the technology section has begun to pay more attention to the news from cyberspace, and in October 2007 the *New York Times Magazine* began running a regular column on online culture called "The Medium," by Virginia Heffernan. It's a start.

Mostly this book will be an annotated compendium of newslore that has been in circulation during the brief time that personal computers equipped with e-mail programs have become fixtures in many American homes and offices, a period bridging the last years of the twentieth century and the first years of the twenty-first. Given how full of incident our times are, and how prolific people are in generating newslore in response, this book can be little more than a snapshot of what was circulating up until the time of its writing. (As I embarked in January 2006, the hot new items on About.com were spoofs of New Orleans mayor Ray Nagin's ill-considered comments about keeping post-Katrina New Orleans "a chocolate city," and send-ups of the disgraced lobbyist Jack Abramoff's relationship with President Bush, which Bush's aides said was nonexistent. A month later that material had been supplanted by jokes about Vice President Cheney's hunting accident.) By the time the book goes to press, new material will doubtless have appeared, and the material that was new as I was writing will long since have dropped out of circulation: though new folklore is almost always recycled from old, it has a short shelf life. No matter. We journos make a distinction between timeliness and currency that may apply here.

Timely stories are breaking news: when Hurricane Katrina made landfall, the dailies had to have the story the next day (the same day, on their Web sites). In contrast, the urban poverty that came to the fore at the Louisiana Superdome and the New Orleans Convention Center was a story that could have—and should have—been told before Katrina. It remains a story that could and should be told as I write and as you read, however wide the temporal gap between my writing and your reading, and, I fear, it will remain a story for some time to come. That is what we mean by currency. Though the e-mails I cite here may have long been spiked and the Web links broken, my hope is that the enterprise of examining and interpreting this material is a worthy enough one for my snapshot to continue to be of interest.

I briefly considered devoting each chapter to a different genre of newslore before deciding that a topical approach made more sense for the simple reason that the news that gets a rise out of people often inspires folklore across genres. If the topic is, for example, President Bush's lack of intelligence, we are likely to see urban legends, jokes, and photoshops that all express that idea. The weakness of this approach is that it can obscure links between similar content adapted to different events. Online folklore exists in fewer versions than oral folklore, but it spawns just as many variants— closely related material adapted to different situations. We have been seeing some of the same jokes told about every president since Jimmy Carter. We also see variants of the same joke—parodies of the "Got milk?" advertising campaign are particularly popular at this writing—applied across topics. The solution, unsatisfactory though it may be, is to cross-reference recycled material as it arises.

We begin, in chapter 1, with jokes about Hillary Clinton, for three reasons. First, some of the jokes date to the earliest days of electronic newslore. Second, my having written a newspaper column about the jokes offers a window into how dangerous it can be for the news media to wade into these waters. And third, the volume and persistence of nasty jokes about Hillary

Clinton are simply astonishing. "No other candidate in history has ever inspired a similar cottage industry of anger—Web sites, books, and movies," wrote Jason Horowitz in a 2008 article called "The Hillary Haters."[97] Chapter 2, in turn, examines the overlapping folklore about Bill Clinton, as well as the material prompted by the men who followed him as the Democratic Party's standard bearers, Al Gore and John Kerry.

Chapter 3 examines the newslore of September 11. Since the September 11 attacks were among the most cataclysmic events in American history, it is hardly surprising that they triggered one of the largest folk responses in the short history of computer-mediated communication. In my own experience as an e-mail recipient, the week following the attacks was a time for the expression of raw anger and sorrow. The spirit of play apparent in so much newslore was wholly absent during this period, which may explain why most of the material came from identified sources and can be thought of only as a sort of proto-folklore. Here is what I mean: A newspaper column would not be considered folklore by anyone's definition. But if it perfectly expresses what many people are feeling, as did the syndicated columnist Leonard Pitts's column on September 12, 2001, it takes on a life of it own.[98] Functionally, we might say, the newspaper column is acting like folklore, and if it had been in circulation before what Walter Benjamin calls "the age of mechanical reproduction,"[99] we might expect to see the sort of variation we see in folklore texts.

The joking about September 11, when it began, was limited in scope. As if by tacit agreement, there was no joking about the victims as there had been with the *Challenger* disaster. The only jokes were really just defiant gestures, humorous only by virtue of their clever vulgarity. Quickly, though, what the Bush administration called the "war on terror" began, which provided a focal point for American anger and fantasies of revenge. As soon as there is an enemy, that enemy can be cut down to size through humor.

Chapter 4 addresses the next cataclysmic event in our troubled times, Hurricane Katrina. As with September 11, there is little focus on the victims. Most of the joking comes at the expense of the public officials, from the president down, who were perceived to have so thoroughly botched the preparations and evacuations. Chapter 5 follows the Hurricane Katrina chapter with more jokes about President Bush. Here the material is tied not to his handling of specific events but to an overall perception of his lack of competence and intelligence.

The next two chapters shift from politics to news from the worlds of business and technology. Chapter 6 deals with the sudden collapse of the Enron

Corporation. Shameless profiteering by the company's executives confirmed some of our worst fears about corporate America, which had long provided fodder for urban legends. This chapter also examines parodies of Master-Card's long-running "Priceless" advertising campaign. Chapter 7 looks at newslore of particular interest to netizens: the folklore that has attached itself to the person of software mogul Bill Gates and the response to business and government warnings of economic upheaval in the event of computer failures on January 1, 2000—the so-called Y2K problem. Chapter 8 covers the jaundiced folk response to media reporting on celebrity deaths. The book's conclusion looks to the most current material up to the date of publication for clues about the future of newslore.

Before we proceed, a word or two about the writing, and about my source material: When I submit papers to scholarly journals, whether they give the work the thumbs-up or thumbs-down or ask me to revise and resubmit, reviewers complain that the writing is "too journalistic" or "too informal" or "too conversational." Well, that's what happens when you write for newspapers for twelve years. In fact, I've always written that way, which is to say that I try to write in such a way that I prove to my peers that I know what I'm talking about while also entertaining them and anyone else who should walk in on the conversation. I believe we have a solemn obligation not to bore each other to death. Or as I tell my journalism students, quoting longtime *Wall Street Journal* editor Barney Kilgore, "The easiest thing for the reader to do is to stop reading."[100] It's especially easy when we use locutions like "the data seem to suggest." The data don't do anything but lie there like loxes, as my dad would say. I will make a special effort to avoid passive-voice constructions like "it will be shown that . . ." I'm going to be doing the showing. Read this book, and for better or worse, you're stuck with me as your chatty guide. My approach, I think, is particularly well suited to the subject matter of this book. Much of the material is outrageous, ridiculous, sophomoric, and mean-spirited. But I think we should take it seriously. So yes, there are endnotes, as you have already seen, but I hope no one will say of this book, as Mary Douglas said of her fellow anthropologist A. R. Radcliffe-Brown, that he "wrote on the subject of joking in a very desiccated perspective."[101]

As for the material: First, netlore is notorious for shoddy spelling and punctuation. Though it pains me, as a journalism professor, to say so, I have not cleaned up the errors in my source material. Second, I cannot vouch for the continuing viability of all my Internet citations. Like the listings in an old phone book, some of the places listed will have moved away.

1

Where Is the Humor?

Anti-Hillary Jokes in the News

Just how indicative of public opinion are jokes? Judging from the number of Hillary Clinton jokes I had collected over the years, I predicted that the former first lady would not be elected president in 2008. (On the other hand, there were enough George W. Bush jokes out there before 2004 to suggest that voters were ready to send him back to Crawford—and we all know how that turned out.) I turned out to be right about Hillary, but much as I'd like to ascribe all this power to folklore, I must acknowledge that Barack Obama's emergence as the Democratic Party nominee may have had more to do with his strengths as a candidate than with the animus toward Hillary expressed in the jokes.

I first learned of the Hillary jokes from a student in a folklore class I taught at UC Davis in the summer of 1995. In keeping with the thesis of this book, the compendium of Internet folklore this student submitted recalls the times. Among the in-the-news celebrities the jokes invoke: David Duke (the Ku Klux Klan leader who ran for governor of Louisiana in 1991), Jeffrey Dahmer (a serial killer arrested in 1991), David Koresh (leader of a religious cult, the Branch Davidians, whose compound in Waco, Texas, was destroyed in a government raid in 1993), Lorena Bobbitt (cut off her husband's penis in 1993), Michael Jackson (charged with child molestation in 1993), Dan Quayle (left office in 1993), Tonya Harding (arranged an attack on her Olympic skating rival Nancy Kerrigan in 1994), O. J. Simpson (accused of murdering his ex-wife and friend in 1994), Newt Gingrich (led Republicans to midterm election victory in 1994 and was at the center of a budget impasse with President Clinton that led to a government shutdown in 1995), Rush Limbaugh (his popularity and influence soared in the mid-1990s), Hugh Grant (caught with a prostitute in 1995), Jerry Garcia (died 1995), Christopher Reeve (paralyzed as a result of an equestrian accident in 1995), Bill Gates (topped *Forbes* magazine's list of the world's richest men in 1995), and, of course, Bill and Hillary Clinton. Compare this list to the Associated Press list of the top ten stories of 1995:

1. The bombing of the Oklahoma City federal building, allegedly by two U.S. Army buddies.
2. The ongoing crisis in Bosnia, a situation brought closer to home by President Clinton's decision to send twenty thousand U.S. troops into the Balkans.
3. The O. J. Simpson case, which delivered a daily dose of race, wealth, fame, and drama into America's living rooms—until the Heisman Trophy–winner-turned-murder-suspect was acquitted of killing his wife.
4. The assassination of Israeli prime minister Yitzhak Rabin, gunned down shortly after speaking to a pro-peace rally in Tel Aviv.
5. An earthquake in Kobe, Japan, that killed more than six thousand people and reduced a city of 1.4 million to rubble.
6. The Washington showdown between Newt Gingrich and President Clinton, a yearlong struggle for control that eventually led to a partial government shutdown.
7. The nerve gas attack by a doomsday cult on the Tokyo subway.
8. Downed Air Force captain Scott O'Grady's escape from behind enemy lines in Bosnia.
9. A killer heat wave that left more than seven hundred dead in Chicago.
10. A jury's decision on Susan Smith: guilty of murdering her two sons, but spared the death penalty.

If my student's compendium is a reliable guide to what was circulating online in the summer of 1995, then eight of the AP's top ten were not considered joking matters. (Just to make sure, I did a Google search for jokes about the Oklahoma City bombing, the war in Bosnia, the Rabin assassination, and so on. There weren't any. Or at least there didn't seem to be any jokes circulating in the United States. Bosnians were telling war jokes, apparently, and Israelis were telling assassination jokes.) The most newsworthy stories of the year are not necessarily the most talked-about stories (see appendix B). For example, Mike Tyson's biting Evander Holyfield's ear makes the category of most talked-about, but not the category of most newsworthy. Were there Mike Tyson jokes? Of course. Here's my favorite:

Q: What did Mike Tyson say to Van Gogh?
A: "You gonna eat that?"

But to return to Hillary jokes: I thought back to my student's selection of these jokes when people began talking her up as a presidential candidate. And when she formally announced her candidacy in early 2007, I devoted my Sunday column, "Frankly Speaking," in the *Centre Daily Times* to them. I reprint the column in full here:

> Hillary Clinton doesn't stand a chance in 2008, and I've got the jokes to prove it.
>
> Some of them go all the way back to 1993, when computer users were just beginning to discover what an efficient grapevine an online network can be. The printable ones are of two types: those that express the idea that Hillary is more powerful or more power-hungry than her husband, and those that express the corollary idea that a powerful woman must be a lesbian (and her husband must be gay).[1] Here's a sampling:
>
> Q: What happened when Bill Clinton got a shot of testosterone?
> A: He turned into Hillary.
>
> Q: What do you get when you cross a lesbian and a gay?
> A: Chelsea.
>
> Q: How did Bill and Hillary Clinton meet?
> A: They were dating the same girl in high school.
>
> Q: Why does the Secret Service guard Hillary so closely?
> A: Because if something happens to her, Bill becomes president.
>
> The idea that Hillary was the real power behind the throne also turned up on bumper stickers:
>
> IMPEACH CLINTON!
> And her husband, too!
>
> I DON'T TRUST PRESIDENT CLINTON
> OR HER HUSBAND ...
>
> It doesn't take a brilliant analyst to figure out what these jokes are about. Even before Bill Clinton was elected, it was clear that his wife was not going to be a traditional first lady, content to serve as White House

hostess and to limit her causes to "women's issues" such as child welfare or funding for the arts. She was as much of a policy wonk as her husband, and the new president had every intention of putting her talents to use.

This, apparently, freaked a lot of people out. Women burning their bras, demanding equal wages, and muscling in on male domains such as the truck cab and the construction site was one thing; a woman helping to run the country was more feminism than they could handle. "Hey, Hillary," shouted one bumper sticker. "Shut up and redecorate!"

Then Mrs. Clinton was tapped to lead the deliberations that would culminate in the administration's proposed overhaul of America's healthcare system. Even now it is unclear whether the proposal was shot down because it was bad policy or if any proposal would have been shot down because of who was in charge of the process.[2]

Consider this 1993 rant against "liberal hypocrisy": "Would you abduct and possibly shoot your neighbors if they refused to buy their health insurance through the same company you do? The IRS will, more so if President Clinton has her way."

Realistically, even if Hillary Clinton exercised more power than any first lady in history, she was still far less powerful than her husband. But the jokes suggest that a man cannot cede any power to his wife without emasculating himself—or that a woman who succeeds in wresting any power from her husband must, perforce, be stronger than he. In the world of these jokes, an emasculated or feminized man is, inevitably, gay; so is a strong woman.

But they're only jokes, right? They don't really mean anything. They're just funny. Or, they're just stupid attempts at being funny. Well, here is a folklorist's advice to the Democratic Party: Take these Hillary Clinton jokes seriously. Yes, 15 years is a long time in American politics, but if you want to take back the White House, don't count on those who sniggered at Hillary jokes in 1993 to vote for her in 2008.[3]

I hope I'm wrong about this, by the way. Think how galling it will be for Hillary's enemies if those snide old bumper stickers turn out to have been prophecies.

The column incurred the wrath of a number of readers, who responded with e-mails of two types. One set of respondents mistook my presentation of Hillary Clinton jokes as an endorsement of them. (My first exposure to this kind of thinking occurred after I wrote a profile of Huey Newton during his stint as an inmate of the local state prison. I thought my treatment of Newton was evenhanded; those who believed the Black Panthers were thugs chastised me for glorifying him.) The other set of respondents understood I was not endorsing, but as far as they were concerned, I might as well have been: by retelling the jokes, I was keeping them in circulation. Here is a sample of an exchange of e-mails of the first type:

> I read your article in the Sunday CDT and I must say that I was appalled. In several short paragraphs, you managed to defame a young lady, insult the gay and lesbian community, attack the dignity of a past President, cast aspersions on a sitting Congressperson and fire off the initial round of gutter trash politics.

> As a fellow writer, I tried to understand your motivation for this piece. Were you trying to create a diversion to change focus from our current Presidential failings? Were you trying to fire-up the anti-Clinton bashers in Centre County? Were you trying to get a reader response to provide you with as the paper put it "grist for your mill" . . . or are you threatened by women in power? What exactly was your motivation?

> I realize that we live in a country where anything and everything is possible including having a biased hate piece published by a local newspaper. If this article is any indication of the content of your book, then my advice to you is to be self published and keep the production run a low as possible.

My response:

I'm sorry you have taken my writing about these jokes as an endorsement of them. My attitude is this: Like it or not, the jokes are out there—and the attitudes that underpin them. That's an important thing to know, especially if you're a Democrat hoping to see your party take back the White House in '08. Hillary's not my first choice for the Democratic nomination, as it happens, though I'm sure I'd vote for her over any Republican nominee. But I worry about her electability, given the antipathy toward her that is expressed in these jokes. This is not to say, by the way, that the country isn't ready for a female president. It's Hillary's supposed "baggage" that I worry about.—RF

At this point, my correspondent switched from chastising me for the views he had mistakenly thought I held to chastising me for perpetuating the views of the Hillary haters:

My 1941 edition of Webster's Comprehensive Encyclopedic Dictionary defines a joke in part as "something said for the sake of exciting a laugh". You keep referring to these statements as jokes. Where is the humor when people who are gay, lesbians, aggressive or who challenge the considered "norm" are attacked by simple minded individuals? What can the readers of the CDT expect for your next column....restatement of attacks on blacks using the "N" word....blind or handicapped.....war vets missing arms or legs how about Jews or Pols? We all hear these quote "jokes" however most of us choose not to perpetuate them or add credibility by restating them.

My response:

The definition of a joke isn't contingent on whether you or the group of people at whose expense it's told think it's funny. I'm quite certain that the people who share this material think it's funny. It's also possible that people who are not in sympathy with the message of the material still think some of it's funny or clever on some level. In any case, I think it's valuable to shine a light in the dark corners of our culture. You, apparently, disagree.

Another writer bypassed me and my editor and went straight to the dean of my college, who then forwarded this missive to me, prefaced with a brief note and followed by the dean's response to the unhappy reader, whose name I have changed:

Russ: Fyi.
Happy New Year!

Dear Sir,

If you did not read Mr. Frank's column in the 1/28/07 edition of the Centre Daily Times then please do. It is by far the most disgusting piece of trash I have ever read in the CDT. IT sickens me and I am not even a Democrat. Are you proud of this? My wife and I sent two sons to Penn State and I really do not feel that this is representative of the true Penn State. What do you think? Best to you in the new year.

Thanks for your e-mail, Mr. Black.

As you likely know, Mr. Frank writes a regular column for the CDT—and his arrangement for doing so is with the newspaper, independent of his teaching here.

Russ, like most opinion columnists, is an engaging man, and, I presume, would welcome feedback from readers.

Thanks again for passing along your thoughts to me.

I hope your new year is off to a good start.

I'm glad my dean thinks I'm engaging. Now here are the e-mails I received that chided me for giving new life to the Hillary jokes:

Dear Russell,

I am very angry and deeply disappointed by the article citing Hillary jokes. The article was in very poor taste and nasty because you were reminding people of the jokes and it is people like you who will keep them alive. Hillary is an extremely intelligent woman whose biggest mistake probably was falling in love and marrying her husband . . . Please stay out of politics in future articles.

Dear RF.

Shame on you! I am REALLY surprised at the childishness of this column. It's not funny; it's not helpful in any way; and it is so dumb in reviving old jokes that maybe people have forgotten or maybe are too young to know . . .

With love to you and yours, a devoted fan otherwise,

Finally, there was an exchange I had with another faculty member:

I am reminded of what Ohio Senator Howard Metzenbaum used to write to constituents who wrote bizarre letters to him, something to the effect of: "Sir: Some crackpot has been writing me letters and signing your name."

Someone wrote a column in Sunday's *CDT* that began in an appalling way and signed your name.

Though I do not read your column regularly, I have done so from time to time and I have found them to be quite good.

I could not believe that you would repeat the hateful comments parading as "jokes" about Senator Clinton.

You could have made your point effectively, which I take it is that there is deep-seated hostility toward women like Hillary Clinton that threaten her electability, without repeating them. By doing so, you put yourself in the service of the right wing hate machine. I can (and even sometimes do) listen to Rush Limbaugh to get a taste of what the latest right wing party-line hate machine is peddling. It does not need to appear in the *CDT* at the hand of a literate and intelligent columnist. Whatever were you thinking? They are no more appropriate than similar jokes about Bush, which also would have no place in your column.

This is not just my reaction. At lunch this noon, a distinguished emeritus professor asked me if I had read it and volunteered that he was appalled. That very word characterized my wife's reaction.

This column goes way beyond "Frankly Speaking".

You owe your readers an apology and much better judgment in the future.

The urge to mock my correspondent's invocation of the "distinguished emeritus professor's reaction" was powerful. I resisted and culled what I thought were Alan Dundes's most persuasive quotes on the subject of offensive jokes instead:

Here are a few excerpts from what the late folklorist Alan Dundes wrote in response to objections to an article he wrote about contemporary Holocaust jokes in West Germany (in the 1980s):

"Censorship, whether imposed from without or self-imposed, is unthinkable in an academic environment of free inquiry and expression. Auschwitz jokes exist and continue to be told in contemporary West Germany—whether or not a sample is published in an American folklore journal . . .

"For those who find Auschwitz jokes offensive (we include ourselves in that group), we ask: Do you really think it would be better not to report on the popularity of such jokes? Do you honestly think that evil, left to its own devices, will somehow disappear? World history suggests otherwise. Prejudices, stereotypes, gross inhumanity, and even ethnic genocide do not appear to be on the wane. Folklorists with a sense of social responsibility have an obligation to do what they can to fight injustice.

"Folklore does not create society; it only mirrors it. If the mirror is unattractive, does it serve any purpose to break the mirror? The ugly reality of society is what needs to be altered, not the folklore that reflects that reality."[4]

I think of it this way: Keeping the lights off doesn't make the cockroaches go away. It just keeps you from seeing them.

Respectfully, RF

His response:

Thank you for taking the time to respond to my email regarding your column.

This is not a question of censorship at all. It is a question of judgment. To argue otherwise is to say that no one has a right to criticize someone else's words, no matter what its content, because that would be censorship.

There is also a difference between what occurs in the academy and in public journalism. In journalism, there is censorship, both formal and self-induced. Indeed, you exercised it when [you] indicated that some of the "jokes" going around about the Clintons could not be printed in the newspaper.

When you say, "Do you really think it would be better not to report on the popularity of such jokes?" you are mischaracterizing my point.

I said, "You could have made your point effectively, which I take it is that there is deep-seated hostility toward women like Hillary Clinton that threaten her electability, without repeating them." It is one thing to report that these jokes exist, and quite another to repeat them. Yes, the "mirror" of folklore, as you put it, is sometimes not pretty. I agree that the ugly reality of society needs to be exposed and altered. But repeating the jokes does not further that goal, especially since (as I recall) your column did not denounce the ugliness of these jokes.

By your reasoning, a column discussing the real and deep seated prejudice against Mexican illegal aliens ought to repeat jokes about wetbacks, and one about mistrust of Muslims anti-Muslim jokes.

It might be convenient to cast criticism of your column in terms of censorship, of keeping the lights off, but it is not the issue here. I can understand how it might be difficult to face up to the fact that your decision to repeat the hate jokes of the right wing was a mistake. But the fact that you damaged your reputation and furthered the right wing agenda is itself something that should not be kept in the dark.

You probably don't regard this as a friendly communication, but in an important sense it is. The fact that I wrote you personally rather than a letter to the editor signifies that I was disappointed in your decision and that I wish for you to exercise better judgment in the future. I hope that you will acknowledge, if only to yourself, that your repeating (multiple) those jokes was a mistake.

My response:

I may have damaged my reputation. I doubt I furthered the right-wing agenda. (They don't need help from the likes of me.) Most people, I'll wager, found these jokes stupid. Perhaps awareness of them will make some of them more vigilant or proactive. Those who did not find them stupid are already Hillary haters.

I confess that as a folklorist, I find this kind of material—wetback jokes, anti-Muslim jokes—interesting. For better or worse, they are my data. It would be odd to discuss the data without presenting the data. I admit

I don't have much patience for those who are too tender-hearted to confront this stuff.

So no, I don't feel like I made a mistake. I do regard this exchange as friendly.—RF

My "friendly" correspondent's point about censorship and the distinction between academic and journalistic contexts deserves to be addressed at some length. Sharing the jokes with other scholars in a journal article is one thing, he said; sharing them with impressionable newspaper readers is quite another. He's right about censorship. I have argued elsewhere that journalists (and critics of journalists) ought to be more careful in their use of the word.[5] Remove the threat of government suppression of news, and censorship or self-censorship does not look much different from the exercise of news judgment. Express some misgivings, as I did, about publication of the Virginia Tech gunman Cho Seung-Hui's "multi-media manifesto" (I questioned whether the negligible amount of understanding we gained from seeing Cho brandishing his weapons outweighed the risk of those images inspiring copycat crimes),[6] and you get taken to task for paternalism—withholding information from the people for their own good—just as I could take my friend to task for academic paternalism: scholars like him and "the distinguished emeritus professor" would understand my point about those Hillary Clinton jokes; newspaper readers might not. Or does it depend on who those newspaper readers are? My column was published in a newspaper that circulates in a college town. Leaving aside the question of whether journalists should ever talk down to their audience, I have never felt the need to talk down to *this* audience. Indeed, some of the readers who complained about my column did so not because they weren't sophisticated enough to understand it but because they were perhaps too implicated in the university's culture of sensitivity: oppressed groups must be protected from hate speech in the same way children must be protected from media representations of sex and violence. More paternalism. Still, I concede my friend's larger point: journalists decide what people need and do not need to know all the time. For better or worse, that's the job. And I concede his smaller point that even I, a defender of journalists' sharing all that they know, withheld the most offensive Hillary jokes. I could argue that an editor would have spiked them anyway, but I didn't even try to sneak them into the paper. Of course, there's nothing to stop me from including them here:

Reporter: "Ms. Co-president, what are your views on capital punishment?"
Hillary: "I like it when women are hung like men!"

Why doesn't Hillary Clinton wear miniskirts?
Because her balls would show.[7]

The key to understanding these jokes is knowing the folk belief that a man's courage, or at least his audacity, resides in his testicles. When women behave audaciously, they are seen as behaving like men, and therefore, at least metaphorically, possess the same anatomical equipment as men. Size matters here as well: the larger the testicles and, by extension (so to speak), the penis, the greater the audacity. According to the first joke, the kind of woman that a "ballsy" lesbian like Hillary Clinton finds attractive, curiously, is one built like a man. All that and a double entendre on the word "hung" as well. The next joke takes an unkind swipe at Hillary's looks:

Bill Clinton was out jogging when he passed by a street walker. She called out "Fifty dollars!" Bill laughed and called back, "Two dollars!" A week later, Hillary has decided to jog along with Bill. They wound up jogging past the same streetwalker who called out, "See what you get for two dollars?"

I also withheld a number of Hillary jokes from my column for the simple but implacable reason that I couldn't fit them in. My column was allotted about six hundred words at the time. Here are a few of those jokes I might have included if I had more space, beginning with another jibe about Hillary's appearance:

When Bill Clinton was President he once walked off of Air Force One carrying a Razorback piglet. One of the secret service agents said, "Interesting animal you have there, Mr. President." Bill replied, "Thanks, I got it for Hillary." The Secret Service agent responded, "Nice trade sir."

Several more jokes suggest that Hillary, as the stronger one, was the real president:

Q: Why were there two presidential limousines in the inaugural parade?

A: The first one held the real president while the second one contained the president's spouse, Bill Clinton.

Q: What is the first thing that President Clinton says after waking up?
A: "Good morning, Bill."

Q: Why did the IRS recently audit Bill Clinton?
A: Because he filed as head of the household.

Q: Why is Chelsea Clinton growing up a confused child?
A: Because dad can't keep his pants on and mom wants to wear them.

Bill, Al, and Hillary all die in a plane crash. Upon reaching Heaven, they are escorted as important personages directly to see God. God looks at Bill and asks, "Bill, you've sinned a great deal. Why should I allow you to enter into Heaven?" "Well, gee, God," replies Bill, "I'm the Pres-ee-dent of the United States. I've been trying to help people—you know, give them universal health care and protect them from those mean-spirited Republicans who want to starve their children and throw sick old people out into the street."

God considers this a moment and says, "Oh, okay. Sit over here on my left." He turns to Al. "Al, why should I let you into Heaven?"

"Well, Lord, I'm the Vice President of the United States. I've tried to protect the environment from abuse by those mean-spirited Republicans and even wrote a very important book about it."

God thinks a moment and says, "All right. Sit over here on my right. Now, Hillary, tell me why I should let *you* into Heaven."

"Well, God, it's like this. I'm the First Lady, the Co-President and, by the way, I think you're sitting in my seat." (In a variant, Bill Gates, a primary joke target in his own right, as we shall see in chapter 7, gets Hillary's lines.)

Where my friend and I continue to disagree over Hillary jokes is on the question of harm. My friend thinks making people aware of the jokes does more harm than good. The harm is of several kinds: to the jokes' supposed victims (homosexuals and feminists, principally; even trying to see this issue from my detractors' point of view, it's hard to get too worked up about the jokes' impact on the Clinton family); to Hillary's supporters, who worry that I have given fresh ammunition to her detractors; to readers impression-able enough to be influenced by the jokes; and possibly to political discourse itself, which these jokes coarsen. I obviously believe otherwise. I took some satisfaction in seeing that in his online column in the *New York Times*, pub-lished almost a year after my column, Stanley Fish remarked on his hesita-tion to write a column about Hillary hatred "because of a fear that it would advance the agenda that is its target."[8]

Jason Horowitz described Hillary Clinton as "an empty vessel into which they [her detractors] can pour everything they detest about politicians, ambitious women, and an American culture they fear is being wrested from their control."[9] The nastiness of the Hillary jokes contrasts sharply with the admiring tone of many of the jokes directed at her husband, as we shall see in the next chapter.

2

I Could Throw All of You out the Window

The Democrats

SLICK WILLIE

Bill Clinton's was the first Internet presidency. Yet for all his talk about "building a bridge to the twenty-first century," he and his supporters, including the famously Internet-savvy Al Gore, made far less use of the information superhighway than their detractors did. The irony here is that the Internet, which began as a tool for intragovernmental communication, wound up being used for political purposes much more quickly by government outsiders than by government insiders. American politics, one supposes, is a tradition-rich system, slow to adapt. Campaigns did not begin to realize the Internet's potential as a mechanism for reaching voters (and donors) until 2004. In the 1990s, the dominant voices were the ones coming from the peanut gallery.

The most irresistible target, not surprisingly, was Clinton's sexual appetites. The history is well known, but to summarize: During his first run at the presidency, Clinton had to answer questions about his alleged involvements with Gennifer Flowers and Paula Jones while he was governor of Arkansas. During his second term in the White House, he had to answer questions about Monica Lewinsky. "If 1998 and 1999 were not favorable years for the person of William Jefferson Clinton," writes Elliott Oring, "they were exceedingly favorable for humor about him."[1] The humor, as it happens, was also surprisingly favorable *to* him. The censorious jokes are mildly so; others might be considered admiring. Some of the jokes are at Lewinsky's expense; others, at Hillary's. Perhaps the least-Clinton-specific jokes allude to the idea that a promiscuous person is one who can't keep his pants on:

> A little boy wanted to be Bill Clinton for Halloween, but he couldn't get door-to-door with his pants around his ankles.

> Q: Did you hear about the Bill Clinton sale at clothing stores on President's Day?
> A: All pants half off.

> Q: Why Does Bill Clinton wear boxer shorts?
> A: To keep his ankles warm!

(During a televised "Rock the Vote" on MTV in 1994, an audience member asked Clinton: "Mr. President, all the world's dying to know. Is it boxers or briefs?" The joke has it wrong: the president's answer was briefs. Here is a Bob Dole version of the joke: "Bob Dole was invited to be interviewed on MTV, much as Bill Clinton was four years ago. They asked him the same question: 'Do you wear boxers or briefs?' 'Depends,' Dole said." Depends, of course, is the name of a brand of adult diapers. This was one of a number of jokes alluding to the possibility that at seventy-three, Bob Dole was too old to be running for president.)

Needless to say, Bill Clinton is not the only politician who became a victim of his own sexual appetites. I found one pants-down joke about Gary Condit, the California congressman who admitted to having an affair with an intern named Chandra Levy but denied any involvement in her death (someone else was eventually charged):

> Q: What will the FBI say when they go to Gary Condit's house to arrest him?
> A: "Mr. Condit, come out with your pants up!"

In this next joke, Clinton is overtly linked to an older generation of philandering politicians, Ted Kennedy and Bob Packwood, and distinguished from Dan Quayle, whose intellectual failings were summed up in his widely publicized misspelling of the word "potato" during a visit to a school spelling bee in 1992.

Q: If Ted Kennedy, Dan Quayle, Bob Packwood, and Bill Clinton all had a spelling contest, which one would win?
A: Dan Quayle. He's the only one who knows that harass is one word.

And while we're on the subject of nudity, who better to come up with the perfect plan to foil hijackers than the former president:

Subject: Suggestions
Federal Aviation Agency
800 Independence Avenue S.W.
Washington D.C. 20591

Dear Sirs;
I have the solution for the prevention of hijackings, and at the same time getting our airline industry back on its feet. Since men of the Muslim religion are not allowed to look at naked women we should replace all of our female flight attendants with strippers.
Muslims would be afraid to get on the planes for fear of seeing a naked woman, and of course, everyone in this country would start flying again in hopes of seeing a naked woman. We would have no more hijackings, and the airline industry would have record sales.
Now why didn't Congress think of this?

Sincerely,
Bill Clinton

A photographic version of this joke (I found it at JibJab.com) goes a step further: everyone on the plane is nude. A May 2008 *New Yorker* cover shows a naked passenger going through airport security. Here, though, the spoof, heading into the summer travel season, is of the ever-more-draconian airport security measures rather than of Islamic prudery.
Next we have a set of what's-the-difference jokes, the humor of which is predicated on what seems to be the distinguishing feature of one of the contrasted entities turning out to be the distinguishing feature of the other. The first couple focus on Clinton; the next five, on Lewinsky:

Q: What's the difference between Bill Clinton and his dog Buddy?
A: One tries to hump the leg of every woman in the White House, the other is a chocolate Lab.

Q: What's the difference between Clinton and a screwdriver?
A: A screwdriver turns in screws, and Clinton screws interns.

This one appears to be a Lewinsky joke but is really another Clinton joke:

Q: What's the difference between Monica Lewinsky and the rest of us?
A: In order for us to get some dick in the White House, we had to go out and vote.

Q: What's the difference between Watergate and Zippergate?
A: This time we know who Deep Throat is.

A variation:

Q: What is Lewinsky's code name in the FBI?
A: Deep Throat.

The thing that's interesting about these last two is the way Deep Throat began as the title for a 1972 pornographic film about oral sex, then was applied to the primary source for Carl Bernstein and Bob Woodward in their reporting on the Watergate scandal for the *Washington Post*. (The identity of Woodward and Bernstein's source was not revealed until 2005, when former FBI deputy director Mark Felt came forward.) The Watergate scandal, in turn, has served as a template for all subsequent "-gate" scandals in Washington. Zippergate permits the merger of Deep Throat's sexual and political meanings.

The flip side of the what's-the-difference joke is the what-do-X-and-Y-have-in-common joke:

Q: What do Monica Lewinsky and soda pop machines have in common?
A: They both have slots which say "Insert Bill Here."

Q: What do Monica Lewinsky and the Buffalo Bills have in common?
A: They both blew the big one several times.

The Bills lost four consecutive Super Bowls from 1991 to 1994. "The big one" can refer both to Clinton as the most powerful man in the world and to his penis. Is there a connection between political power and sexual potency?

There is this sense that a powerful sexual appetite goes hand in hand with other kinds of power, and perhaps a folk belief that phallic power is a source of political power—or at least explains Bill Clinton's power over women. Probably the other reason the Lewinsky scandal lent itself to jokes is that our endless euphemisms for sex and sexual parts make it so easy to pun on the literal and figurative meanings. Note the clumsy pun in this next riddle joke:

Q: What was the first thing Monica saw in government?
A: The Executive Branch.

Inevitably we come to the lightbulb jokes.[2] Note the inversion of responsibility from the first joke to the second, which may reflect the view that, far from being the victim of a power-abusing boss, Lewinsky was the aggressor and wound up causing no end of trouble for poor old Bubba:

Q: How many Bill Clintons does it take to screw in a lightbulb?
A: Zero. He only screws interns.

Variation:

Q: How many White House Interns does it take to screw in a lightbulb?
A: None, they are too busy screwing the President.

Some other riddle jokes:

Q: What does Clinton say to interns as they leave his office?
A: "Don't hit your head on the desk."

Q: How do you know Bill Clinton is done having sex?
A: You have to wipe the "White-Water" off your blouse . . .
[Whitewater is a reference to the Clintons' investment in a shady Arkansas real estate deal.]

Q: What does Bill Clinton say to Hillary Clinton after having sex?
A: "I will be home in 20 minutes, dear."

Q: How will history remember Bill Clinton?
A: The President after Bush.

Q: Why is Clinton so interested in events in the Middle East?
A: He thinks the Gaza Strip is a topless bar.

Q: What did Clinton say when asked if he had used protection?
A: "Sure, there was a guard standing right outside the door."

In contrast to Bill Clinton's own hair-splitting definition of sex, the jokes, as a cycle, don't seem to make any meaningful distinction between screwing around and screwing. If sex between Clinton and Lewinsky was limited to her performing oral sex on him, he would have had little interest in her "bush" or "slot" (except, perhaps, as a place to put his cigar) and did not need to worry about "protection" against an unwanted pregnancy.

The next set of story jokes is less interested in the president's sexual immorality than in his sexual prowess—and his brazenness. In these jokes, Clinton becomes a trickster of Herculean sexual appetites (and in a remarkable turnabout, Hillary becomes a sympathetic dupe). The logic is this: if the Flowers, Jones, and Lewinsky dalliances are the ones we know about, might there be countless others that Clinton got away with? If so, more power to him.

When Bill and Hillary first got married Bill said, "I am putting a box under the bed. You must promise never to look in it." In all their 30 years of marriage Hillary never looked.

However, on the afternoon of their 30th anniversary, curiosity got the best of her and she lifted the lid and peeked inside. In the box were 3 empty beer cans and $81,874.25 in cash.

She closed the box and put it back under the bed. Now that she knew what was in the box, she was doubly curious as to why.

That evening they were out for a special dinner. After dinner Hillary could no longer contain her curiosity and she confessed, saying, "I am so sorry. For all these years I kept my promise and never looked into the box under our bed. However, today the temptation was too much and I gave in. But now I need to know, why do you keep the cans in the box?"

Bill thought for a while and said, "I guess after all these years you deserve to know the truth. Whenever I was unfaithful to you I put an empty beer can in the box under the bed to remind myself not to do it again."

Hillary was shocked, but said, "Hmmm, Jennifer, Paula and Monica. I am very disappointed and saddened but temptation does happen and I guess that 3 times is not that bad considering the years."

They hugged and made their peace.

A little while later Hillary asked Bill, "So why do you have all that money in the box?"

Bill answered, "Well, whenever the box filled up with empty cans, I took them to the recycling center and redeemed them for cash."

The details make this an odd joke. Using beer cans seems a peculiar way to keep count of one's extramarital affairs (apart from the beer cans' conformity to Clinton's "bubba" image) until we learn that there are enough of them to recycle. Why that dollar amount, apart from the verisimilitude lent by exactitude? And how likely is it that the occupant of the White House would do his own recycling (though it would make an excellent photo opportunity) or go out to dinner? Somewhat endearingly, the joke does not recognize the uniqueness of the Clintons' positions in the world but portrays them as Everycouple, celebrating their anniversary and doing routine household chores just like everyone else. Here is a less successful version, updated for the next presidential election cycle and reflecting the belief in some quarters that Al Gore tended to exaggerate his achievements:

Al Gore was entertaining Joe Lieberman and decided to show off his new home. Upon entering the bedroom, Joe noticed a very large wooden box with 5 empty beer cans and about $1500.00 in cash.

Out of curiosity, Joe asked "Al, I see you're a beer drinker, I am too! you see, we DO have something in common"

With a condescending voice, Al quipped, "yes, of course we do Joe"

Joe then asked "Al, why the 5 empty cans and all that cash"

Al gladly told Joe about his new program. "Joe, since last month, I have decided to turn a new leaf and become a more accountable person, while at the same time rewarding myself for my efforts. Whenever I tell a lie, I drink a beer and put the can in this box"

"That's really impressive", Joe replied, "only 5 beer cans in a whole month, but tell me, where did all that cash come from"?

Without missing a beat, Al responded, "Whenever the box gets full of beer cans, I take it down to the recycling center, you know how concerned I am about environmental issues."

The next joke is predicated on the happy linguistic coincidence whereby we use the same word to mean both a notice of payment due and a draft piece of legislation:

President Clinton looks up from his desk in the Oval Office to see one of his aides nervously approach him. "What is it?" exclaims the President.

"It's the Abortion Bill, Mr. President—what do you want to do about it?"

"Just go ahead and pay it."

The flip side of congratulating Bill Clinton for getting so many women to have sex with him is blaming Hillary Clinton for being an inadequate partner:

Chelsea had the most exciting news. She burst into the room shouting, "Dad! Mom! I have some great news! Nick asked me to marry him. He is like the biggest hunk in Washington. We are supposed to get married next month."

Bill took Chelsea in the back and said, "Chelsea, you're mother, although an ideal administrator and public speaker, has never had much to offer in the sack, so, as you might have heard, I have been known to fool around with other ladies on occasion. Your boyfriend Nick happens to be the product of one of my love making sessions. He is my son and thusly, he is your half-brother."

Chelsea ran out of the office screaming, "Not another brother!"

The next joke, referencing the 1997 movie about the sinking of the Titanic, covers most of the titillating details of the Lewinsky scandal, including the semen stain on Monica's dress, the cigar Clinton inserted in her vagina, and his lying under oath about the affair, and concludes with a dig at poor Hillary, whose sexual frigidity must be the cause of her husband's philandering, as the earlier half-brother joke suggests.

PROBLEM: Two Videos are for sale—Which to Buy? Titanic or the Clinton Video?

TITANIC VIDEO: $9.99 on Internet.
CLINTON VIDEO: $9.99 on Internet.

TITANIC VIDEO: Over 3 hours long.
CLINTON VIDEO: Over 3 hours long.

TITANIC VIDEO: The story of Jack and Rose, their forbidden love, and subsequent catastrophe.
CLINTON VIDEO: The story of Bill and Monica, their forbidden love, and subsequent catastrophe.

TITANIC VIDEO: Jack is a starving artist.
CLINTON VIDEO: Bill is a bullshit artist.

TITANIC VIDEO: In one scene, Jack enjoys a good cigar.
CLINTON VIDEO: Ditto for Bill.

TITANIC VIDEO: During ordeal, Rose's dress gets ruined.
CLINTON VIDEO: Ditto for Monica.

TITANIC VIDEO: Jack teaches Rose to spit.
CLINTON VIDEO: Let's not go there.

TITANIC VIDEO: Rose gets to keep her jewelry.
CLINTON VIDEO: Monica's forced to return her gifts.

TITANIC VIDEO: Rose remembers Jack for the rest of her life.
CLINTON VIDEO: Clinton doesn't remember Jack.

TITANIC VIDEO: Rose goes down on a vessel full of seamen.
CLINTON VIDEO: Monica . . . uh, never mind.

TITANIC VIDEO: Jack surrenders to an icy death.
CLINTON VIDEO: Bill goes home to Hillary . . . basically the same thing.

Compare this quickie:

An official Gallup survey polled over 1,000 women with the question: Would you sleep with Bill Clinton?
1% said, "No"
2% said, "Yes"
97% said, "Never Again."

This joke is more ambivalent than the previous ones. On the one hand, President Clinton managed to charm his way into a thousand beds. On the other hand, his partners apparently didn't enjoy it much. Perhaps as the details of Clinton's encounters with Lewinsky emerged, and we learned of his reluctance to "go all the way," or even to allow himself to climax during oral sex, he started to sound oddly priggish, and not all that much fun. On the other hand, it may be that the joke takes the female point of view, while some of the more appreciative jokes about oral sex take the male view that oral sex is preferable to intercourse insofar as the entire focus is where men would prefer it to be, and they don't have to worry, at least for the moment, about their partner's pleasure. From this point of view, it's a feather in Clinton's cap that he got Monica to pleasure him without his having to reciprocate. Implicit also, perhaps, is an appreciation of the way Clinton, by limiting his relations with Lewinsky to oral sex, was later able to say that (technically) he did not have sex with her. One might say he grew into his nickname, Slick Willie, with its double-double meaning (slick = shrewd/slippery; Willie = diminutive of his name/penis).

This next set of jokes clearly came later, insofar as each references Hillary's election to the Senate:

> Hillary Clinton goes to her doctor for a physical, only to find out that she's pregnant. She is furious. Here she's in the middle of her first term as Senator of New York and this has happened to her. She calls home, gets Bill on the phone and immediately starts screaming; "How could you have let this happen? With all that's going on right now, you go and get me pregnant! How could you? I can't believe this! I just found out I am five weeks pregnant and it is all your fault! Your fault! Well, what have you got to say?"
>
> There is nothing but dead silence on the phone.
>
> She screams again, "Did you hear me?"
>
> Finally she hears Bill's very, very quiet voice. In a barely audible whisper, he says, "Who is this?"

The next joke takes the blaming of Hillary a step further: Bill cheats on her because she is a lesbian. As with many letter jokes, the punch line is the identity of the writer, withheld until the end.

> Dear Abby,
>
> My husband is a liar and a cheat. He has cheated on me from the beginning, and when I confront him, he denies everything. What's

worse, everyone knows he cheats on me. It is so humiliating. Also, since he lost his job four years ago, he hasn't even looked for a new one.

All he does is buy cigars and cruise around and bullshit with his pals, while I have to work to pay the bills. Since our daughter went away to college, he doesn't even pretend to like me and hints that I am a lesbian. What should I do?

Signed, Clueless

Dear Clueless:

Grow up and dump him. For Pete's sake, you don't need him anymore.

You're a United States senator from New York. Act like it!

This joke has Hillary taking far more drastic action:

Senator Hillary Clinton snuck off to visit a fortuneteller of some local repute. In a dark and hazy room, peering into a crystal ball, the mystic delivered grave news.

"There's no easy way to say this, so I'll just be blunt: Prepare yourself to be a widow. Your husband will die a violent and horrible death this year."

Visibly shaken, Hillary stared at the woman's lined face, then at the single flickering candle, then down at her hands. She took a few deep breaths to compose herself. She simply had to know. She met the fortuneteller's gaze, steadied her voice, and asked her question.

"Will I be acquitted?"

Our last joke neatly wraps up the Clinton years, suggesting, rightly, that the real harm of the Lewinsky scandal was that defending himself prevented the president from dealing with far more pressing problems, while also summarizing Hillary's image problem:

Bill Clinton was walking along the beach when he stumbled upon a Genie's lamp. He picked it up and rubbed it and lo-and-behold, a Genie appeared. Bill was amazed and asked if he got three wishes.

The Genie said, "Nope . . . Due to inflation, constant downswing, low wages in third world countries, and fierce global competition, I can only grant you one wish. So . . . What'll it be?"

Bill didn't hesitate. He said, "I want to be remembered for bringing peace to the Middle East, instead of that other stuff with Monica, and

Jennifer, and the rest of those women. See this map? I want these countries to stop fighting with each other."

The Genie looked at the map of the Middle East and exclaimed, "Jeez,
Fella! These people have been at war for thousands of years. I'm good,
but not THAT good. I don't think it can be done. Make another wish."

Bill thought for a minute and said, "You know, people really don't like
my wife. Even though she got elected, they call her a carpetbagger. They
think she's mean, ugly, and pushes me around. I wish for her to be the
most beautiful woman in the world and I want everybody to like her.
That's what I want."

The Genie let out a long sigh and said, "Lemme see that map again."

It should be noted, parenthetically, that there are several variant forms
of the genie-with-a-map joke, which is itself a subgenre of the enormous
corpus of genie-grants-three-wishes jokes. The versions of the map joke I
ran across are, in turn, examples of the even larger corpus of jokes about the
war between men and women. In one, a woman is seeking the right man,
"one that's considerate and fun, likes to cook and help with the house clean-
ing, is great in bed, and gets along with my family, doesn't watch sports all
the time, and is faithful." In the other, a man wants to understand women.
In both cases, the genie decides it might be easier to bring about peace in
the Middle East after all. The Y2K (see chapter 7) problem gave rise to yet
another variation:

An executive is vacationing on the beach. A bottle washes up. He picks
it up and uncorks it. A genie oozes out and says, "Look. It's been a tough
week and I'm all tuckered out. I can only grant you one wish."

The exec thinks for a moment and says, "Well, I've always wanted a
bridge from California to Hawaii."

Genie says, "Gimme a break. No can do a bridge. Try again."

The exec says, "OK. Tell me everything I need to know to keep my
business from failing in the Year 2000."

Genie sighs and says, "Alright. Do you want that bridge two lanes or
four?"

And returning to our earlier jokes about Monica Lewinsky performing
oral sex on President Clinton, there's this genie joke:

Monica Lewinsky was walking on the beach when she found a lantern
washed up on the shore. She started to rub it and out popped a genie.

"Oh goodie, now I will get three wishes!" she exclaims.

"No," said the genie, "You have been very bad in recent years, and because of this, I can only give you one wish."

"Let's see," says Monica, "I don't need fame, because I have plenty of that due to all of the media coverage. And I don't need money, because after I write my book, My TV show, and do all my interviews, I'll have all the money I could ever want. I would like to get rid of these love handles, though . . . Yes, that's it, for my one wish, I would like my love handles removed."

POOF!!!!

And just like that . . . her ears were gone!

GORE LORE

Years from now, if one wanted to know why the 2000 election finished in a virtual dead heat despite Al Gore's being the more experienced and intelligent candidate and his having been the vice president during an era of peace and prosperity, one could do worse than to look at the more popular jokes about him. The jokes represent distillations, however unfair, of what became the conventional wisdom about him: First, Gore was considered boring, wooden, and stiff, attributes that do not play well on television.[3] Second, as we saw earlier, he was thought to have a penchant for overstating his contributions, an idea that took hold after an interview in 1999 with CNN's Wolf Blitzer where Gore said that as a member of Congress he "took the initiative in creating the Internet." Gore's defenders say that what he clearly meant was that he took the lead formulating policies that made the Internet possible. His detractors said he was claiming to have invented the Internet.[4] The Gore's-a-stiff jokes:

A man died on a subway train in New York City and his body rode the train for five hours before anyone noticed it. Apparently they thought it was just Al Gore in town to campaign for Hillary Clinton's Senate bid.

Baseball great Ted Williams is endorsing George W. Bush for president. However his bat is endorsing Al Gore.

News Flash: Al Gore was admitted to a hospital yesterday in Washington. Sources tell us that termites thought that Al Gore was an old bed post.

Q: What's the difference between Al Gore and a slab of formica?
A: Absolutely nothing.

On July 8, 1947, witnesses claim a spaceship with five aliens aboard crashed on a sheep-and-cattle ranch outside Roswell, an incident they say has been covered up by the military. March 31, 1948, nine months after that day, Al Gore was born.

That clears up a lot of things.

[This is the most plausible version of this implausible joke. In more grandiose versions, every leading Democrat—or Republican—was born nine months after the UFO landing, which is patently false. Too bad. It would be a fine explanation for why the people who lead our country aren't up to the task—because they're not people at all but the progeny of extraterrestrials and sheep.]

More bad news for Al Gore's quest to become president in 2000. Paula Jones claims he exposed himself to her in a hotel room and he has no distinguishing characteristics whatsoever.

This joke is a sly reference to Jones's sexual harassment lawsuit against President Clinton, which included the lurid tidbit that she could prove Clinton exposed himself to her by describing "distinguishing characteristics" of his penis.

Researchers at Stanford University say they may have found the gene that causes narcolepsy, the disease where people suddenly fall asleep at odd times. If they can find a pill that cures it, the Gore campaign promised to buy the entire supply to spike the punch at his next campaign dinner.

A list of the world's thinnest books had Gore's "The Wild Years" in thirteenth place. (Clinton's "My Book of Morals" took the top spot.) On to the invention jokes:

Vice President Al Gore is supporting a $7.8 billion rescue plan for the Florida Everglades that is being studied by Congress. Al has a special attachment for the Everglades. He didn't invent them, but he does claim to be the first person to ever say, "See you later, alligator."

Vice President Al Gore has a campaign ad showing him and his son Albert Gore III climbing Mount Rainier last year. A mountain-climbing expert in the ad says the qualities needed to climb mountains are the same ones needed in a president. However, when interviewed later, he wouldn't verify Gore's claim that he invented yodeling.

Vice President Al Gore and Hillary Rodham Clinton shared the stage in New York at a rally held by the Young Men's Hebrew Association. They both have personal connections to the members of this organization. Hillary says she has some Jewish ancestors and Al claims he invented bagels and lox.

Hillary Clinton is trying to appeal to Jewish voters in New York by revealing that the second husband of her grandmother was a Russian-born Jew named Max Rosenberg. If that works for her, Al Gore plans to announce he invented the matzo ball.

HANOI JOHN

Four years later, John Kerry was also perceived as wooden, which prompted this joke:

The sci-fi thriller "I Robot," starring Will Smith was a box office hit this summer with its stunning tale of how stiff, but somewhat lifelike automatons try to take over the world. Of course, half the people paying to see the film thought it was about the Kerry campaign.

But most of the newslore about Kerry took the form of photoshops. One of the ways his foes sought to discredit him was by belittling his service in Vietnam and emphasizing his opposition to the war after his return from Vietnam. One of the best ways to cast his opposition in the worst possible light was to link him with other antiwar activists who were thought to be subversives or even traitors. Little wonder, then, that two photos of Kerry with "Hanoi Jane" Fonda were so widely circulated during the campaign. In one photo, Fonda is sitting in the foreground at an antiwar rally, and Kerry is in the background. In the other, Kerry and Fonda share the speaker's

John Kerry and Jane Fonda appear to share a speaker's platform at an antiwar rally in 1971. In fact, the photo is a fake. Jane Fonda was added by a photoshopper to discredit Kerry during the 2004 presidential campaign.

Ken Light's original photograph of Kerry at the rally in Mineola, New York. Jane Fonda did not attend. Photograph © Ken Light, 2004.

platform. The photo appears to have been clipped from a newspaper with headline and caption, including photo credit, attached.[5]

After watching all this Internet traffic, the photographer Ken Light had seen enough. He wrote an opinion piece for the *Washington Post* in which he explained what he knew about the speaker's platform photo. Which turned out to be quite a lot: Light had shot it. He was still in his teens at the time, just getting started as a photographer. He attended the antiwar rally in Mineola, New York, and took a photo of Kerry on the speaker's platform. He didn't get Jane Fonda into the frame for one simple reason: Jane Fonda wasn't there. Light had the negative to prove it. A photo thought to be true turned out to be a fake.[6] Also fake, therefore, were the headline, cutline, and photo credit. The photo was not a joke but a hoax: it was meant to be believed. Given the belief in some quarters that Fonda's trip to Hanoi in 1972 was treasonous, this was photoshopping at its most pernicious.

Naturally, Light's photo cast doubt on the authenticity of the other Kerry-Fonda photo. Naturally, that photo turned out to be the real deal. Unfortunately for Kerry's opponents, the real image wasn't nearly as effective as the fake one. A photo of Kerry and Fonda sitting several rows apart didn't prove they were two peas in a pod. It just proved what everyone already knew— that both Kerry and Fonda strongly believed that the United States needed to bring its troops home from Vietnam. Unfortunately for Kerry, the challenges to his record as a war hero stuck.

A good way to end this chapter is with jokes about the phenomenon that came to be known as Clinton fatigue—the feeling that after eight years of Bill and Hillary and Monica and Paula and Gennifer, the country was ready to turn the page.

A Marine Colonel on his way home from work at the Pentagon came to a dead halt in traffic and thought to himself, "Wow, this traffic seems worse than usual, nothing is moving."

He notices a police officer walking back and forth between the lines of cars, so he rolls down his window and asks, "Excuse me, Officer, what seems to be the hold up?"

The officer replies, "The President is just so depressed that Hillary has moved to New York, and may leave him altogether that he just stopped his motorcade in the middle of the Beltway, and he's threatening to douse himself in gasoline and set himself on fire.

He says his family absolutely hates him and he doesn't have the $33.5 million he owes his lawyers for that whole Monica and Paula thing.

So I'm walking around taking up a collection for him."

"Oh really? How much have you collected so far?"

"So far about three hundred gallons, but I've got a lot of folks still siphoning."

[This became a Hillary joke during the 2008 presidential campaign.]

Bill looks at Al, chuckles and says, "You know, I could throw a $10,000 bill out the window right now and make one person very happy."

Al shrugs his stiff shoulders and says, "Well, I could throw ten $1,000 bills out the window and make 10 people very happy".

Hillary tosses her perfectly sprayed hair and says, "Of course, then, I could throw one-hundred $100 bills out the window and make a hundred people very happy."

Chelsea rolls her eyes, looks at all of them and says, "I could throw all of you out the window and make the whole country happy."

This joke was later updated as a Bush-Cheney-Rumsfeld joke, with the pilot of the plane they're on playing Chelsea's part. But you have to love the detail about Al Gore's stiff shoulders. If we look back at the catastrophic presidency of George W. Bush and wonder how such a lightweight could have served not one but two terms in the White House, the Gore and Kerry jokes remind us that the two Democratic nominees, for all their intelligence and experience, were two singularly ungifted politicians.

3

When the Going Gets Tough
Newslore of September 11

"IT RAISED MY SPIRITS SO I'M PASSING IT ON"

A premise of this book is that we can learn more about how "ordinary Americans" respond to national and world affairs from the mass e-mails they exchange than we can from the news media. In this chapter, I would like to illustrate this point via a chronological look at the e-mails I received in the days and week following the suicide attacks of September 11, 2001. The e-mails suggest that after a brief period of stunned and perhaps respectful silence in the aftermath of the attacks, cybercitizens resumed joking. Most of the jokes played it safe by targeting the Muslim world in general and Osama bin Laden in particular. While some of these jokes were straightforward fantasies of by-the-sword revenge, in the darkest ones, not even obliteration was enough: bin Laden needed to be scatologically and sexually humiliated. The jokes' subversiveness, then, lay not in the challenge they posed to the Bush administration's response to the attacks—if anything, the jokes suggested that a substantial number of citizens supported a military response—but in the challenge they posed to the dispassionate language of the news reports. The hegemony of journalism's objective tradition has been challenged precisely on the grounds that the affectless tone of news reports gives the public the impression that reporters and the news organizations they work for are disengaged from the communities they cover.

The first e-mail I received on September 11 was a forwarded "MESSAGE FROM DR. SPANIER" from the dean of my college. Penn State president

Graham Spanier's message to the faculty urged us to "stand together and do our utmost to provide mutual support and comfort," to meet with our classes as scheduled, to report "safety-related concerns," and to apprise our students of the counseling services available to them. I also received a message from a colleague who knew I grew up in New York and wanted to know if I was "OK."

Then came the mass e-mails, most of which were forwarded to me by my mother. The first of them came with the subject line "Fwd: [Fwd: FW: TRIBUTE TO AMERICA]," the three "forwards" providing the first indication of how widely distributed the messages were. I was one of twenty people who received my mother's forward. (I could see, from the other e-mail addresses, that I was related to at least eight of these people.) But my mother is one of those forwarders who pass a message along as is, without trimming any of the redundancies. So after her group of addressees came the group she was part of, which consisted of another forty-two people. Beneath that group was a third layer of 22 addressees, followed by a fourth set of 15, and a fifth group of 3. That's 102 people, but there's no reason to think it either began or ended with the first group or the fifth. If any of these 102 people forwarded in turn to their own set of e-mail correspondents, we can only guess at the exponential growth in the number of recipients. This is what I mean by a mass e-mail.

"Tribute to America," by the Canadian radio commentator Gordon Sinclair, extolled Americans as "the most generous and possibly the least appreciated people on all the earth."[1] It included lines that sounded, given the timing, as if they were alluding to the September 11 attacks: "They will come out of this thing with their flag high. And when they do, they are entitled to thumb their nose at the lands that are gloating over their present troubles." In fact, though, another "Tribute" e-mail forwarded by a friend explained that Sinclair's commentary was originally broadcast in 1973. Its opening sentence, deleted from the first version I received, made clear what had occasioned it: "The United States dollar took another pounding on German, French, and British exchanges this morning hitting the lowest point ever known in West Germany." Not terribly earth-shaking compared to 9/11.

In any case, an anonymous link in the long chain of forwarders added the following peevish postscript:

This is one of the best editorials that I have ever read regarding the United States. It is nice that one man realizes it. I only wish that the rest of the world would realize it. We are always blamed for everything and never even get a thank you for the things we do.

I would hope that each of you would send this to as many people as you can and emphasize that they should send it to as many of their friends until this letter is sent to every person on the web. I am just a single American that has read this.

One of the e-mails I received ended there. The other continued, "I am just a single American who has read this, but I SURE HOPE THAT A LOT MORE READ IT SOON," which suggests that this tag end was inadvertently cut off the other version.

The second mass e-mail I received from my mother on September 13 was essentially a condolence card to America from the assistant manager of a hotel in Baja California. "This note I've forwarded can be viewed as a clever marketing tool," a forwarder named Karen wrote. "I choose, however, to feel warmed, moved and refreshed by the thoughts shared here."

My mother received the next mass e-mail from my sister, who commented, "This one's intense!" The message, authored by a Floridian named Charles Bennett, was a paean to America's freedom and Americans' spirit. The accompanying note, from someone preceding my sister in the chain:

> i received this early this morning........it raised my spirits a bit so i'm passing it on.
> xoxo
> jo-anne

The Bennett piece bore some resemblance to one written by Leonard Pitts in his popular 9/11 column. Here are the last lines of Bennett's essay: "Wait until you see what we do with that Spirit, this time. Sleep tight, if you can. We're coming." And here is how Pitts's column ends: "You don't know my people. You don't know what we're capable of. You don't know what you just started. But you're about to learn."[2] If the twenty-six-thousand e-mails Pitts received in response to the column are any indication, the column reflected a widespread thirst for vengeance that provided political cover for the Bush administration's subsequent invasions of Afghanistan and Iraq.

The next day, September 14, I received a rather more scholarly forward from my wife with the subject line "Sources of Terrorism Against the US." Attributed to Steve Niva, a professor of international politics and Middle East studies at Evergreen State College—I verified that Niva is, in fact, on the faculty at Evergreen State—the message outlines, at considerable length, some of the causes of Islamist anger at the United States while stressing that "there is no justification for the horrendous attacks on innocent American civilians in New York or Washington." Commented one of the forwarders: "I thought this analysis of US policies and Middle East politics might be useful to members of the Family Medicine and Community Health list. I know I need all the information I can get about this situation."

The same day as the Niva essay landed in my in-box, I received what my sister labeled "Another weird one!" before she passed it on to my mother. Here is that e-mail in its entirety:

> for those of you who are not familiar with this, within jewish mysticism is the study of numerology. the letters all have number values. though i don't know what the significance of all this is, i have to admit that it piques my curiosity.
> i remember years ago, when israel was being attacked by scud missiles, we received a letter from a girl from israel, who showed us the numbers of the "patriot" missiles and that they had the same number value of "shom-er", which means watchman, and is one of the hebrew names for god.
> this may mean nothing to you, and i am not suggesting that it should. enjoy it for what it is worth, and delete it if it seems meaningless to you.
> always wondering,
> jo-anne

> The date of the attack: 9/11 - 9 + 1 + 1 = 11
> September 11th is the 254th day of the year: 2 + 5 + 4 = 11
> After September 11th there are 111 days left to the end of the year.
> 119 is the area code to Iraq/Iran. 1 + 1 + 9 = 11
> Twin Towers - standing side by side, looks like the number 11
> The first plane to hit the towers was Flight 11
> I Have More.......
> State of New York - The 11 State added to the Union
> New York City - 11 Letters
> Afghanistan - 11 Letters
> The Pentagon - 11 Letters
> Ramzi Yousef - 11 Letters (convicted of orchestrating the attack on the WTC in 1993)
> Flight 11 - 92 on board - 9 + 2 = 11
> Flight 77 - 65 on board - 6 + 5 = 11
> The date of the attack: 9/11 - 9 + 1 + 1 = 11
> September 11th is the 254th day of the year: 2 + 5 + 4 = 11
> After September 11th there are 111 days left to the end of the year.

119 is the area code to Iraq/Iran. 1 + 1 + 9 = 11
Twin Towers - standing side by side, looks like the number 11
The first plane to hit the towers was Flight 11

A mass e-mail that arrived on September 16 exhorted the receiver to "keep the message going," though unlike other chain e-mails, it threatens no consequences as a result of not doing so:

We are keeping this candle burning for all the people & their families who were in the planes, buildings and anywhere near the explosions today. May God be with them and help them through this terrible time.

God Bless

Keep The Candle Going

I asked God for water, he gave me an ocean.
I asked God for a flower, he gave me a garden.
I asked God for a tree, he gave me a forest.
I asked God for a friend, he gave me YOU.

"There is not enough darkness in the world to put out the light of one candle."

The Candle of Love, Hope and Friendship

```
()
||
||
||
||
||
————
```

This candle was lit on the 11th of September, 2001. Someone who loves you has helped keep it alive by sending it to you.

Don't let The Candle Of Love, Hope and Friendship die!

"A candle loses nothing by lighting another candle"

What can this partial collection of mass e-mails from the first week after the attacks tell us? In contrast to the brevity and frivolity typical of so much computer-mediated communication, all the material shared in the immediate aftermath of September 11 was serious, and much of it was remarkably long. People were angry, sad, and bewildered, and they were willing to read whatever best expressed those states of mind. Even Dan Kurtzman, the steward of the vast About.com humor Web site, posted the following message to regular visitors on September 13:

> In light of recent events, there will be no new humor material posted to this site this week.
>
> Eventually, laughter will have an important role to play in helping heal our national psyche, but now is clearly not the time.
>
> For the latest news and commentary, I recommend you check out About.com's special coverage of America under attack, as well as some of the other useful links and resources listed on this page.
>
> If you would like to be notified when About Political Humor returns with new material, feel free to sign up for my newsletter and I'll drop you a line.
>
> My heart goes out to all those who perished in this terrible tragedy and to all those mourning the loss of loved ones.
>
> To find out ways you can help, click here.[3]

The revival of Sinclair's Canadian tribute and the condolence message from Baja suggest a need for reassurance, after being stunned by Islamist hatred, that not everyone hates us. The Bennett piece gives voice to America's anger and thirst for vengeance, while Professor Niva's remarks counsel a more temperate response. If Bennett represents the hawkish and perhaps conservative response to September 11, and Niva the dovish and possibly liberal response, together they tell us that the world of computer-mediated communication is the domain of neither the political right nor the political left.

If this small sampling is representative of the totality of what was swirling around cyberspace from September 11 to 17, the numerological analysis and the chain candle would indicate a shift from positivistic to mystical responses. After all the tough talk and calls to action, it may have begun to sink in that there wasn't much we civilians could do about what had happened. And as the anthropologist Bronislaw Malinowski pointed out in his landmark study of magic in the Trobriand Islands in the 1920s, when rational explanations and behaviors are less than satisfying, we become receptive to less rational approaches.[4] Numerology assures us that there is an internal logic to events that on the surface seem inexplicable. In the absence of the comfort of action, the candle chain offers the comfort of virtual communion, which is the comfort of e-mailing itself.

But then, on September 18, it was as if a barrier had been lifted: It became okay to joke and to spread stories of dubious veracity.

WHEN THE GOING GETS TOUGH, THE TOUGH GO PHOTOSHOPPING

The first September 11 joke I received, one week after the attacks,[5] was a visual one: a digitally altered photographic design for a new World Trade Center with five towers, the middle one taller than the rest.[6] To build an even more imposing structure on the site of the towers would already be an act of defiance. To build it in the shape of the *digitus impudicus* is to give symbolic form to that act of defiance. The folklorists Joseph Goodwin and Bill Ellis both suggested that America suffered a symbolic castration when the Twin Towers were toppled.[7] "The finger" would signal a return to potency. On another level, the *digitus impudicus* is simply a gesture of impotent rage: it's about all a driver can do to express his displeasure with another motorist who has cut him off—although it could be argued that even here the expression "to cut someone off" suggests that to be thwarted in one's forward automotive progress is to suffer a symbolic castration.

The other photoshopped image I received on this theme (on September 29) substituted the finger for Lady Liberty's torch. In keeping with the folk penchant for recycling images and motifs,[8] Lady Liberty's obscene gesture recalls folk cartoons of Mickey Mouse making the same gesture in response to Iranian students' seizure of the U.S. Embassy in Tehran in 1979.[9] The cartoon, photocopied and faxed, expressed the feeling that after Vietnam, America had become too innocent, too cuddly, and so risk-averse that we gave our enemies the impression that if they hit us, we would not hit back. (One argument for keeping our troops in Iraq after Saddam Hussein had been overthrown was that the Iraqi insurgents were counting on Americans to weary of war before the country had been stabilized.) The cartoon said, in

NEW DESIGN FOR REBUILDING THE WORLD TRADE CENTER

Within days of the September 11 attacks, photoshoppers began circulating their design suggestions for a new World Trade Center.

effect, hey, don't underestimate us. Mickey gave way to Lady Liberty, perhaps because the Statue of Liberty appeared in some of the New York harbor photos and video footage of the World Trade Center site and is as much a New York symbol as it is an American symbol. As Dundes and Pagter say, "Stressful and traumatic events of national or international scope often stimulate the generation of new folklore—although the new folklore may turn out to be old folklore in disguise."[10]

Returning to our chronology, on September 20 I received a warning from my brother-in-law about the Klingerman virus, an item that I had already received from my mother back on February 10, 2001, but which seemed to take on new life after September 11 amid speculation that the terrorists might follow up with biological or chemical attacks. (The anthrax mailings did not happen until October.) To a student of urban legends, much about this e-mail was immediately familiar. There was a disclaimer from a sender who felt compelled to express some skepticism lest any of his or her addressees think him a fool for believing such obvious nonsense: "Could be a scam but anything is possible, as we all know." The subtext seems to be

This much-recopied piece of photocopier-and-fax-machine lore circulated after Iranian militants stormed the U.S. Embassy in 1979 and held seventy Americans hostage for 444 days.

A lot of the photocopier lore from the Iranian hostage crisis reappeared during Operation Desert Storm in Iraq in 1991 and again—in updated digital form—in response to the September 11 attacks.

that the idea of terrorists using American passenger planes as missiles to attack American buildings would also have seemed farfetched before September 11. There was the acknowledgment that people might dismiss this as another wacko e-mail if one did not slap on a "WARNING" label—in capital letters—and exhort the recipient to "PLEASE READ" and "PLEASE FORWARD TO ALL YOU KNOW."

> Subject: Warning - Do Not Open Blue Envelopes in your U.S. Mail
> ONCE YOU HAVE READ THIS PLEASE FORWARD TO ALL YOU KNOW.
>
> This is from Schwab corporate headquarters—so it's no joke.
> Very scary.

Be careful Just when you thought you were safe, now we have the following to deal with ... please read, it definitely is a serious threat to our lives and health. This is an alert about a virus in the original sense of the word ... one that affects your body, not your hard drive.

The body of the message goes on to warn that blue envelopes labeled "A Gift from the Klingerman Foundation" contain sponges laced with "a strain of virus they have not previously encountered." Journalistic verisimilitude is attempted via a quote attributed to "Florida police sergeant Stetson," though a journalist would look askance at the lack of a first name, the lack of a specific reference to a city police force or the state police, and that name Stetson, which would be a good choice for a southern lawman in a work of fiction. The other interesting thing about the Klingerman virus warning is that, as the "please read" preamble suggests, it restores the literal meeting of virus in a realm that has been dominated by figurative use of the word "virus" to refer to "contagious" computer problems and "viral" to refer to the computer-to-computer spread of the material in this book. If your computer can catch an electronic virus by opening an e-mail, it makes sense that your body can catch a biological virus by opening a piece of snail mail.[11]

Another wave of warning e-mails arrived in mid-October, timed to connect September 11 to Halloween. I received the first on October 11 from a student who had been in a class where we had talked, among other things, about urban legends. The message begins thus: "What you are about to read is a letter that was forwarded to me by a close and honest friend." And here is how the letter begins: "My friend's friend was dating a guy from Afghanistan up until a month ago." The letter explains that the Afghan boyfriend "stood up" the friend's friend. When she went to his apartment to confront him, she found that he had cleared out. Then she got a letter from him in which he said he could not explain why but "BEGGED her not to get on any commercial airlines on 9/11 AND TO NOT GO TO ANY MALLS ON HALLOWEEN." The letter concludes with the writer attesting to the warning's authenticity:

This is not an email that I've received and decided to pass on. This came from a phone conversation with a long-time friend of mine last night.

I may be wrong, and I hope I am. However, with one of his warnings being correct and devastating, I'm not willing to take the chance on the second and wanted to make sure that people I cared about had the same information that I did.

A second version, also passed along by a student, was attributed to "a friend of someone I work with." This is a less detailed version, and it ends thus: "I just heard this tonight, and the source in the company here is pretty credible (one of the partners), so I thought I'd pass the word of caution on to all of you about Halloween, just in case there's any truth to it."

Yet another of my students wrote his own introduction to a third version:

> Dear Professor Frank,
> I received the following email from a friend a week or so ago. I found it interesting at first because it wasn't sent as a "FWD: fwd: fwd: FWD: Read This!!!: Fwd: Possible terrorist attack on Halloween" but written as if he knew the girl personally. I checked up on it, and two of my roommates had received the exact same email, except as a "FWD: fwd:...." message. I don't know if you've already seen this message floating around or not, but I thought you might find it intriguing. In the wake of September 11th, such "warnings" seem inevitable, given our discussions on Urban Legends. When I asked one of my roommates what he thought about the "Halloween email," he replied "I guess there's no shopping for me on October 31st." When further questioned, he admitted he didn't really believe the email was true, but he'd rather be safe then sorry. He admitted he doesn't shop all that much anyway, so staying in wouldn't be too much of a problem.

Here is the text of his version:

> The last thing I want to do is scare you guys but last night one of my friends was telling me that her friend's bf was from the middle east and dissapeared on Sept 8th. He left her a note telling her to stay away from planes on the 11th and not to go to the malls on Halloween.
> Just for my sake please be careful on halloween and use your judgement. I can't be sure this is completely true but I care about you guys so I'd prefer you stayed away from shopping on halloween. Buy your things a day or 2 early instead.
> I hope that this is all a big lie but i just wanted you to be safe.

About.com's Netlore Archive offered a version that began with a quintessential urban legend disclaimer:

Hi All—

I think you all know that I don't send out hoaxes and don't do the reactionary thing and send out anything that crosses my path. This one, however, is a friend of a friend and I've given it enough credibility in my mind that I'm writing it up and sending it out to all of you.

The Netlore Archive provides links to a *New York Times* story[12] and offers four variants labeled "My friend Colleen . . . ," "My friend Jill . . . ," "From Someone Who Works at Sprint . . . ," and "Her friend that lives right here in Baltimore . . ."[13]

Readers unfamiliar with the strange world of urban legends will readily see from this sampling why folklorists sometimes refer to these stories as "foaflore"—short for friend-of-a-friend lore. The warnings to avoid malls on Halloween may have been a response to speculation that the terrorists might next strike in the American heartland to further demoralize Americans with the message that no place is safe. (I remember hearing a loud, low-flying plane while raking leaves on a football Saturday that fall and becoming convinced that it was going to crash into Penn State's Beaver Stadium, where it could potentially kill many more people than were lost in the World Trade Center attacks.) The warnings also bear an interesting relation to politicians' exhorting Americans to defeat the terrorists by going about their business—including the business of shopping. "Go to restaurants," said New York City mayor Rudolph Giuliani. "Go shopping. Do things. Show that you're not afraid. Show confidence in yourself and the city."[14]

The shopping mall warnings also partake of a larger tradition of Halloween legends, from warnings about pins or razor blades in Halloween treats to rumors that circulate on college campuses from time to time that a costumed psychopath is planning to kill dorm residents on Halloween.[15] (In some versions, a psychic reveals this plot to Oprah Winfrey, who has become a category of urban legend in her own right. Supposedly she booted the fashion designer Tommy Hilfiger [or Liz Claiborne] off her show when he confirmed rumors that he never intended for blacks to buy his clothes. Calls for a boycott ensued.)[16]

In a variation on the mall warning story sometimes referred to as "The Grateful Terrorist," an Arab warns someone who has done him a favor (like chipping in a small amount of money for his groceries when she learned he was short of cash) not to drink Coke or Pepsi after a certain date. The stories don't say why drinking the colas would be a bad idea, but presumably plans were afoot to contaminate them. The story thus connects both to the Klingerman legend and to classic urban legends about contaminated products, especially tales of mice in Coke bottles.[17] Why Coke and Pepsi? What better way to sow terror than to tamper with the most ubiquitous consumer product on earth? *Forbes* reported in 2003 that 1.2 billion eight-ounce servings of Coke are consumed daily worldwide.[18] The Web site of the Coca Cola Bottling Company's Indonesia branch devotes considerable space in its FAQ section to debunking "myths and rumours."[19]

But back to our chronology. On September 22, my mother forwarded "Flight to Washington," an anonymous note from someone who flew from Denver to Washington with a captain who gave the passengers a strength-in-numbers pep talk about how to subdue hijackers, if any should happen to be on board, and a crew member who urged the passengers to introduce themselves to each other and show each other family photos. The sender and forwarder comments were "The following is from a letter by a professional friend and her return flight to D.C. this week" and "This was passed along to me by a friend. Interesting."

Here, I think, we're seeing two influences coming into play. One is the stirring tale of the passengers on Flight 93 who tried to wrest control from the hijackers and succeeded to the extent that the plane crashed into a field in rural Pennsylvania rather than into its intended target, which might have been the White House or the U.S. Capitol. The other is the recognition that, for all the tough talk about revenge, the only opportunity most of us would have to confront the terrorists would be if we met up with them on a flight. Sooner or later, we were all going to have to resume normal activities, including flying. This was a way to steel ourselves for the experience.

An e-mail with a related message arrived on September 27. Called "I Forgot," it places responsibility for September 11 on our own shoulders. Each time Osama bin Laden revealed his intentions in bombings throughout the 1990s, it says, we expressed outrage, then "forgot." This time, the piece concludes, we must not forget:

> Please, Please, Please, if you are reading this, don't look away when they show the airplanes flying into the buildings on TV, look at it over and over again !! Don't stick your head in the sand! Remember how despicable the act was, remember the loss of life, don't shield your children, use restraint, but help them understand it, and remember it! They are our future! You will go back to work, and resume your daily duties, but, PLEASE, PLEASE, PLEASE, DON'T EVER FORGET! I assure you the

terrorists around the world are counting on us to! AGAIN! I fear the next time we will see a mushroom cloud on our beautiful horizon! Then it will be too late! All because WE FORGOT!

"THIS ONE WILL MAKE YOU CRINGE"

My brother-in-law sent me an unforgettable image on September 28, along with a noncommittal message: "Check this out." Also included were prior forwarders' similarly neutral messages: "If you haven't seen" (September 26) and "This is interesting" (September 25). But the message that appears to have accompanied the original transmission goes like this: "This picture was developed from film in a camera found in the rebble of the wtc!!!!!! person in picture still not identified." A tagline at the bottom of the photo said, "SUPPORT YOUR POLICE, FIRE, AND EMS PERSONEL."

Another version of the accompanying message, reproduced on the Netlore Web site, appeared under the subject line "Different Perspective on the New York Tragedy":

> Attached is a picture that was taken of a tourist atop the World Trade Center Tower, the first to be struck by a terrorist attack. This camera was found but the subject in the picture had not yet been located. Makes you see things from a very different position. Please share this and find any way you can to help Americans not to be victims in the future of such cowardly attacks.

And a third version, on Snopes.com:

> We've seen thousands of pictures covering the attack. However, this one will make you cringe. A simple tourist getting himself photographed on the top of the WTC just seconds before the tragedy . . . The camera was found in the rubble!!

"For just the briefest split-second of gut reaction," wrote the *Chicago Sun-Times* columnist Richard Roeper, "we thought we were seeing one of the most astonishing photos in recorded history."[20] On closer inspection, one sees that there are enough holes in this image to fly several airplanes through. Netlore enumerated most of them:

Many people were taken in by the original Tourist Guy image, which was usually accompanied by a message asserting the camera was found in the rubble and urging support for the troops.

- Why isn't the fast-moving aircraft blurry in the photo?
- Why doesn't the subject (or the photographer, for that matter) seem to be aware of the plane's high-decibel approach?
- The temperature was between 65 and 70 degrees that morning. Why is this man dressed for winter?
- How did the camera survive the 110-story fall when the tower collapsed?
- How was the camera found so quickly amidst all the rubble?
- Why has this one-of-a-kind, newsworthy photo not appeared in any media venue?

Those were the obvious illogicalities. Roeper, who aptly referred to the images as "photographic urban legends," pointed out more arcane clues to the images' inauthenticity: "There was no observation deck on the north tower, and the deck on the south tower wasn't scheduled to open until 9:30 a.m. that day." Also, "The American Airlines jet shown in the photo is a Boeing 757, but the American Airlines plane that struck the tower was a Boeing 767."[21]

And so Tourist Guy, as he came to be called (or alternatively, the Ground Zero Geek, which I prefer), was revealed to be a hoax. Did that cause him

Once Tourist Guy was debunked as a fake, a succession of spoof versions followed.

In this version of Tourist Guy, the World Trade Center is menaced by the Stay Puft Marshmallow Man from the movie *Ghostbusters*.

An alternative tradition developed wherein Tourist Guy appears at the scene of various earth-shattering events, such as the assassination of President Kennedy in Dallas in 1963.

The joke-within-the-joke in this image of Tourist Guy at the crash of the *Hindenburg* in Lakehurst, New Jersey, in 1937, as with the Kennedy motorcade image, is the faux-digital date in the right-hand corner.

In another twist on the Tourist Guy tradition, the variable is Tourist Guy himself, here replaced by Osama bin Laden.

to disappear from view? Hardly. As with e-mailed warnings, the hoax gave way to parodies of the hoax.[22] We see the same guy on the same observation platform. Only now a subway car is coming at him. Or a hot-air balloon. Or the Stay Puft Marshmallow Man from the 1984 movie *Ghostbusters*. Then, instead of the disaster coming to him, the Ground Zero Geek goes to the disaster: the crash of the Concorde in 2000, the bombing of the USS *Cole* at port in Yemen in 2000, the Kennedy motorcade in Dallas in 1963, the crash of the *Hindenburg* in 1937, the sinking of the *Titanic* in 1912, the sinking of the *Titanic*—the movie—in 1997, and President Lincoln's box in Ford's Theatre in 1865. He also drives the bus in the 1994 movie *Speed* and feels the hot breath of Godzilla on his neck. In a later version that only a New York Yankees fan can appreciate, Tourist Guy joins the Boston Red Sox in celebrating their 2004 World Series victory, their first since 1918.[23]

Finally, we go back to the observation platform and the looming menace of the plane, only now it's not the disaster that has morphed into something else, but Tourist Guy himself. He becomes the owner of a giant cat named Snowball in one meta-parody—an image that was almost as popular on the Internet in 2001 as Tourist Guy—and none other than Osama bin Laden in another.

The news media devoted an enormous amount of attention to the seeming arbitrariness of fate. There were countless tales of people who were supposed to be on one of the four planes or at the World Trade Center but were delayed or had to change their plans. The stories emphasized the gratitude and guilt of these survivors. The dominant attitude was awe in the face of so many reminders of the slender thread on which our lives hang. Consider the following headlines:

- Running Late Saved Them from Trade Center Death[24]
- Fiery Escapes, Surreal Stories at Trade Center[25]
- She Got Laid Off, He Missed a Train; Such Lucky Breaks[26]

The photoshoppers were also aghast at the precariousness of life but took a darker view. Sudden death makes a mockery of our plans. It is the ultimate cruel joke. Where the news media dwelled on the solemnity of it all, the newslore focused on the absurdity. If Osama bin Laden was the face of evil, Tourist Guy became the face of absurdity. He is the quintessence of being in the wrong place at the wrong time. In his ignorance of what is about to befall him, he represents all of us on the morning of September 11.[27] The stories about the real victims of that terrible day struggle to particularize them, to assert the meaningfulness of all their lives, in Jack Lule's words, "to make sense of life in the face of the seeming randomness of human existence."[28] Victims became heroes. Death became sacrifice. In contrast, newslore counters the pious approach with an anonymous, fictitious victim that allows for the expression of the subversive, unspeakable view. These deaths were senseless, absurd. We're here one minute, gone the next. What's heroic about it? We're geeks, tourist guys, on planet Earth. As is often the case, the folkloric response may have been the more honest response.

The original Tourist Guy image was plausible, at least at first glance, more urban legend than joke. The apparent motive of the first wave of e-mailers was not to amuse but to appall. Once the picture had been debunked, however, the sense of victimization gave way to relief: Tourist Guy, like the rest of us, had survived. The endless permutations of Tourist Guy that followed, coinciding with the reduced sense of imminent threat as the days and weeks after September 11 passed without follow-up attacks, seemed to place September 11 in historical context: as horrific as it was, we had come through other horrific events. We would come through this one as well. The jokes do more than express anxiety; they grapple with it.[29]

The substitution of Osama bin Laden for Tourist Guy on the observation deck provides us with a segue into the trove of newslore that shifts the focus from the attack on "the homeland," as it was suddenly being called, to the counterattack on Afghanistan and Iraq.

VENGEANCE

As soon as Osama bin Laden's name surfaced in connection with the September 11 attacks, the faceless enemy had a face. Following President Bush's lead, much of the post–September 11 newslore was directed specifically at bin Laden, just as it had been directed at the Ayatollah Khomeini during the Iranian hostage crisis of the late 1970s and at Saddam Hussein during the Gulf War of the early 1990s.[30] Here is where our material becomes unprintable, at least by newspaper standards. In devising suitable punishments for bin Laden, the newslore brings together the contemporary meaning of cursing—using four-letter words—and the ancient meaning of wishing harm upon another person.[31]

My collection of September 11 newslore includes a cycle of six photoshops that centers on the idea of targeting. Just as in 1979 Khomeini's face appeared in a gun sight's crosshairs in a photocopied cartoon that circulated via fax machine, so bin Laden's face appeared behind a shooting-range target, on a dartboard, and in two pop-cultural parodies in a series of images that circulated by e-mail in fall 2001. In one, bin Laden appears in the crosshairs with the caption "Who wants to bomb a millionaire?" on the perimeter of the circle—a reference to the popular television program *Who Wants to Marry a Millionaire?* In the other, bin Laden appears in the crosshairs in a parody of a MasterCard company ad that offers an opportunity to assassinate him (we'll look at the "Priceless" parodies in chapter 6). The parodying of commercial messages is consistent with what Elliott Oring found in the *Challenger* joke cycle, with its plays on well-known TV spots for beer (Bud Lite), shampoo (Head and Shoulders), and soft drinks (7UP).[32] Paraphrasing Dorst,[33] Bill Ellis, who includes the credit card spoof in his study of 9/11 lore, writes that topical jokes appropriate "mass media imagery in order to challenge official definitions of reality."[34]

Another set of target images turns scatological. Just as the face of the president of Iraq appeared on a cartoon titled "Saddam Hussein Urinal Target" that was widely photocopied and faxed during the Gulf War in 1991, bin Laden's face was emblazoned on a photoshopped urinal ten years later.[35]

NOVEMBER   197

OPEN SEASON'S the NAME –
KHOMEINI's the "GAME"

Like the Mickey Mouse image we saw earlier, this item of photocopier lore featuring the Grand Ayatollah Ruhollah Khomeini, spiritual leader of the Iranian revolution, dates back to the Iranian hostage crisis.

trip to afghanistan: $800
high powered sniper rifle: $1000
hotel stay with accessible roof: $100
scoring a head shot on osama bin laden: priceless

For everyone else there's:

Cruise Missiles

The updated, digital version of the 1979 image of Ayatollah Khomeini puts Osama bin Laden in the crosshairs.

This photocopied cartoon hints at public frustration that America could be victimized by such a technologically inferior adversary.

Both parody the targets designed to help in the potty training of little boys. Echoing the credit card parody's characterization of bin Laden as "a piece of shit," another photoshop depicts a dog using bin Laden's face as a target.[36] In a similar vein are the punning photoshops of bin Laden's face on a roll of toilet paper. One carries the slogan "Get Rid of Your Shiite." Another says, "Wipe Out Terrorism."

References to defecation lead, in turn, to an array of images that follow a chain of associations connecting defecation, military assault, and homosexual assault. Symbols of military and sexual aggression, Dundes and Pagter point out, are often interchangeable.[37] In combat, including the ritual combat of sports, Dundes writes, "one proves one's maleness by feminizing one's opponent. Typically, the victory entails some kind of penetration."[38] To begin with antecedent material, there is the Gulf War cartoon of an American military plane chasing an Iraqi camel. Just as the plane "rides the camel's ass"—with the appropriate "Holy shit!" response—so a warplane tails Osama bin Laden's flying carpet or appears in the *rearview* mirror of his car in at least three variants that circulated in 2001.[39] A photoshop of the bat-wing B-2

Here the image of the flying carpet rather than the camel is invoked as an icon of the Middle East to highlight the disparity in military might between the United States and its latest enemy in the Islamic world.

bomber is inscribed with a parody of the bumper sticker designed to tweak tailgaters: "If you can read this, you're fucked."[40] Another photoshop shows a cache of missiles on the deck of the aircraft carrier USS *Enterprise* with the words "Taliban-Brand Extra-Strength Suppository" stenciled on them.

Another set of images expresses the theme of homosexual assault through the use of the upraised middle finger. As Oring points out, the news anchors may offer reassurance and a sense of control in times of national trauma, but when it comes to expressing anger, they are too constrained by decorousness to be up to the task.[41] A final image with a more overt homosexual theme shows the martyr's supposed reward in heaven: seventy virgins, only the virgins are gay men.

In yet another cycle of photoshops, which corresponds to Ellis's second wave of 9/11 lore,[42] the humiliations are heterosexual rather than homosexual, which reflects news reports of the puritanism and misogyny of fundamentalist Islamic movements such as the Taliban and the Wahaabi sect in Saudi Arabia, of which bin Laden is a member. One photoshop showed bin Laden being squashed by a large female bed partner. Depicting

Photoshoppers gleefully devised suitable punishments for Osama
bin Laden. This one responds to what appeared, at least to
Western sensibilities, as a strong misogynistic streak in Islamic
fundamentalism.

the al-Qaeda leader in any sort of sexual encounter shows disrespect for
his religious beliefs. Showing the woman crushing him violates patriarchal
folk ideas about man-on-top male dominance. A second image showed
bin Laden pinned beneath a woman flexing her muscles while waving an
American flag.

In the following genie joke, bin Laden is dominated in another way by
three strong women who themselves were the subjects of a considerable
outpouring of newslore in the 1990s:

Osama bin Laden found a bottle on the beach and picked it up. Suddenly, a female genie rose from the bottle and with a smile said, "Master, may I grant you one wish?"

"Infidel, don't you know who I am? I need nothing from a lowly woman," barked bin Laden.

The genie pleaded, "But master, I must grant you a wish or I will be returned to this bottle forever."

Osama thought a moment. Then, grumbling about the inconvenience of it all, he relented. "OK, OK, I want to wake up with three white, American women in my bed in the morning. I have plans for them." Giving the genie a cold glare, he growled, "Now, be gone!"

The genie, annoyed, said, "So be it!" and disappeared back into the bottle. The next morning, bin Laden woke up in bed with Lorena Bobbitt, Tonya Harding, and Hillary Clinton. His penis was gone, his leg was broken and he had no health insurance.

The backstory: Lorena Bobbitt experienced her brief brush with fame in 1993 when she cut off her husband's penis. Tonya Harding had hers in 1994 when she hired a hit man to injure her Olympic figure-skating rival Nancy Kerrigan. As we saw in chapter 1, Hillary Clinton's image suffered long-term damage when her husband made her chair of a task force charged with developing some sort of national health insurance. It is a measure of celebrity when veterans of old newslore resurface in new newslore.

In two final humiliating images, Osama bin Laden is not feminized but infantilized. One image parodies milk carton campaigns on behalf of missing children. On a container of "Afgan Farms" goat milk ("already expired") it says: "Last seen: Mounting his donkey before crawling his skinny little pajama, towel headed lanky ass into some elusive Afghan cave." The other image, a poster version, asks: "Have you seen me? I'm about to get my ass nuked off the face of the planet."[43] This echoes an earlier milk carton parody of the Mars *Explorer* spacecraft with which NASA briefly lost contact in 2004.

The bin Laden connection also provided a geographic target: he was believed to be hiding in Afghanistan. The *San Diego Union-Tribune* columnist Joseph Perkins may have been one of the first to suggest that Afghanistan be "bombed back to the Stone Age."[44] The next day, the *New York Times* reporter Barry Bearak grimly joked that the war-torn land was "already there."[45] The idea of bombing back to the stone age, which the *San Francisco*

Chronicle columnist Rob Morse reminded readers was a recycled Vietnam-era quote from General Curtis LeMay,[46] and the observation that Afghanistan was already there, appeared in scores of newspaper columns and stories. The newslore was more creative. The desire to lay waste to Afghanistan found pictorial expression in cybercartoon maps showing the country transformed into either a lake or a parking lot (the radio talk show host Howard Stern reportedly made the same suggestion on the air).[47] Dundes and Pagter found similar maps of Iraq-as-parking-lot during Operation Desert Storm.[48] As Ellis noted,[49] the urge to flatten Afghanistan also found expression in several riddles:

> Q: How is Bin Laden like Fred Flintstone?
> A: Both may look out their windows and see Rubble.

Remember that the Flintstones were a "modern Stone Age family" and that Fred Flintstone's neighbor and pal was Barney Rubble. Some other riddles and jokes with annihilation themes:

> Q: What do Osama bin laden and General Custer have in common?
> A: They both want to know where those Tomahawks are coming from!

> Q: How do you play Taliban bingo?
> A: B-52 ... F-16 ... B-1 ...

> Q: What do Bin Laden and Hiroshima have in common?
> A: Nothing, yet.

> Q: What's the five-day forecast for Afghanistan?
> A: Two days.

A variant:

> Forecast weather for; Kabul, Karachi, Baghdad and Damascus for the week of 9/24/2001: Very brief period of extremely bright sunlight followed by variable winds of 2000 knots and temperatures in the mid to upper 6000 degrees range with no measurable moisture. SPF 12000 sun block highly recommended if standing near an outside structural wall of less than one meter thick.

Q: What is the Taliban's national bird?
A: Duck.

NOTHING SACRED

Until this point, the only 9/11 jokes we've seen have been at the expense of the perpetrators and their allies (or supposed allies)—Osama bin Laden, the Taliban, Afghanistan, Iraq, the Arab world in general. For a long time, I had the impression that jokes about victims of the 9/11 attacks were off-limits. Alas, they were not. In the interest of completing the record, I offer the following examples:

Q: What does WTC stand for?
A: "What Trade Center?"
[This is a common riddle type. After the *Challenger* disaster, for example, we learned that NASA stood for "Need Another Seven Astronauts," among other things. After the bombing of the Branch Davidian compound in Waco, Texas, we leaned that Waco stood for "We Ain't Comin' Out," "We All Cremated Ourselves," etc.]

At the World Trade Center restaurant, they offered three seating areas: smoking, non-smoking and burned beyond recognition.

They dont need any more volunteers to help at the WTC: they have found 5000 extra pairs of hands . . .

Q: What is world most efficient airline?
A: American Airlines, leave Boston 8:15 . . . be in your office in New York 8:48!

America's new math:
Q: Now how many sides to a Pentagon?
A: 4.

If one side of the Pentagon has collapsed, will it now be renamed "The Square"?

Q: Why are police and firemen New York's finest?
A: Because now you can run them through a sieve.

A man goes to the World Trade Center. He says, "I want to buy a jumbo jet."
    "We don't sell jumbo jets here, sir," was the reply.
    "Well, you've got one in the window!"

Q: What's the difference between 9/11 and the Oklahoma City Bombings?
A: Once again, foreigners have proven that they can do it better and more efficiently.

I should note that these jokes did not come my way as e-mail forwards. I found them on various humor Web sites. The jokes aggressively refute the notion that there are some things one just does not joke about. While the knee-jerk reaction would be to deplore the insensitivity of this material, it could also be looked at as an ostentatious display of tough-mindedness and defiance. "If I laugh at any mortal thing," Byron writes, "'Tis that I may not weep."[50] I think of the scene in the film *Monty Python and the Holy Grail* where the Black Knight refuses to surrender even after King Arthur lops his arms off. "Just a flesh wound," he says.

Giselinde Kuipers wisely cautions that interpreting the sick 9/11 jokes as a coping mechanism assumes that everyone was traumatized by the attacks—which may not be warranted. Doubtless there were those who didn't see what all the fuss was about and said as much in the jokes. (After all, as a *New York Times* story noted in 2008, "the chances of the average person dying in America at the hands of international terrorists [is] comparable to the risk of dying from eating peanuts, being struck by an asteroid or drowning in a toilet.")[51] The jokes, Kuipers writes, "defy the moral discourse of the media, provide the pleasure of boundary transgression, and block feelings of involvement."[52] The defiance, in other words, is not of the terrorists but of the taboos against offensive humor.

UNFIT TO PRINT

When big news happens, reporters, as a matter of course, will report what happened and how people reacted to what happened. If the event is deemed to be of major importance, a separate reaction story will run alongside the main news story. By any measure, the September 11 attacks were the biggest story in the history of American journalism. Beginning with extra editions that hit the streets on the afternoon of September 11, coverage included not just one-story roundups of the latest developments but multiple stories, including stories that focused exclusively on the reaction—from world leaders, from members of Congress, from military personnel, from terrorism experts, from clergy, from people in the street at home and abroad, and so on. The *New York Times* devoted an entire section to 9/11 follow-up stories throughout the fall of 2001.

The stories are inevitably balanced. The rituals of objectivity require reporters to present, if not a range of viewpoints, at least representative expressions of opposing views. The message to readers is that, in its news columns, the paper does not privilege one view over another. It does, however, limit its sampling of views to those that do not violate the canons of good taste. The dual imperatives of balance and taste produce a muting effect. There is anger in the post–September 11 reaction stories, but it seems restrained compared to the revenge fantasies that are played out in the folklore.

On September 19, for example, *USA Today* asked, "Do we seek vengeance or justice?" and noted that "the sentiments of Americans run the gamut." Four voices calling for rage and retribution followed, including one who said, simply, "Nuke 'em." Then came the balancing act: "Others prefer the guidance of the old saying 'Revenge is a dish that is best served cold.'"[53]

The *St. Petersburg Times* noted that polls showed "overwhelming support for a military response" and illustrated the point with a quote from a local official that was as risqué as most general-circulation American newspapers ever get: "I think we need to go kick some ass big time." After three other blustery quotes, though, the story turns to the more measured responses: "While most Americans support whatever action is necessary, not everyone is quite ready for what that could mean."[54]

A September 14 story in the *New York Times* began thus: "Having donated more blood than victims needed, having wallpapered their towns with flags, and with little choice but to stew over television reruns of terror in their homeland, more than a few Americans are beginning to obsess about how to get even." One interviewee suggested that we find and kill "these Arab people," then "wrap them in a pigskin and bury them. That way they will never go to heaven." Another said, "If I could get my hands on bin Laden, I'd skin him alive and pour salt on him." Such talk, the reporter Blaine Harden noted, "also alarmed many Americans."[55]

Another *New York Times* story, "Fantasies of Vengeance, Fed by Fury," on September 18, included calls for parading bin Laden's head through the city on a pike, burning him alive, and "nuking" Kabul.[56] Then President Bush himself weighed in, invoking "Wanted: Dead or Alive" posters from the old West. The *Times* disapproved, taking the president to task in its lead editorial for his "overly bellicose" language.[57]

Taken together, these stories and others like them offer specific evidence of American anger. But that anger found its fullest and most profane expression in the newslore that circulated among friends and acquaintances via e-mail. Americans weren't just angry about the September 11 attacks, they were cursing angry. Studies of the sick jokes that greeted the explosion of the space shuttle *Challenger* in 1986 suggest that the jokes were a response not only to the disaster itself but also to the disaster story—in other words, to the solemnity and piousness of the news media's narrative of the disaster.[58]

While it may seem obvious that much contemporary folklore responds to current events, it is easy to forget that, strictly speaking, the lore responds not to the events themselves but to accounts of the events. As countless sociological and rhetorical studies of news have pointed out, the news is a story about an occurrence.[59] As such, it is important to recognize that newslore may be a response to how that story is told—to what is left out as well as what is included—as much as it is a response to the occurrence itself.

No one, other than people who were close enough to the launch site to see it in person, could have known about the *Challenger* explosion other than by seeing it on television, hearing about it on the radio, reading about it in the newspaper the next day (this was before newspapers had Web sites), or hearing about it from someone who had been paying attention to the mass media.[60] For those of us who watched the disaster on TV, the experience was visually framed and reduced by the screen itself, bracketed by the commercial messages that underwrite the news programming, and filtered through the personality of whichever news anchor told us the story. The juxtaposition of extraordinary tidings with the business-as-usual production values and fiscal imperatives of network news was jarring and more than a little absurd.

Oring argues that the *Challenger* jokes were a "strategy of rebellion" against the slick media packaging of the disaster. Part of that strategy was to effectively bar the news media from appropriating the jokes by making them unspeakable according to the news media's canons of good taste.[61] Oring infers public attitudes toward the "packaging" of disaster from the content of the jokes themselves—and from the cultural knowledge one would need to possess to understand the content. Here, contrasting the newslore of September 11 with the expressions of rage and dismay that were deemed fit for public consumption has shown how newslore functions as an alternative discourse on disaster. Like the accused miscreant who makes an obscene gesture at the cameras during his perp walk, those with a taste for newslore can fight off news media co-optation and thereby maintain the world of computer-mediated communication as a parallel or underground universe of discourse simply by making the material "unspeakable."

Sure enough, as exhaustive as news coverage of September 11 and its aftermath was, when I searched for stories about the newslore of September 11, I found that the American news media mostly ignored or toned down "tasteless" expressions of public anger so as not to offend their audiences. A *USA Today* story about humor on the Web noted that the goat milk carton emblazoned with the image of Osama bin Laden contained "language unsuitable for a family newspaper."[62] A *Rocky Mountain News* story mentioned photos of bin Laden "in none-too-flattering poses."[63] Anything more explicit, presumably, was simply not fit to print. As Christie Davies wrote of jokes about the death of Princess Diana, "Such jokes never appear on radio or television or in established newspapers, for media executives stringently censor out any such material lest an influential or vociferous segment of their audience feel offended."[64] (I would note that the media executives need not get involved; the canons of good taste are widely shared among the newsroom rank and file.)

The Pew Internet and American Life Project, incidentally, also gave the folklore of 9/11 a wide berth. The project's sixty-five-page study of how Americans used the Internet in the aftermath of September 11 noted that "the Internet became a channel for anguished and prayerful gatherings, for heartfelt communication through email, and for vital information"[65] but made no mention of jokes or humor apart from observing the presence of rumors and other "fanciful tales."[66] Snopes got a mention for its role in debunking rumors, as did Fark.com for abandoning its usual comedy format to deliver straight news.

Elsewhere, the Pew report acknowledged that the Internet "provided a virtual public space where grief, fear, anger, patriotism and even hatred could be shared,"[67] but only addressed direct statements of those sentiments and not their expression in the more stylized or artistic forms of folklore. Similarly, a section on images listed six kinds of images but ignored cartoons and photoshops.

Meanwhile, with the acquiescence of a shockingly docile news media and Democratic opposition, the Bush administration ordered the invasion of Iraq and toppled Saddam Hussein—so far, so good—but U.S. forces were unable to restore order once Saddam's army had disbanded and dispersed. Though polls showed that a majority of Americans continued to believe that Saddam had his hand in the September 11 attacks and possessed weapons of mass destruction long after conclusive evidence to the contrary came to light, eventually the sense that we were bogged down in Iraq while Osama bin Laden remained at large eroded popular support—and the change seems to have been reflected in the newslore.

A good starting point for a discussion of antiwar—and therefore anti-Bush—newslore is the juxtaposition of two wildly contradictory Bush statements:

September 13, 2001: "The most important thing is for us to find Osama bin Laden. It is our number one priority and we will not rest until we find him."

March 13, 2002: "I don't know where he is. I have no idea and I really don't care. It's not that important. It's not our priority."

In one version, the two quotes are set in speech bubbles, each coming from a reversed image of the president and labeled "The Two Faces of George Bush Jr."[68] Another, parodying the "Where's Waldo?" series of children's books, is labeled "Where's bin Laden?"

A similar juxtaposition of Bush quotations was captioned "Two-Faced Bush":

May 29, 2003: "We've found the weapons of mass destruction. And we'll find more weapons as time goes on."

February 7, 2004: "There's theories as to where the weapons went. They could have been destroyed during the war."

The other major contributor to turning the tide of public opinion against the war was the set of photographs taken—and shared, folklore-like—by American military personnel detailed to the Abu Ghraib prison. The visual evidence of prisoner abuse shocked the public—and lent itself to pointed photoshops, including images where a smirking Bush (and, in some instances, Secretary of Defense Donald Rumsfeld) was substituted for the faces of guards at Abu Ghraib. The most searing image, the hooded prisoner with electrodes attached to his fingers, appeared as the White House Christmas tree, under the "Mission Accomplished" banner under which Bush appeared on the aircraft carrier USS *Abraham Lincoln* in the original photo taken on May 2003, and on the Statue of Liberty's pedestal, among other places. As we will see in chapter 5, Bush had been skewered before his election—and before September 11—as a stooge, a chimp, a dunce, and a puppet of his father or of Dick Cheney or his friends in the oil industry. But when things began to go wrong in Iraq, the newslore took on a harder edge. Bush's supposed lack of qualifications for the highest office in the land became more disturbing—and the newslore more condemnatory—as the stakes rose, as they did again in 2005 when the Bush administration seemed woefully inept in its response to Hurricane Katrina.

4

Got Fish?
Newslore of Hurricane Katrina

"DISGUSTING"

On September 12, 2005, a colleague down the hall forwarded an e-mail to me with the subject line "Got Fish?" (the subject line in the Urbanlegends.about.com version is "Some people find good in EVERYTHING!!!!"). "Disgusting," Ken Yednock commented in the body of the e-mail. "But funny."

What followed was a photograph of the two presidents Bush on what appears to be the deck of a sportfishing boat. George Bush the elder, smiling in cap and windbreaker, is holding a fishing rod. George Bush the younger, grinning in leather jacket and sunglasses, is holding a striped bass. That's the foreground. In the background we see nine or ten people, most if not all of whom appear to be African American, wading through waist-high water on a city street.

Here is some of what one needed to know to understand why the photograph was disgusting but funny: The Bushes are members of the leisure class, which likes to engage in high-end recreational pursuits such as sportfishing. The streets of New Orleans had flooded when Hurricane Katrina made landfall the week before. Many African American citizens of New Orleans are poor and therefore lacked the ways and means to heed the order to evacuate the city. They were trapped. President Bush in particular and authorities at all levels of government in general were perceived as being catastrophically and criminally slow to respond to the gravity of the situation. Message of the photo: the Bushes are so out of touch with the plight of the poor, especially poor blacks, that they saw the flooding of New Orleans

The two presidents Bush appear to be taking advantage of the flooding of New Orleans by Hurricane Katrina to do a little sportfishing.

as nothing more than an opportunity to do a little fishing. The name of the file is BushVaca.jpg—an abbreviated version of "Bush Vacation." The subject line "Got fish?" refers to the "Got Milk?" advertising campaign, more parodies of which we will see in chapter 7.

The bass-fishing photo can also be read as a response to Barbara Bush's "Let them eat cake" moment at the Houston Astrodome, which was serving as a temporary evacuation center for New Orleans's poorest and least-mobile residents. "What I'm hearing, which is sort of scary," the wife of the first President Bush and mother of the second one told a reporter, "is they all want to stay in Texas. Everyone is so overwhelmed by the hospitality. And so many of the people in the arena here, you know, were underprivileged anyway, so this is working very well for them."[1] John Nichols blogged in the *Nation*: "Finally, we have discovered the roots of George W. Bush's 'compassionate conservatism'"[2]

Other people made the "let them eat cake" connection. A piece of commentary on Politicalhumor.about.com juxtaposes a photo of a black man standing amid the wreckage of his house and a photo of President Bush and Senator John McCain standing behind a white cake and superimposes both photos over a dictionary definition of the word "negligence." The caption asks, "Where were you on August 29, 2005? They were eating cake."[3] A similar collage juxtaposes the cake photo, a photo of Bush playing a guitar given to him by the country singer Mark Wills, a photo of Bush looking out the window of Air Force One, and a pink "While You Were Out" pad with the message "FEMA called." The collage is labeled "Operation: Enduring Vacation," which parodies the slogan "Operation Enduring Freedom," coined for the invasion of Afghanistan in fall 2001.[4]

Comparisons with Nero fiddling while Rome burned were also popular, as the following letter to the editor of *Newsday* shows (while connecting Bush's mishandling of Katrina with his mishandling of 9/11):

> Yet, as the country cries and mourns for those who have died, our president found time to ape for the cameras, strumming a guitar with country singer Mark Wills for a photo op. He also managed to get in a round of golf before deciding to cut short his five-week vacation. Four years ago when disaster struck he sat dumbstruck and continued to read a children's book so as not to "frighten the students." What excuse can he possibly have this time for strumming away on his guitar as catastrophe strikes? He truly has become a modern-day Nero, fiddling as the nation burns. President Bush, who's not big on the classics, probably wasn't thinking about this when he mugged for the cameras Tuesday, playing a guitar presented to him by country singer Mark Wills. But with the photo now Exhibit A for many liberal bloggers, he may find the comparison hard to shake.[5]

Thus far, the meanings I have teased out of this photo explain only why it is disgusting. To understand why it's funny, you have to know that the photograph is a fake, which is to say you have to know that it is possible to digitally alter or combine photographs in ways that make the altered photo almost indistinguishable from a photograph of a scene as it appeared to the photographer through the camera's viewfinder. Snopes.com says it received many "is this real?" inquiries about both "Got Fish?" and another photo of President Bush the Younger strumming the guitar for a weeping woman outside the New Orleans convention center. Snopes displayed the original photos from which the spoof versions were made.[6]

That some people believed these images to be true tells us two things: even though we are routinely exposed to and aware of realistic digital "fauxtos," our knee-jerk response to the physically plausible image (as opposed to, say, a horse's head on a man's body, which would be a physically implausible image) is to accept it at face value; and we are likelier to believe a physically plausible image if the content accords with beliefs we already hold. In the present instance, I suspect the believers were those whose boundless contempt for George W. Bush made them susceptible to almost any calumny. That "Got Fish?" hadn't appeared in any newspapers would not have surprised them. If you believe "Got Fish?" it's no stretch to believe in conspiracies to suppress news. Presumably these people did not find the photograph amusing.

Those who laughed at "Got Fish?" recognized it as a fake not because they were able to spot the telltale signs of a cut-and-paste job but because the conduct depicted in the photo was so breathtakingly inappropriate to the situation. One of the phrases that recurs in the humorless scholarly literature about humor is the idea of "appropriate incongruity." "Got Fish?" is incongruous in multiple ways: though digitally altered photographs have become commonplace, we continue to marvel at how realistic a fake can look. The disconnect between the visual plausibility of the image and the implausibility of the conduct is startling, but it would not be funny if the conduct, though literally false, did not express a figurative truth. If we laugh at "Got Fish?" we laugh because someone has cleverly brought together these disparate scenes to craft a false, yet maliciously apt, representation of the Bushes' perceived insensitivity and disengagement.

The day after Ken Yednock forwarded "Got Fish?" to me, I received another copy from my friend Michael Yonchenko in California. Michael correctly surmised that he was trafficking in old news. His subject line read: "You may have already seen this, but . . ." I was one of thirty-five addressees. "Got Fish?" came up in conversation several times in the next few days. Everyone, it seemed, had seen the picture, which is why it became my shorthand explanation of what this book was going to be about. "You know that photo of the Bushes?" I'd say. "The book is going to be about 'stuff like that.'"

"Got Fish?" may have been the most popular bit of Katrina newslore. There were others. One photoshop showed Bush putting the Presidential Medal of Freedom around the neck of FEMA director Michael Brown. Brown bore the brunt of the blame for FEMA's poor performance, at first. (He later testified to Congress that he tried in vain to convey the severity of the situation to White House staffers and his boss, Michael Chertoff, secretary of the Department of Homeland Security.) But Bush, who has often been accused of being loyal to a fault, was famously quoted as saying that "Brownie" was doing "a heck of a job." (Giving Brown the Medal of Freedom would have been consistent with what Bush had done the year before when he awarded the Medal of Freedom to former CIA director George Tenant, despite Tenant's key role in the use of faulty intelligence about Saddam Hussein's weapons of mass destruction to justify the invasion of Iraq.)

Another bit of newslore that addressed Bush's apparent obliviousness to the plight of ordinary citizens displaced by the hurricane was a bumper sticker that said, "I want to sit on Trent Lott's porch." Lott was the junior senator from Mississippi at the time. Here is what the president said while surveying the damage:

> The good news is—and it's hard for some to see it now—that out of this chaos is going to come a fantastic Gulf Coast, like it was before. Out of the rubbles of Trent Lott's house—he's lost his entire house—there's going to be a fantastic house. And I'm looking forward to sitting on the porch.[7]

Here are three more jokes that poked fun at Bush's racial insensitivity:

> In response to accusations that he doesn't care about black people, George Bush replied, "Of course I care about black people, every home should have one."

> What's all this talk about the poor people in New Orleans? There ain't none, from what I hear most everyone has got prime waterfront property, and swimming pool in the backyard.

> Q: What is George W Bush's position on Roe v. Wade?
> A: He doesn't care how the blacks get out of New Orleans.[8]

This joke recalls an earlier Dan Quayle joke:

> After the 1989 earthquake struck Northern California, President Bush dispatched Vice President Quayle to the epicenter. The vice president flew to Orlando.

To get this joke, you had to know that Quayle, like Bush, was widely thought to be lacking in the brains department, in large part because he frequently misspoke; and that Quayle must have mistaken "epicenter" for "Epcot Center," which is part of Disney World, located in Orlando, Florida.

Here are two more jokes that recall the "shake-up" puns that greeted the 1989 Loma Prieta earthquake in northern California:

Black men in Purple Dinner jackets & bow ties were found floating
under a pier in New Orleans today . . . D.N.A Tests have revealed they
were indeed the DRIFTERS.

I heard from my brother who has reopened his bar in the French Quarter, he said business was a little quiet but was picking up now that some
of his regulars have been drifting back in.

I ran across a similar joke about Thai bar owners saying business had
been slow since the 2004 tsunami. This next joke makes sly reference to
France's unwillingness to support the invasion of Iraq:

Did you hear which part of New Orleans was the first to surrender to
the Hurricane Katrina flood waters? The French Quarter.

Finally, Katrina provided grist for those who can tie any newsworthy
occurrence to the sexual misconduct of Michael Jackson and Bill Clinton:

Why did Michael Jackson volunteer to help Hurricane Katrina victims?
Because New Orleans now has the highest concentration of children
wearing wet underwear.

Bill Clinton says, "The hurricane season in New Orleans is no big
deal . . . last time I was there I got blown up a back alley in the French
Quarter."

As with the Loma Prieta quake, newspaper coverage of Katrina included stories about gallows humor, not immediately after the disaster but months later,
when reporters returned to New Orleans to cover the first post-Katrina Mardi
Gras. Most of a *Washington Post* column by Linton Weeks was about the "edgy"
humor of the parade floats and costumes, T-shirts, and bumper stickers. Several
T-shirts and bumper stickers parodied the city's slogan "New Orleans—Proud
to Call It Home": "Proud to Crawl Home," "Proud to Swim Home," and, with a
sketch of a FEMA trailer, "Proud to Call It Home." Another T-shirt joked about
the looting that went on amid the chaos: "I Stayed in New Orleans and All I Got
Was This Lousy T-shirt, a New Cadillac and a Plasma TV."
    Oddly, Weeks asks if such flippancy is appropriate and concludes that
"the jury's still out," without asking anyone. I must admit I was tickled to see
Weeks describe a supposedly unintentionally funny moment:

> A tour guide said that she heard a TV reporter ask a New Orleans woman if she was devastated by the destruction of all the churches in the area and the woman replied: "Not really. I eat at Popeyes."
>
> That's a local fried chicken reference. If you don't get it, ask a New Orleanian.[9]

What Weeks means is that Church's, liked Popeyes, is a chain of fried chicken restaurants. What he apparently didn't know is that this is a variation on an old joke—nothing unintentional about it at all. The story pops up on Snopes.com as an urban legend.[10]

As with jokes about celebrity deaths (see chapter 8), there were those who thought Hurricane Katrina was no laughing matter:

> This Joke Line or whatever it is, should stop I had 10 family members to die out there in new orleans and you have people on here using the N word thats not funny im black proud of it and there were alot of people to die out there including whites and its not about color anyway there or whites on welfare just like blacks so the comments on here about welfare is just down right stupid. And who ever started this katrina joke shyt, I see you weren't the one waiting for days for food or water you weren't the one preying not to get raped or have your family that you found lost again seperated again have some compasion, God Bless all the people that did write these stupid jokes because your day is coming, because paybacks a bytch.

THE MAYHEM LEGEND

As if reports of the conditions in the Louisiana Superdome and the New Orleans Convention Center weren't horrifying enough—overcrowding, no air conditioning or plumbing, insufficient food and water—the news media reported that evacuees were being raped and killed. Some of the rumors came from people inside the two evacuation centers, who may have been reporting what they had heard rather than what they had seen, but some came from officials, including the mayor and the city's police superintendent. Mayor Ray Nagin went on *The Oprah Winfrey Show* and told of people "in that frickin' Superdome for five days watching dead bodies, watching hooligans killing people, raping people."[11] Police Superintendent Edwin P. Compass III talked about rapes and beatings in the convention center and added that tourists were also getting raped and beaten. In some accounts, the rape victims were as young as seven years old; in some they were as young as two. The *New York Times* acknowledged that some of these stories had not been verified.[12] Other papers reinforced the accounts with quotes like the following, from Sgt. Tony Small of the New Orleans Police Department: "That's not rumors," Small said of the mayhem at the convention center. "It was horrendous."[13]

A couple of weeks later, the press began reporting that most of the accounts of violence were either false or had never been confirmed. Even Eddie Compass said as much. "We have no official reports to document any murder," he told the *New York Times*. "Not one official report of rape or sexual assault."[14]

A *Washington Post* story dated September 15 began: "Rumors were treated as fact—both inside the convention center and out."[15] The *Times* described the stories as "figments of frightened imaginations."[16] *Times* columnist David Carr called it "a game of toxic telephone."[17] Many reporters and sources turned to the vocabulary of folklore to describe the unverified stories:

I think it was urban myth. Any time you put 25,000 people under one roof, with no running water, no electricity and no information, stories get told.
—Lieutenant David Benelli, New Orleans Police Department[18]

[The Superdome] morphed into this mythical place where the most unthinkable deeds were being done.
—Major Ed Bush, Louisiana National Guard[19]

And many of the urban legends that sprang up—the systematic rape of children, the slitting of a 7-year-old's throat—so far seem to be just that.... Even now, the real, actual events in New Orleans in the past three weeks surpass the imagination. Who needs urban myths when the reality was so brutal?
—David Carr, *New York Times* columnist[20]

That the nation's front-line emergency management believed the body count would resemble that of a bloody battle in a war is but one of scores of examples of myths about the Dome and the Convention Center treated as fact by evacuees, the media and even some of New Orleans' top officials, including the mayor and police superintendent.
—Brian Thevenot and Gordon Russell, *New Orleans Times-Picayune*[21]

There was plenty of blame to go around. Officials blamed sensation-mongering journalists. Journalists blamed officials—and each other. Print journalists, for example, blamed television journalists,[22] irresponsible Web sites, and talk radio. Columnists blamed sensation-mongering reporters and, buttressed by academic sources, racism. Carl Smith, a professor of English and American studies at Northwestern University, told the *Times* that stories of "a city in chaos and people running loose" offered "the fulfillment of some timely ideas and prejudices about the current social order."[23] *Times-Picayune* editor Jim Amoss was more blunt: "If the dome and Convention Center had harbored large numbers of middle-class white people, it would not have been a fertile ground for this kind of rumor-mongering."[24]

Carl Lindahl, a folklorist and codirector of the Surviving Katrina and Rita in Houston project, presented a paper at a conference I attended about another set of rumors that swept through New Orleans's black community after Katrina: the government had deliberately sabotaged the levees protecting the city's Ninth Ward, both to divert the water away from more-affluent white neighborhoods and to have a pretext for razing the Ninth Ward and turning it over to developers who would put the land to more upscale use.

The racial dimension of the rumormongering was seemingly confirmed by the treatment of two photos that appeared on the Yahoo! News Web site. The people in one of the photos were white. The caption:

> Two residents wade through chest-deep water after finding bread and soda from a local grocery store after Hurricane Katrina came through the area in New Orleans, Louisiana.

The person in the other photo was black. The caption:

> A young man walks through chest deep flood water after looting a grocery store in New Orleans on Tuesday, Aug. 30, 2005.[25]

Students in my journalism ethics class got worked up about the seemingly overt racism of the word choices. They were responding to forwards of posts such as these:

> The captions on two photos from flood victims show very clearly the sinister and subtle ways that racism thrives in this country. . . . What's the difference between "looting" and "finding?" Apparently it's as simple as the color of your skin.[26]

My job was to challenge their knee-jerk responses. I noted (as did many other commentators) first that the photos came from two different sources, so it wasn't as if the same photographer was distinguishing the behavior of the white flood victims from the behavior of the black flood victims along racial lines; and second that the use of the word "looting" does not necessarily entail a moral judgment. "Looting" *describes* taking items from stores during a breakdown in order; it doesn't address the question of whether the taking of the items may be justified. Ultimately the episode told us less about racism in the news media than about how racially charged life remains in America.

As the controversy over the juxtaposed looting photos died down, another looting photo, of a black man carrying a plastic tub filled with bottles of beer, took on a life of its own, appearing in a wide variety of contexts, just as Tourist Guy did before him.[27]

DISASTER OVERSEAS

I mentioned a tsunami joke earlier; there was other tsunami lore. Some involved real photos that were given phony backstories. One showed spectators calmly watching the wave come in. "Not too smart!" commented one of the forwarders. "Here is why sooo many people died. . . . They just stood there and watched the wave come." The casting of aspersions on the intelligence of the Southeast Asian victims of the tsunami is similar to some exasperated reactions to the failure of black residents to evacuate New Orleans. An About.com page titled "Stupid Quotes About Hurricane Katrina" includes one from former Pennsylvania senator Rick Santorum: "I mean, you have people who don't heed those warnings and then put people at risk as a result of not heeding those warnings. There may be a need to look at tougher penalties on those who decide to ride it out and understand that there are consequences to not leaving."[28] In fact, according to Snopes, the purported tsunami photo actually showed a high tide that at regular intervals causes a river in China to rise dramatically. Another photo of the tsunami supposedly taken from a high-rise building in Phuket, Thailand, was actually an altered photo of a city in Chile.[29] Then there were the sick jokes:

How can you tell an Indonesian prostitute?
She's the one in the fish nets.

How do you stop a tsunami?
Throw 160,000 Asians in front of it.

The Australian Gold Coast Surf Classic was won this week under controversial circumstances........by a Burmese on a wardrobe.

According to published reports, immediately following the Tsunami in January of 2005, all of the sharks in the Indian Ocean came down with a terrible case of diarrhoea.
You try eating Thai for a whole week!

Jokes about the 2008 earthquake in China also reveal a continuing Western distrust of Asian cuisine. In the 1980s, the folklorist Florence Baer wrote about stories circulating in Stockton, California, that Asian immigrants were stealing pets and cooking them. Such was the furor over these tales that the city council considered an ordinance that would specifically ban the practice. Cooler heads prevailed. No documented instance of petnapping in Stockton ever materialized.[30] Here are the China earthquake jokes:

Torrential rain has been hampering relief efforts in the Chinese earthquake zone.... Luckily for survivors, it's been raining cats and dogs.

Apparently they are flying in food aid for victims of the earthquake in South-Western China ... Battersea dogs home is completely out of stock, in response to the emergency.

The meagerness of the crop of jokes about the Loma Prieta and China earthquakes and the tsunami when compared to jokes about September 11 and Hurricane Katrina may partake of a larger pattern: when unfunny things happen, we are likelier to joke if we have someone to blame. One might think that we would be likelier to joke about catastrophes that happen on the other side of the world than ones that happen close to home, but the paucity of jokes about the Asian disasters suggests that when it comes to sick joking, distant disaster doesn't have enough shock value.

5

It Takes a
Village Idiot

Bushlore

Alan Dundes regarded jokes as "socially sanctioned outlets for expressing taboo ideas and subjects."[1] Thus, he claimed, political jokes are far more plentiful in dictatorships than they are in democracies, where the press can openly lampoon political leaders in opinion columns and editorial cartoons. In America, Dundes found, instead of joking about politics, we joke about sex and race because those are the topics we feel least comfortable discussing openly.[2]

Is Dundes's claim, made in 1987, no longer true? In cyberspace, political jokes seem at least as plentiful as jokes about sex and race. Why should this be? Has our political culture changed, or is there something about computer-mediated communication that lends itself to political humor?

A couple of tentative answers: With the notable exception of the 2008 presidential election, voter turnout has been declining steadily. The standard explanation is that voters are increasingly disgusted with the way politics works, and that disgust inevitably leads to apathy. But the disgust-apathy link may not be as automatic as is generally supposed. To be disgusted with the way politics works, you have to care about it, a lot. The assumption seems to be that if you care about something a lot, are unhappy about it, but can't do anything about it, you give up on it. It may be, though, that disgust is not a precondition of political apathy. While a society like ours gives us the freedom to criticize our political leaders, it also affords us the luxury of ignoring them. I don't agree with those who say that every election offers us a choice between Tweedledum and Tweedledee: The differences between Democrats and Republicans may not be as stark as those between, say, liberals and libertarians, but they are real, and they matter. At the same time, American politics is so fundamentally centrist, and American society so stable, that one can tune out the whole process, confident that whoever wins elections, one's own life is not going to change much either way. People don't stay home on Election Day, in other words, because they've lost confidence in the system but because they have an abundance of confidence. The disgusted people, I would wager, are conscientious voters, and the most zealous jokers come from their growing ranks. The only reason I assert this is that the jokes themselves offer evidence of a high degree of engagement. The jokes make sense only if you follow the news, and I can't imagine why a nonvoter would follow the news.

The other reason why political jokes are flourishing has to do with the nature of the medium in which the jokes are crafted. Political leaders and celebrities dominate news photographs, just as they dominate news stories. Those photographs comprise a trove of near-at-hand raw materials for the photoshopper's art. News photos are on the Web for the taking—and faking. If Bill Clinton was unfortunate to be president when e-mail became the dominant joke exchange medium, George W. Bush was unfortunate to occupy the White House during the evolution of the computer from a predominantly text-driven medium to a text-and-graphics-driven medium.

Bushlore hammers away at four themes:

1. Bush is not intelligent.
2. He has a substance abuse problem.
3. He is a huckster.
4. He should never have gotten as far as he has, and therefore his demise would be no great loss.

While all this material has overlapped in terms of its currency in cyberspace, it should be noted that concerns about Bush's intelligence and his misspent youth were voiced even before his ascension to the White House following the disputed election of 2000, and disgust with Bush's role as a shill for policies widely seen as the work of Cheney or Rumsfeld on behalf of their cronies in industry (Halliburton, et al.) mounted as the war in Iraq began to bog down. Once it became clear that Bush was not equal to the task of presiding over a much more dangerous world than the one he faced when he took office in 2001, the jokes got meaner. As I suggested in the previous chapter, the last straw, for many who might previously have given the president the benefit of the doubt, was the administration's mishandling of Hurricane Katrina. Before Katrina, the argument over the war in Iraq was largely ideological: was it an appropriate use of American power to topple a dictator and preside over the ensuing chaos? After Katrina, the issue was competence. Those who may have disagreed on whether the interference in Iraqi affairs was justified readily agreed that the invasion and occupation were poorly planned and poorly executed.

BUSH IS NOT INTELLIGENT

The President Can't Read

George W. Bush took the national stage with a reputation for not being articulate, scholarly, thoughtful, or well-read. It didn't help matters when he named Jesus as his favorite philosopher and couldn't name a favorite children's book. His detractors went further. The guy isn't just a nonreader. He doesn't even know how to read. He received all those "gentleman's C's" at Yale because of his pedigree. The photograph of Bush holding a book upside down at an elementary school illustrates that rumor. The photo is identical to one that appeared in newspapers except that the book has been inverted in Photoshop. (A photoshop of Bill Clinton uses the same situation—he is reading to a group of schoolchildren—but to spoof the forty-second president's reputation as a sex fiend, the book is open to photographs of naked women.) Apparently a number of people got taken in by the upside-down book photograph. The Web site Idealog ("Where technology, politics, media and snowboarding collide") ran a correction—"Apparently, the photo of Bush reading upside down that we posted last week . . . was a manipulated image"—and linked to Snopes.com.[3] A personal Web page, anvari.org, posted the photo along with two comments:

> anonymous: ITS PHOTOSHOPPED YOU IDIOTS!
> Chris: You all know Bush is that stupid to read a book upside down
> [Presumably the more recent comment appears above and responds to the comment below it.][4]

A related illustration of Bush's ineptitude shows him talking into an upside-down phone receiver. (Newer photoshops show Barack Obama doing the same thing. A digitally reversed photo from the opposite side of the political spectrum shows former Senate majority leader Tom Daschle saluting the flag with the wrong hand. The caption says: "He's so left of center, he pledges backwards!") Another photoshop shows Bush in a trench

George W. Bush entered the national political spotlight with a reputation as an intellectual lightweight. The rumor illustrated by this photoshop took it a step further: Bush did not know how to read.

with two soldiers, looking through binoculars with the lens caps still on. According to Snopes, it's not clear whether the image is a photoshop or the president was caught raising the capped binoculars to his eyes—as many of us have done—before he removed them.[5]

If Bush can read, his abilities—or tastes—are so infantile that his preferred reading is comic books: one photoshop shows him carrying X-Men, Donald Duck, and Superman comics under his arm. Then there's a joke that references the belief that Vice President Cheney was the real brains of the outfit:

> George Bush and Dick Cheney are having lunch at a fancy Washington restaurant. Their waitress approaches their table to take their order and she is young and very attractive.
> She asks Cheney what he wants, and he replies, "I'll have the heart-healthy salad." "Very good, sir," she replies.
> Turning to Bush she asks, "And what do you want, Mr. President?"
> Bush answers, "How about a quickie?"

Taken aback, the waitress slaps him and says, "I'm shocked and disappointed in you. I thought you were bringing in a new administration that was committed to high principles and morality. I'm sorry I voted for you." With that, the waitress departed in a huff.

Cheney leans over to Bush, and says, "Mr. President, I believe that's pronounced 'quiche.'"

Part of what is interesting about this joke is that it plays on the contrast between President Clinton's reputation for sexual indiscretion and President Bush's reputation for butchering the language. When Bush makes a sexual overture toward the waitress, it appears to be a recycled Clinton joke, very much out of keeping with most other Bush jokes. But then it turns out he is not making an out-of-character proposition but committing an altogether in-character verbal gaffe.

Or is he? Months after running across the quiche joke with Bush and Cheney as the dramatis personae, I ran across a version that suggests the joke may originally have been a Clinton joke after all. In this version, Clinton is the mispronouncer, and Al Gore the corrector.

The President Is Unsophisticated
Bush's unfamiliarity with quiche also marks him as a bit of a bumpkin, as do the next two jokes:

George W. says to an aide, "I need to do better in south Florida four years from now. I've got to see what all this Jewish stuff is about."

So off they go to a kosher restaurant. The first course set in front of them is matzoh ball soup. George W. is grossed out and reluctant to taste this strange-looking brew. Gently, the aide says, "Just have a taste, Mr. President. If you don't like it, you don't have to finish it."

George W. gingerly lowers his spoon into the bowl, picking up a small piece of matzoh ball with some broth. He hesitates, then swallows, and a grin slowly appears on his face. George W. digs in, quickly finishes off the entire bowl of soup and all of the matzoh balls.

"That was delicious," George W. says to his aide. "Do the Jews eat any other parts of the matzoh, or just the balls?"

What you need to know to get the next joke is that during the 1992 campaign, President Clinton received a lot of attention for playing the saxophone on television on *The Arsenio Hall Show*.

George W. Bush was invited to the White House for a foreign policy orientation session. After drinking several glasses of iced tea, he asked Bill Clinton if he could use his personal bathroom. He was astonished to see that the President had a solid gold urinal.

That afternoon, W. told his wife Laura about the urinal. "Just think," he said, "when I am President, I'll get to have a gold urinal!"

The next day Laura Bush had lunch with a group of female Senators. She told Hillary Clinton how impressed W. had been with his discovery that the President had a gold urinal in his private bathroom.

That evening, Bill and Hillary were getting ready for bed. Hillary turned to Bill and said, "Well, I found out who peed in your saxophone."

At least two other urban legends about Bush's cluelessness made the rounds. In one, he is supposed to have said that "the problem with the French is [that] they don't have a word for entrepreneur." In another he is supposed to have waved to musician Stevie Wonder, who is blind. According to Snopes, neither tale is true.[6]

The Crayola Presidency

I have run across three photoshops that show President Bush writing or drawing with crayons. In one, he is using a thick crayon to draw a stick figure with bombs falling and the words, written in a childish scrawl, "Bad, Bad Saddam." Another shows the president, sitting at a desk with four men standing behind him, signing a bill or declaration. But instead of signing the document with a pen, he is drawing with an oversize crayon. The third image shows the same scene from a different angle, but here we also see a box of "Payola" crayons and a Mr. Potato Head. Clearly the images portray the president as childlike, which correlates with editorial cartoonists' and columnists' depictions of Bush's relationship with Vice President Cheney as a father-son relationship. Then there's this phony news story:

Fire Destroys Bush Presidential Library

WASHINGTON—A tragic fire on Monday destroyed the personal library of President George W. Bush. Both of his books have been lost. Presidential spokesman Scott McLelland [sic] said the president was devastated, as he had not finished coloring the second one.

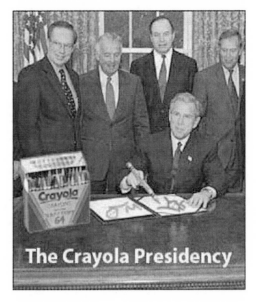

The Crayola Presidency

Bush's lack of intellectual sophistication was also portrayed with images of him using crayons.

The President Can't Talk. Or Write.

Another example of the durability of newslore is a rebus that first circulated as photocopier lore during the 1991 Gulf War. The words, originally attributed to President George H. W. Bush, then to President Clinton, and then to President George W. Bush, incorporate the logos of the major oil companies to indicate what U.S. military intervention in the Middle East is really about: "We [Shell] not [Exxon]erate Saddam Hussein for his actions. We will [Mobil]ize to meet this threat to vital interests in the Persian [Gulf]. Our best strategy IS TO [BP]repared. Failing that, we [ARCO]ming to kick your ass." The George W. Bush version includes an addendum: "Let me explainify the war against Iraq a little bit in Texas terminologragy."

A similarly exaggerated send-up of the president's tortured syntax and mangled pronunciations cropped up in a parody of the Nigerian scam—the attempt, most often from Nigeria, but also from other African countries, to enlist the help of a gull with a bank account in securing monies for both parties, provided that the gull puts up a considerable chunk of change up front. The scam has received a fair amount of attention from the news media—a LexisNexis search of the fifty largest English-language newspapers summoned almost seven hundred stories over twenty-five years—and with that kind of exposure, parody was sure to follow:

HIGHLY CONFIDENTIAL:URGENT ASSISTANCE
Dear Sir / Madam / Other,

I are GEORGE WALKER BUSH, son of the former president of the United State of Americas, George Herbert Walker Bush, and are currently serving as a President of the United State of Americas. This letter might surprise you because we have not met neither in person nor by being there in person. I am writing you in absolute confidence primarily to seek your assistafication in acquiring oil funds that am presently trapped in the Republic of Iraq.

My partners and me solicit your assistancy in completing transaction begun by my father, who have long been engaged in the extraction of petroleum in the Untied States, and bravely serve his country as director of the Central Intelligent Agency. In the decade of the nineteen-eighty, my father, then vice-president of the United State, sought to work with good offices of the President of Republic of Emirate of Iraq to re-get lost oil revenue sources in the neighbor Emerate of Iran.

These unsuccessful venture was soon followed by a falling-off with his Iraqi partner, who sought additional oil revenue source in the neighboring Kuwait, a whole-owned U.S.-British subsidiary. My father re-unsecured the petroleum asset of Kuwait in 1991 at the costimigation of sixty-one bajillion u.s. dollars ($61,000,000,000). Out of that cost, thirty-six bajillion dollars ($36,000,000,000) were supplied by his partners in the Kingdom of Saudi Arabian and other Persia Golf monarch butterflies, and sixteen bajillion dollar ($16,000,000,000) by German and Japanic partners.

But my father's former Iraqi businesses partner remained in control of Iraq and its petroleums. My familys is calling for you urgent assistantfication in funding the removal of the so-called President of Irak and acquiring the petroleum assets of his country, as compenation for the costs of removing him from powers.

Unfortunately, our partners from 1991 are not willing to shoulder the burdenicate of this new ventures, which in it upcoming phase may cost the sum of 100 bajillion to 200 bajillion dollars ($100,000,000,000 –$200,000,000,000), both in the initial acquisitionism and in long-term managementation.

That is why my family and our colleagues are urgently seeking your graciousness assistance. Our distinguished colleaguers in this business transaction include the seated vice-president-in-hiding, Richard C Heney, who is an original partners in the Iraq venture and former heads the Halliburton oil company, and Condoleeza Rice, who professional dedications to the venture was demonstratified in the naming of a Chevron oil tanker after her.

I would beerseech you to transfer a sums equaling ten to twenty-five percents (10–25 %) of your yearly incomes to our account to aids in this important ventured. The internal revenue service of the United State of Americas will function as our trust intermediary-ness. I pray that you overstand our plight. My family and our colleagues will be forever graceless. Please reply in strict confidencency.

With Sincere and Warmest Regardations,

George Walker Bush[7]

This is actually a second-generation parody. It is identical to the original, composed by Zoltan Grossman, a geography professor at Evergreen State College, except Grossman's contains no grammatical or spelling errors.[8] Here, that the war in Iraq was really about oil is a given. While we're on the subject of Nigerian scam parodies, here is a solicitation from Laura Bush:

My dear Friend!!

I hope this letter is finding you well, and those in your family! Pardon me in advance for my informality in contacting you, you see I am hoping for your personal assistance in a matter of Most Confidential importance and sensitivity. My name is Mrs. Laura Bush, wife to the President of the American United States. I am having in my possession and in my reach some large sums Totaling 24 millions of US dollars.

The monies in regard to this of which I am speaking of which came to us through my husband's service to our Country after he took control during a bloodless coup. During which he and his Partner, Prime Minister Dick Cheney, accumulated this very vast sum through a deal with our Government and Halliburton, a company which Mr. Cheney was still in the service of although no one noticed or cared, in as of that we secretly killed a peasant fishwife named Laci Peterson in order to distract the public and had his husband blamed for it, a man who is too stupid to defend himself in our Courts of Lawfulness.

All of this seemed well yet in as of that we had the money well-guarded until recently, when a local warlord from the Province of Massachusetts, Generallisimo Johann Kerry, took up arms against my husband the rightful President and raised an army of blacks and jews and black jewish movie stars and began the great Super Tuesday Trek towards the Capitol City. He is seeking to take control of these United States and force our children to worship his half-man half-monkey deity, Charles Darwin. And I pray that he does not also seize our money, which he would give to Barbara Streisand, who is secretly a negress and also kind of pretentious.

Of which of and towards in the end to of for wherein by these monies are held in an security company and are now untraceable for the moment, as I agreed to perform sexual deeds with Minister of Money Greenspan so that he would keep the transaction secrets. I will not go into these deeds and what they consisted of in their nature, because I am still in confusion about how I am feeling about these things. It is like, I am supposed to love only my Husband, In our union under God, but this Greenspan, he was like a great and terrible beast in the bed chamber, and it made me feel under his control, but safe at the same time. He was not like my Husband at these things, in as of that he did not giggle during the act or cry afterwards. But this is not for what I am writing to you about.

At any rate of things, this money is being held in an account to which I have access, but it is necessary to safely transmit these funds into a locale where I know my husband and I are well-loved and will be kept safe, Baghdad. But for this to occur, it is imperative that you my friend assist in this transaction with a small fund transfer fee. After completion, I shall be rendering you a 20 percentage portion of the 24 million US dollars, which my husband has calculated is 90 trillion US dollars. Please to be hearing from you soon!
Allahu Akbar, Laura Bush[9]

Rather pointed, no? We have references to the 2000 election as a bloodless coup, Dick Cheney's Halliburton ties (to which, we may infer, the press paid insufficient attention), the convenient distraction of a lurid murder case (another swipe at the press), the characterization of the Democratic Party as the party of blacks and Jews (and the implication that the Republican Party is decidedly not "the big tent" its image makers tried to pretend it was during the 2000 national convention in Philadelphia), and, most bizarrely of all, the love affair with former Federal Reserve chairman Alan Greenspan.

The President Has a Low IQ
In fact, according to a report from the Lovenstein Institute in Scranton, Pennsylvania, "President Bush Has Lowest IQ of All Presidents of Past 50

Years." Specifically, the president has an IQ of 91, a figure, arrived at via examination of Bush's writings, speaking, and schoolwork, that is "accurate to within five points." In a column in which she also took on rumors that Teresa Heinz Kerry had contributed to a foundation that gives money to terrorist groups, Margie Boule of the *Oregonian* assured readers that there is no Lovenstein Institute in Scranton, or anywhere else.[10]

"This must be a joke," Boule wrote, thereby establishing that she is no folklorist, for the item in question is clearly a legend, not a joke. But it started as a joke.[11] Using David Emery of About.com as her source, Boule traces the IQ story to a Lovenstein Institute Web site, the spuriousness of which is immediately apparent from the site's slogan: "Somewhere in Texas, a village is missing its idiot." Which brings us to a book cover parody of Hillary Clinton's *It Takes a Village* called *It Takes a Village Idiot*. (The title of Hillary's book also lent itself to jokes about her husband: Q: How do you satisfy Clinton's sexual appetite? A: It takes a village.)

In a similar vein, I have miscellaneously run across photoshops of Bush in a dunce cap, as a member of the Three Stooges, as *Mad* magazine's Alfred E. Neuman, and as a chimp or a monkey. A few years later, comparisons of Barack and Michelle Obama to monkeys were viewed as racist.

Other Jokes about Bush's Intelligence

The next joke partakes of the hoary tradition of numbskull jokes. One of the hallmarks of the numbskull, as exemplified in the Amelia Bedelia series of children's books and the character Zero in the *Beetle Bailey* comic strip, is literal-mindedness:

> This just in: In an attempt to thwart the spread of bird flu, George W. Bush has just ordered the bombing of the Canary Islands.

This joke, like the *Roe v. Wade* joke we looked at in chapter 4, recalls the 1989 Loma Prieta earthquake joke where Vice President Quayle flies to Epcot Center rather than to the epicenter. Other numbskull jokes:

> An airplane was about to crash; there were 5 passengers on board but only 4 parachutes.
>
> The first passenger said, "I'm Kobe Bryant, the best NBA basketball player, the Lakers need me, I can't afford to die. . . . So he took the first pack and left the plane.

The second passenger, Hillary Clinton, said, "I am the wife of the former president of the United States, I am also the most ambitious woman in the world and I am a New York Senator and a potential future president." She just took the second parachute and jumped out of the plane.

The third passenger, George W. Bush, said: "I'm President of the United States of America, I have a great responsibility being the leader of a superpower nation. And above all I'm the cleverest President in American history, so America's people won't let me die." So he put on the pack next to him and jumped out of the plane.

The fourth passenger, the Pope, says to the fifth passenger, a 10-year-old school boy, "I am old and frail and I don't have many years left, so I will sacrifice my life and let you have the last parachute."

The boy said, "It's OK. There's a parachute left for you. America's cleverest President has taken my schoolbag."

In one variation on this joke, Britney Spears is assigned the numbskull's role, with Bill Clinton, the NBA player Antoine Walker, and the pope playing the parts of the other parachutists. In another, Bill Gates is the numbskull, and the other dramatis personae are Michael Jordan, the Dalai Lama, and a hippie. And in a third, the parachutists are a Boy Scout, a priest, and Bill Clinton—who argues that he's too sexy to die—and the person who gets stuck with the schoolbag is "the smartest woman in the world," Hillary Clinton.

George W. Bush, Albert Einstein and Pablo Picasso have all died. Due to a glitch in the mundane/celestial time-space continuum, all three arrive at the Pearly Gates more or less simultaneously, even though their deaths have taken place decades apart.

The first to present himself to Saint Peter is Einstein. Saint Peter questions him. "You look like Einstein, but you have NO idea the lengths certain people will go to, to sneak into Heaven under false pretenses. Can you prove who you really are?"

Einstein ponders for a few seconds and asks, "Could I have a blackboard and some chalk?"

Saint Peter complies with a snap of his fingers. The blackboard and chalk instantly appear. Einstein proceeds to describe with arcane mathematics and symbols his special theory of relativity.

Saint Peter is suitably impressed. "You really *are* Einstein! Welcome to heaven!"

The next to arrive is Picasso. Once again Saint Peter asks for his credentials. Picasso doesn't hesitate. "Mind if I use that blackboard and chalk?"

Saint Peter says, "Go ahead."

Picasso erases Einstein's scribbles and proceeds to sketch out a truly stunning mural. Bulls, satyrs, nude women: he captures their essences with but a few strokes of the chalk.

Saint Peter claps. "Surely you are the great artist you claim to be! Come on in!"

The last to arrive is George W. Bush. Saint Peter scratches his head. "Einstein and Picasso both managed to prove their identity. How can you prove yours?"

George W. looks bewildered, "Who are Einstein and Picasso?"

Saint Peter sighs, "Come on in, George."

Jokes about St. Peter deciding whether the new arrival at the Pearly Gates will spend eternity in heaven or in hell are ubiquitous. Here is a Bill Clinton version that mocks the fine distinctions he apparently made between intercourse and oral sex when he asserted that he did not have sex with Monica Lewinsky:

Clinton died and was standing at the Pearly Gates. After knocking at the gates, St. Peter appeared.

"Who goes there?" inquired St. Peter.

"It's me, Bill Clinton."

"And what do you want?" asked St. Peter.

"Lemme in!" replied Clinton.

"Soooo," pondered Peter. "What bad things did you do on earth?"

Clinton thought a bit and answered, "Well, I smoked marijuana but you shouldn't hold that against me because I didn't inhale. I guess I had extra-marital sex—but you shouldn't hold that against me because I didn't really have 'sexual relations.' And I lied, but I didn't commit perjury."

After several moments of deliberation St. Peter replied, "OK, here's the deal. We'll send you someplace where it is very hot, but we won't call it 'Hell.' You'll be there for an indefinite period of time, but we won't call it 'eternity.' And don't abandon all hope upon entering, just don't hold your breath waiting for it to freeze over."

Another Clinton variation plays with his reputation as a ladies' man:

Bill Clinton and the Pope died on the same day, and due to an adminis-
trative foul up on the part of Yama, Clinton was sent to heaven and the
Pope was sent to hell.

The Pope explained the situation to the devil, who checked out all
of the paperwork, and the error was acknowledged. The Pope was told,
however, that it would take about 24 hours to fix the problem and correct the error.

The next day, the Pope was called in and the devil said his good-bye
to the Pope as he went off to heaven.

On his way up, the Pope met Clinton who was on his way down, and
they stopped to chat.

Pope: Sorry about the mix up.

Clinton: No problem!

Pope: Well, I'm really excited about going to heaven.

Clinton: Why is that? It's not that great.

Pope: All my life I've wanted to meet the Virgin Mary.

Clinton: Sorry, your Holiness—but you're about a day late.

Before leaving the subject of Bush's intelligence, I should point out that
the Center for Media and Public Affairs annual survey of late-night TV jokes
for 2005 found that more than 40 percent of the Bush jokes were about the
president's intelligence.[12]

THE PRESIDENT HAS SUBSTANCE ABUSE PROBLEMS

It became well known during the 2000 presidential campaign that Bush had
a drinking problem when he was younger. Among many voters, this was
a point in his favor: recognizing the problem and overcoming it showed
strength of character. That he also embraced religion at the time he gave up
drinking improved his standing with some voters as well. But to some jokers
in cyberspace, once a drunk, always a drunk. And when Bush sidestepped a
reporter's question about rumors that he had used cocaine, his nonanswer
was treated as being tantamount to a confession.

One of the jokes parodies the "Got Milk?" ad campaign. Bush is posed
with his bag of cocaine at the Republican National Convention. The text
preceding the "Got Coke?" tagline: "I'm not saying I've used cocaine. But if

Another rumor had Bush "experimenting" with cocaine in his younger days. The question "Got Coke?" references the "Got Milk?" advertising campaign.

I did, it was merely a 'youthful indiscretion.' Today I'm clean. And I'm tough on crime. So if I catch you using coke, I don't want to hear any of that 'youthful indiscretion' nonsense. I'm throwing your crack-addicted ass in prison. That's not hypocrisy. That's politics."

A second coke-themed photoshop is a Kentucky Fried Chicken sign with the words "GW Bush Inaugural special / bucket of right wings / unlimited coke party hats." Compare this version, with its unkind focus on a woman's appearance: "Hillary special / 2 Fat thighs with small breast and a left wing."

An alcohol-themed photoshop shows Bush in a similar signing scene to the Crayola scenes described earlier. In this one, the president's head is on the desk, a drink is in his hand, and a bottle of Glenlivet scotch is nearby. A billboard for Miller Genuine Draft bears the legend "One Draft George Dubya Didn't Dodge," an allusion to Bush's service in the Air National Guard, which was widely seen as a ploy to avoid service in Vietnam. A billboard for "Bush" beer with a photo of Bush and his twin daughters, Barbara and Jenna, features the slogan "Puts the 'W' in DWI!" A photoshop shows Bush in a Yale sweatshirt, guzzling from a bottle of Jack Daniel's.

During the 2000 presidential campaign, Bush acknowledged "drinking too much" before the age of forty, when he quit.

THE PRESIDENT AS HUCKSTER

One of the hallmarks of the Bush presidency was his highly scripted appearances before friendly crowds in settings that were "dressed" to emphasize the White House message of the day. Far and away the most famous of these was the "Mission Accomplished" banner that was hung on the USS *Abraham Lincoln* in May 2003 when President Bush flew in to announce that "major combat" in Iraq was at an end. When Bush left the White House in 2009, despite repeated assurances from Vice President Cheney that the Iraqi insurgency was in its "last throes," the administration had still not figured out how to extract itself from Iraq without the country collapsing into civil war. "Plan for Victory" wallpaper that was used for a speech the president delivered a year and a half after "Mission Accomplished" was particularly amusing, in the disgusting sort of way that my colleague found "Got Fish?" disgusting. It is all eerily reminiscent of the Newspeak banners in *1984*. Little wonder, then, that there are photoshop parodies like "Ignorance Is Strength." Here are some others, which together form a bill of particulars outlining the case to be made against Bush as one of the nation's worst presidents:

- Corporate Criminal
- Credibility Deficit

The Bush White House predilection for "dressing the set" with slogans for a presidential appearance gave rise to countless parodies.

- Crippling the Economy
- Destroying the Environment
- Neglecting the Homeland
- Protecting the Wealthy
- Protecting my Imbecile Lying Ass
- Consolidated Unchecked Power Through Fear
- Liar Tyrant Thief Puppet Idiot Fraud

The other approach to parodying the banners and wallpaper is to keep the original message but superimpose it on a different scene, much as Tourist Guy pops up in multiple locations. An example would be the "Mission Accomplished" banner placed on the Superdome (a green highway sign pointing the way to "Interstate 10—New Orleans" makes the identity of the building clear) with Bush smiling and giving the thumbs-up sign among grieving New Orleans residents.

One of the things folklorists like best about what they study is its mix-and-match quality. Claude Lévi-Strauss used the term *bricolage* to describe the way cultural artifacts are assembled from whatever lies near at hand and seems apposite to the purpose.[13] A good example is a set of parodies of a notorious photo of Michael Jackson dangling his child off a hotel balcony in Berlin in 2002. It's the sort of bizarre behavior that people came to expect from Jackson, which is one of the reasons why "Jackolore" would be a fertile field of study in its own right (see chapter 8 for a sampling). The Jackolore that fits the theme of this chapter substitutes Saddam Hussein for Jackson's baby. In one, Jackson dangles Saddam off the balcony; in the other, President Bush has replaced Jackson, and a caption has been added: "Time to fly, dickhead."

THE PRESIDENT SHOULD NEVER HAVE GOTTEN AS FAR AS HE HAS

The next set of jokes is closely related to the numbskull jokes but differs from them by making Bush's dimwittedness the implicit premise rather than the punch line. Given what we know about Bush's intellect, the jokes marvel that such a manifestly unqualified candidate could wind up in the Oval Office. One joke, which may be found in both verbal and visual versions, references the reality-TV program *Extreme Makeover*. The show indulges the fantasy that even the plainest person can be transformed from ugly duckling to beautiful swan. Beauty, according to this fantasy, is less a matter of genetic inheritance than of professional intervention. One's chance of being plucked from obscurity to be made over by the show's plastic surgeons may be slim, but at least it's possible, just as one is likelier to become wealthy by winning the lottery than by inheriting a fortune. And of course, if one were to win the lottery, one could then purchase all the plastic surgery one needs. The jokes suggest that nothing less than an extreme makeover could make Bush fit for the presidency.

> Three Texas plastic surgeons were playing golf together and discussing surgeries they had performed. One of them said, "I'm the best plastic surgeon in Texas. A concert pianist lost 7 fingers in an accident, I reattached them, and 8 months later he performed a private concert for the Queen of England." One of the others said. "That's nothing. A young man lost both arms and legs in an accident, I reattached them, and 2 years later he won a gold medal in 5 field events in the Olympics." The third surgeon said, "You guys are amateurs. Several years ago a cowboy who was high on cocaine and alcohol rode a horse head-on into a train traveling 80 miles an hour. All I had left to work with was the horse's ass and a cowboy hat. Now he's president of the United States."

| George W. "Horse Tail" Bush, before | George W. "Horse Tail" Bush, after |

Dismay over what Bush's detractors saw as his woeful lack of qualifications for the presidency coincided with the widespread use of e-mail and the World Wide Web to circulate photographs.

The joke echoes a photoshop labeled "Never Underestimate the Power of Makeup" that features a series of before-and-after photos of women who look plain before, then glamorous after. The last pair of images shows a horse's rear end before and the face of George W. Bush after.

In this next set of jokes, instead of explaining how such an unlikely candidate made it to the White House, the jokes call our attention to his predicament now that he is there. The first one also alludes to Bush's seeming discomfort with his role, never more apparent than when he was called on to speak without a script:

> While suturing a laceration on the hand of a 90-year-old man (he got his hand caught in a gate while working his cattle) a doctor and the old man were discussing Bush's health care reform ideas.
>
> The old man said "Well, ya know, old Bush is a post turtle."
>
> Not knowing what he meant, the doctor asked him what a "post turtle" was.
>
> And he said, "When you're driving down a country road, and you come across a fence post with a turtle balanced on top, that's a post

turtle. You know he didn't get there by himself, he doesn't belong there, he can't get anything done while he's up there, and you just want to help the poor thing down."

This joke, needless to say, was subsequently applied to Barack Obama, Sarah Palin, and Supreme Court nominee Sonia Sotomayor and may go back at least as far as the Clinton years, given that health care reform was not the priority for Bush that it was for Clinton before him and Obama after him. I ran across one recent reference to Obama as the "Post-Turtle-in-Chief."

In the post turtle joke, the accidental president is high and dry, unable to stand on solid ground. In the next joke, he has the opposite problem. You might say he is literally in over his head:

I have a moral question for you. This is an imaginary situation, but I think it is interesting to decide what one would do.

The situation: You are in the Midwest, and there is a huge flood in progress. Many homes have been lost, water supplies compromised and infrastructures destroyed.

Let's say that you're a photographer out getting still photos for a news service, traveling alone, looking for particularly poignant scenes. You come across George W. Bush who has been swept away by the floodwaters.

He is barely hanging on to a tree limb and is about to go under.

You can either put down your camera and save him, or take a Pulitzer Prize winning photograph of him as he loses his grip on the limb.

So, here's the question and think carefully before you answer the question below:

Which lens would you use?

Does this joke challenge journalists to come out from behind their objective lens and tells us what they really see when they look at President Bush? Here is a shorter version from the 2008 presidential campaign:

Here is a tough question: If you came across Hillary Clinton struggling in a raging river and you had a choice between rescuing her or of getting a Pulitzer prize-winning photograph, what shutter speed should you use?

In a couple of less effective versions, Osama bin Laden and Yasir Arafat are the drowning victims. For photographers it's enough of a joke to make the victim a nameless drowning man. Here is a different drowning joke:

> One day there were three boys walking down the street, and suddenly they heard cries for help. When the boys got to the noise they saw Bill Clinton in a lake drowning. The three boys saved him from drowning.
> Dubya asked the boys how he could ever repay him. The first boy said, "I want a boat."
> The second boy said, "I want a truck."
> And the third boy said, "I want three tombstones with our names all on them." Dubya asked, "Why is that, son?"
> The little boy said, "Because when my Dad finds out that we saved you, he is going to kill us all!"

This joke offers the best evidence I have ever seen of folkloric recycling—the tendency to update old folklore by simply changing the names of the dramatis personae. Here the name Dubya appears in two places, but the name Bill Clinton was inadvertently kept. In the famous urban legend about the black man in an elevator with a big dog and a white woman (the man says, "Sit, Lady," and the frightened woman obeys, not realizing that Lady is the dog's name), the man has been identified as Reggie Jackson, Joe Greene, Magic Johnson, and others.[14] Similarly, as we saw in chapter 3, the Ayatollah Khomeini, Saddam Hussein, and Osama bin Laden have been interchangeable in certain jokes about America's stormy relationship with the Islamic world over the past three decades. And the name of the current president has been routinely substituted for the name of his predecessor on such faxlore as the "Simplified Tax Form" (Step 1: How much money did you make last year? Step 2: Send it in) and this "quadrennial perennial," as one Web site calls it:

> Five thousand years ago, Moses said, "Hitch up your camel. Pick up your shovel. Mount your ass. I will lead you to the promised land."
> Five thousand years later, Franklin Roosevelt said, "Light up a Camel. Lay down your shovel. Sit on your ass. This is the promised land."
> Today, George Bush will lay off your camel, tax your shovel, kick your ass and tell you there is no promised land.

6

You Can't Raffle
Off a Dead Donkey

Newslore of Commerce

The pervasive power of corporations has been a consistent theme in contemporary American folklore. In studies of the Kentucky Fried rat and other legends of foreign or harmful substances in our food and drink (feces in refried beans, mice in Coke bottles, sterility drugs in fried chicken), and of legends of companies with ties to sinister forces or ideologies (Procter and Gamble and devil worship; Tommy Hilfiger or Liz Claiborne or Reebok and racism), Gary Alan Fine[1] and Patricia Turner,[2] among others, have proposed that such tales of contamination and conspiracy express anxiety about how much control of what we consume we have ceded to faceless corporations and how much economic power we fritter away buying overpriced products that we cannot afford and do not need. As we have seen, countless disaster jokes invoke product names, advertising slogans, and commercial punch lines to cast a jaundiced eye on the commodification of tragedy while mocking the triviality and trivializing impact of consumer culture. This chapter looks at two cycles of newslore aimed at the corporate world. One is a set of parodies of MasterCard's long-running "Priceless" campaign. The second is a set of jokes about the collapse of the Enron corporation.

PRICELESS

There are a number of obvious reasons for the popularity of commercial parodies and jokes. Our lives are saturated with these messages, so they spring readily to mind to the creator of a parody and are readily recognized by the receiver of the parody. Plus they cry out for parody because they are so inherently cynical. Whatever they purport to be about, they are always ultimately about one thing: selling goods or services. The more "warm and fuzzy" they are, the more cynical they seem to be. MasterCard's "Priceless" campaign, which debuted in 1998, is among the warmest and fuzziest. Therefore it is among the most often parodied. The commercials show people having a delightful time and the prices of the various goods and service they are enjoying. What it all adds up to, though, is not the sum of the costs but the pricelessness of the experiences. "There are some things money can't buy," says the voice-over. "For everything else, there's MasterCard." The parodies hinge on the dual meaning of the word "priceless." MasterCard uses it to mean "worth more than money can buy." As parodists use it, it's an all-purpose superlative, as in "too funny" or "too perfect." A Google search for "priceless parodies" yields dozens of sites. Here are a dozen news-related examples.

Columbine
The version I found was all text, no photo.

Eric and Dylan's American Express Commercial

AMMO, 200 Rounds: $75
Semi-Automatic Rifle: $675
Kenneth Cole Trench Coat: $400
Ski Mask: $10.00
Look on classmates face just before you blow his head off: Priceless

The backstory: Eric Harris and Dylan Klebold were the two perpetrators of the 1998 Columbine High School massacre. At first blush, the tone of this parody seems quite callous, but the expensive trench coat tells a different story. The message is that these were spoiled kids who had nothing to complain about. The joke takes Eric and Dylan's point of view: They would have found their classmates' expressions priceless, which only goes to show how messed up they were. The parody, I would argue, expresses disgust. Odd that it's mistitled "American Express Commercial."

Elian
The photo, which is untouched, shows two armed men in helmets, goggles and olive-drab uniforms. The one in the foreground appears to be

confronting a frightened-looking civilian who is holding a young boy in his arms.

A Rubber Inner Tube and Trip to America ... $17.38
A Plane Ticket from Cuba for Dad ... $325.00
A FULL SWAT Team w/Automatics ... $75,000
The look on the little bastards face ... Priceless

The backstory: The photo, taken in April 2000, would be recognizable to most people. It appeared on the front page of many newspapers as the culminating moment in a long tug-of-war over a six-year-old Cuban boy named Elian Gonzalez. Elian had fled Cuba in a motorboat with his mother, who died en route to Florida. The boy, found floating on an inner tube, then went to stay with his relatives in Miami. The boy's father wanted him to return to Cuba. On one side were those who thought Elian should be reunited with his father; on the other were those who thought the boy would be better off remaining in the United States. Finally, Immigration and Naturalization Service agents were ordered to seize the boy from his Miami relatives and take him to his father. The photo of their doing so with its stark contrast between the armed INS agent and the frightened-looking child was a public relations disaster for President Clinton and Attorney General Janet Reno. (Reno had to address accusations that a subsequent photo of a smiling Elian with his father was a fake.) Naturally, the parodists didn't see what all the fuss was about. In their view, this was one of those mediathons where the coverage was out of all proportion to the importance of the story. The parody put the boy, but really, the story, in its place. This was not the final battle in the great twentieth-century war between communism and democracy. It was a custody battle. The joke suggests the government should never have gotten involved.

Bush/Cocaine

The photo shows a smiling President Bush in the cabin of an airplane, presumably Air Force One, with a plastic water pipe in his hand. The wording on the familiar overlapping red and gold circles of the MasterCard logo has been changed to read "MasterRace."

New Bong: $50
Cocaine Habit: $300

Finding Out That the Good-Old-Boy Network Can still Rig an Election in the Deep South: Priceless
For the Rest of Us there's honesty.

The backstory: When reporters asked candidate Bush in the summer of 1999 whether he had ever used cocaine, he declined to answer, apart from alluding to his "irresponsible youth." Many drew their own conclusions. The rest of the parody links Bush's lack of candor about drug use with the way he allegedly stole the 2000 election by stealing votes in Florida.

Gore Supporters
The photo is a close-up of Al Gore.

> Haircut at the Mall: $10
> Suit Off the Rack: $300
> Losing the Presidential Election Because Nineteen Thousand of Your Supporters Are Too Damned Stupid to Follow Directions and Fill Out the Ballots Properly: Priceless
> For Everyone Else There's George W. Bush

The backstory: The parody alludes to the infamous "butterfly ballots" that were used in Palm Beach County, Florida. The ballot was arranged in a verso-recto format, with six presidential candidates listed on the left, four on the right, and corresponding holes to be punched for the candidate of one's choice down the middle. The first name on the verso was Bush's; so was the first hole. The confusion arose because the second name on the verso was Gore's, but the second hole corresponded to the first name on the recto, which was Buchanan's. Thus many voters (including my mother) who intended to vote for Gore punched the second hole and later learned they had voted for Buchanan. The design was immediately scrapped for future elections.

Nader Supporters
The photo shows a group of protesters holding signs with messages such as "War no more" and "War isn't working."

> Poster board: $3.00
> Bus ticket to the march: $1.75

Failing to see the irony of voting for Nader and putting Bush in power: Priceless!

The backstory: Ralph Nader and his supporters contend that he drew votes from those who would not have voted for Bush or Gore in 2000. Others believe that he mostly siphoned Democratic votes, thus costing Gore the election. He is thus partly to blame for the war in Iraq.

Bush/Poverty

The photo shows President Bush waving at the White House press photographers while carrying one dog and walking another on a leash.

Percent of low-income working American families whose taxes will not be reduced by the Bush tax plan: 60%
Children under the age of 18 without health insurance: 10 million
Money borrowed by the government to pay for the Bush "tax rebate": $51 billion
Heading to your ranch for 30 days off after 6 months on the job: Priceless
There are some things money can't buy.
Real compassion is one of them

The backstory: Though there's no aircraft in the photo, the parodist has inferred, or possibly knew from seeing the photo in the newspaper, that the president was about to fly to his spread in Crawford, Texas, for a little vacation time. The contrast between the problems of ordinary Americans and Bush's immunity and seeming indifference to such problems—does he care more about his pets than the people?—speaks for itself. Here, too, the expense report style of the commercial lends itself to criticism of the government's handling of the nation's finances.

Bush/Iraq

The photo shows Bush lifting a baby, probably during a campaign stop.

Military deployment . . . $79 billion
Military occupation: $105 billion
Reconstruction/Recovery . . . $105 billion
Debt/Claims/Reparation . . . $361 billion

Humanitarian Aid ... $10 billion
Aid to allies ... $10 billion
Governance ... $12 billion
Getting future generations to pay for your oil war ... priceless

The backstory: There are three versions of why the United States invaded Iraq and deposed Saddam Hussein. The Bush administration's version, now widely discredited, posited that Saddam had links to the September 11 attacks, was developing weapons of mass destruction, and therefore posed a threat that had to be removed. The second version had it that the Bush administration knew very well that Saddam had nothing to do with 9/11 and that sanctions and inspections were keeping him in check. But after 9/11, the Bush administration felt it needed a win to bolster the confidence of a shaken populace. Unlike Osama bin Laden, whose whereabouts were unknown, Saddam Hussein, much weakened by his war with Iran and by the 1991 Gulf War, made an easy target. The third and most cynical version was that Bush and Cheney were oilmen, and Iraq is an oil-rich land. The 9/11 attacks provided a perfect pretext for seizing Iraq's oil and lining the pockets of the president and vice president's friends. The parody reminds us of the war's staggering cost—and of who is going to pay for it.

Bin Laden
The next three examples are similar. One shows Osama bin Laden in the crosshairs.

Trip to Afghanistan: $800
High powered sniper rifle: $1,000
Hotel stay with accessible roof: $100
Scoring a head shot on Osama bin laden: priceless
For everyone else there's: CruiseMissiles

The next version shows photos of a bullet, a rifle, a commercial jet, and a head shot of Osama bin Laden.

Ammunition: $12
New rifle: $385
Airline travel to Afghanistan: $1,349
Clear line of sight: priceless

The photo shows a bomb.

Gross weight: 15,000 lbs.
Aluminum powder explosive = 12,000 lbs
Unit cost = $27,318
The look on their faces when this ugly motherfucker falls into their
tent . . . Priceless

The backstory: These parodies come across as criticisms of the Bush
administration's failure to bring Osama bin Laden to justice, though such
criticism may not have been the intent of the creators. The fake ads suggest
that getting bin Laden is so clearly desirable and should be such a simple matter, in terms of both logistics and expense; why, then, is he still at large? And
why are we spending billions on a war in Iraq when we could send an assassin
to the Afghanistan–Pakistan border, where, supposedly, bin Laden remains in
hiding? Perhaps the parodists did not believe Bush's tough talk about wanting
bin Laden "dead or alive." The more typical American approach would be to
capture and try in a court of law, as was done with Saddam Hussein. Seizing
someone, which can only happen with troops laying hands on him, is a lot
more complicated than killing him, which can be accomplished at a distance.

Terrorist
Two photos. The first shows a crowd in Middle Eastern dress and a bearded
figure setting fire to an American flag. The second shows the man's clothes
on fire.

American flag: $25
Gasoline: $2
cigarette lighter: $2.50
Catching yourself on fire because you are a terrorist asshole: priceless

The backstory: This parody uses the MasterCard ad as the basis for some
straightforward commentary on a news photo.
And a variation: Another photo of a crowd in Middle Eastern dress.
Some participants are carrying banners with the following slogans: "We Are
Idiots," "Bomb Us Next," "Please Kick Our Asses." Perhaps these parodies are
meant to reassure us: just as it is said that the biggest advantage the police
have in the war on crime is the stupidity of most criminals, so can we perhaps view the September 11 attacks as a lucky shot that made the terrorists
look much more formidable than they really are.

Bus fair to anti-war protest rally—$.50
Paint and canvas protest signs—$32.00
Asking a retired US Army Sergeant to translate your anti-American slogans—Priceless

The backstory (as told in the accompanying e-mail, which bore the subject line "Syrian geniuses"):

POSITIVELY PRICELESS!!!
Read the following explanation before looking at the picture!
Most Syrians struggle to even read Arabic, much less have a clue about reading English.
So, how do a group of Syrian protest leaders create the most impact with their signs by having the standard 'Death To Americans' (etc.) slogans printed in English?
Answer:
They simply hire an English-speaking civilian to translate and write their statements into English.
Unfortunately, in this case, they were unaware that the 'civilian' insurance company employee hired for the job was a retired US Army Sergeant! Obviously, pictures of this protest rally never made their way to Arab TV networks, but the results were PRICELESS!
This picture is not doctored.

Snopes, after pronouncing the photo an obvious fake, offers a parody where the signs read "Spam Us," "We Forward Anything," and "We Never Check Snopes.com," and the "Priceless" copy goes like this:

Access to the Internet: $14.95
Adding an informational site to your favorites: Free
Getting flooded with urban legends and glurge because your friends know you're gullible enough to believe and forward everything you read? Priceless.[3]

Bush/NASCAR
The news photo shows President Bush shaking hands with a man in a jump-suit emblazoned with patches from makers of various automobiles and automotive parts. A number of similarly attired men look on. A crowded grandstand is in the background.

Air Force One Flight: $1,000,000
Extra Secret Service: $200,000
Having the Taxpayers Foot the Cost of Your Campaign Stop: Priceless

The backstory: NASCAR dads—white men who tended to be culturally conservative but receptive to Democratic appeals on economic issues—were identified as "the election cycle's hottest new constituency" during the 2004 presidential race. President Bush dropped in on the Daytona 500 in February 2004, greeted the 180,000 spectators, and said, "Gentlemen, start your engines." Both engines and spectators roared.

One of the marvels of Bush's career is that an Ivy League–educated scion of a wealthy New England family succeeded at representing himself as a regular guy from west Texas. The creator of this parody wasn't buying it. The parody could have served as an illustration of Ellen Goodman's column in the *Boston Globe*: "All this was billed—and I do mean billed—as a presidential, not a political, visit."[4] The purpose of Bush's drop-in, Marc Cooper wrote in the *Nation*, was "to burnish the Everyman cultural pose that Bush has so successfully honed, and this was a ripe audience."[5] As with the Elian Gonzalez parody, our attention is drawn to the extravagant and irresponsible expenditure of the taxpayer's money.

Hillary Clinton

The photo shows Hillary Clinton shaking the right hand of a soldier who has crossed the middle and index fingers of his left hand, signifying that he is not as pleased to be meeting the senator as it would appear.

Haircut: $8
BDUs: $100
Knowing You Just Mocked The "Smartest Woman On Earth" Right Under Her fat Elitist Nose: PRICELESS!!!

The backstory: According to Snopes, the photo, taken in Iraq in 2003, has not been altered. An alternative version, sans the Priceless parody, offers the following explanation:

Picture shows that this guy has been thru Survival School. He's giving the sign of "coercion" with his left hand. These hand signs are taught in survival school to be used by future POW's to send messages back to our intelligence services viewing the photo or video. This guy was being coerced to holding hands with Hillary. Little did she know that he would tell us.

Snopes says there is no evidence of outright coercion.[6] Oh, and BDU means battle dress uniform (I had to look it up).

Enron
The image shows the Enron logo, leaking oil.

> Paper shredder: $100
> Debt hidden in off-balance-sheet subsidiaries: $500 MILLION
> Stock cashed in by executives while encouraging employees to keep buying: $1.3 BILLION
> Sitting in front of a congressional committee and claiming ignorance of any wrongdoing with a completely straight face: PRICELESS
> There are some things money can't buy.
> Integrity is one of them.

The backstory: In 2001, Americans were appalled to learn that the top executives of a major corporation, some with uncomfortably close ties to the Bush administration, had used fraudulent accounting practices to conceal company losses and had then cashed out while encouraging rank-and-file employees to invest in the company, which, when it collapsed, wiped out those employees' retirement funds. The scandal so captured the public imagination—the comedy writer Ben Karlin referred to Enron as a "cultural touchstone" that confirmed "your creepy, horrible suspicions about just how government and the corridors of power work"[7]—that newslore pertaining to it warrants its own section.

ENRON

Most jokes and urban legends about corporations are about unmasking: beneath the friendly faces the companies that feed and clothe us present in their commercials and advertisements lurk unsanitary food-handling practices or unholy alliances with racist organizations. Enron was something different. The fraud was there for all to see, which is why the folk reaction was not the whisper campaign of an urban legend cycle but the open derision of a joke cycle. Although the great recession of 2008 and 2009 affected many more people than the collapse of Enron, it inspired much less folklore, perhaps because, apart from the swindler Bernard Madoff, the key players did not become public figures to the extent that Enron executives Ken Lay and Jeffrey Skilling did. For this reason, I include jokes from the later financial crisis where it dovetails with the Enron material. As for Bernie Madoff, in keeping with a larger trend away from verbal jokes and toward photoshops and video clips, there are a few obvious puns on his name, but mostly what one finds are song parodies on YouTube (and one movie trailer parody, "Scumbag Billionaire," based on *Slumdog Millionaire*, which won the Oscar for Best Picture in 2009). The Madoff puns:

Q: Why are 13,000 investors mad at Bernie?
A: Because he made off with their money!

Q: Why did Bernie choose the name, "Madoff?"
A: Because "Ripoff" had already been taken.

The first Ken Lay joke reflects our fondness for stories about our heroes' youth that foreshadow future greatness.

How Ken Lay Got Started

A city boy, Kenny, moved to the country and bought a donkey from an old farmer for $100.00.

The next day the farmer drove up and said, "Sorry son, but I have some bad news, the donkey died."

Kenny replied, "Well then, just give me my money back."

The farmer said, "Can't do that. I went and spent it already."

Kenny: "OK then, just unload the donkey."

Farmer: "What ya gonna do with him?"

Kenny: "I'm going to raffle him off."

Farmer: "You can't raffle off a dead donkey!"

Kenny: "Sure I can. Watch me. I just won't tell anybody he is dead."

A month later the farmer met up with Kenny and asked "What happened with that dead donkey?"

Kenny said, "I raffled him off. I sold 500 tickets at two dollars a piece and made a profit of $998.00."

The farmer asked, "Didn't anyone complain?"

Kenny replied, "Just the guy who won. So I gave him his two dollars back."
Kenny grew up and eventually became the chairman of Enron.

Raffling off a dead donkey is a fair metaphor for Enron executives' ability to persuade investors to sink money into a worthless company. Seven years later, when the stock market tumbled and banks began to fail—or required propping up by the federal government—a similar, though rather more labored, joke about the buying and selling of monkeys purported to explain how the stock market works. Like the previous Ken Lay joke, this next one is predicated on the surprise revelation of the identity of the wheeler-dealer at the end.

Valentine's Day

A few weeks ago, I was rushing around trying to get some Valentine's Day shopping done. I was stressed out and not thinking very fondly of the weather right then. It was dark, cold, and wet in the parking lot as I was loading my car up. I noticed that I was missing a receipt that I might need later.

So, mumbling under my breath, I retraced my steps to the mall entrance. As I was searching the wet pavement for the lost receipt, I heard a quiet sobbing. The crying was coming from a poorly dressed boy of about 12 years old. He was short and thin. He had no coat. He was just wearing a ragged flannel shirt to protect him from the cold night's chill. Oddly enough, he was holding a hundred dollar bill in his hand.

Thinking that he had gotten lost from his parents, I asked him what was wrong. He told me his sad story. He said that he came from a large family. He had three brothers and four sisters. His father had died when he was nine years old. His Mother was poorly educated and worked two full time jobs. She made very little to support her large family. Nevertheless, she had managed to skimp and save two hundred dollars to buy her children some Valentine's Day presents (since she didn't manage to get them anything on Christmas). The young boy had been dropped off, by his mother, on the way to her second job. He was to use the money to buy presents for all his siblings and save just enough to take the bus home. He had not even entered the mall, when an older boy grabbed one of the hundred dollar bills and disappeared into the night.

"Why didn't you scream for help?" I asked.

The boy said, "I did."

"And nobody came to help you?" I queried.

The boy stared at the sidewalk and sadly shook his head.

"How loud did you scream?" I inquired.

The soft-spoken boy looked up and meekly whispered, "Help me!"

I realized that absolutely no one could have heard that poor boy's cry for help. So I grabbed his other hundred and made a dash for my car.

Signed,
Kenneth Lay
Enron CEO

Here we have yet another subgenre of newslore, the fake letter. Classics include the "College Girl's Letter Home," in which she reveals an escalating series of calamities that add up to her being pregnant, married to a black man, and infected with a venereal disease, only to say at the end that really, the only thing that's amiss is that she's failing her classes, which is not nearly as bad as what could have befallen her;[8] a "Dear Abby" letter written in an increasingly wobbly handwriting on the subject of the writer's husband being a sex maniac;[9] and various parodies of hillbilly speech. This one is doubly caustic, first because it uses synecdoche to bring Enron's slipshod and fraudulent business practices down to a human scale by having Ken Lay lose a receipt and then rob a child of a poor family just as Enron execs essentially robbed rank-and-file employees of their pensions, and second by underscoring Enron's shamelessness by having Lay boast about his nefarious deed. The surprise ending is set up beautifully by the details of the family's plight, which cry out for a compassionate response.

The next item takes the form of a mock school handout.

How to Explain Enron to Your Children

Feudalism - You have two cows. Your lord takes some of the milk.

Fascism - You have two cows. The government takes both, hires you to take care of them, and sells you the milk.

Communism - You have two cows. Your neighbors help take care of them and you share the milk.

Totalitarianism - You have two cows. The government takes them both and denies they ever existed and drafts you into the army. Milk is banned.

Capitalism - You have two cows. You sell one and buy a bull. Your herd multiplies, and the economy grows. You sell them and retire on the income.

Enron Venture Capitalism - You have two cows. You sell three of them to your publicly listed company, using letters of credit opened by your brother-in-law at the bank, then execute a debt/equity swap with an associated general offer so that you get all four cows back, with a tax exemption for five cows. The milk rights of the six cows are transferred via an intermediary to a Cayman Island company secretly owned by the majority shareholder who sells the rights to all seven cows back to your listed company. The annual report says the company owns eight cows, with an option on four more.

Handouts like this one that purport to define and highlight differences among competing ideologies or religions made the photocopier and fax machine rounds for years before finding new life on the Internet. In this version, "Enron Capitalism" is clearly an add-on, but the multiplying cows nicely capture Enron's essential modus operandi of selling assets that it did not have. A favorite of mine in this genre, as a journalism instructor, is the following, which I have received multiple times over the past couple of years:

NEWSPAPER READERS

1. The Wall Street Journal is read by the people who run the country.
2. The New York Times is read by people who think they run the country.
3. The Washington Post is read by people who think they ought to run the country.
4. USA Today is read by people who think they ought to run the country but don't understand the Washington Post.
5. The Los Angeles Times is read by people who wouldn't mind running the country, if they could spare the time.
6. The Boston Globe is read by people whose parents used to run the country.
7. The New York Daily News is read by people who aren't too sure who's running the country.
8. The New York Post is read by people who don't care who's running the country, as long as they do something scandalous.
9. The San Francisco Chronicle is read by people who aren't sure there is a country, or that anyone is running it.
10. The Miami Herald is read by people who are running another country.

Another oft-updated piece of office copier lore places the Enron scandal in the context of a broader cultural decline.

Teaching Math

Teaching Math in 1950:
A logger sells a truckload of lumber for $100.
His cost of production is 4/5 of the price.
What is his profit?

Teaching Math in 1960:
A logger sells a truckload of lumber for $100.
His cost of production is 4/5 of the price, or $80.
What is his profit?

Teaching Math in 1970:
A logger exchanges a set "L" of lumber for a set "M" of money. The cardinality of set "M" is 100. Each element is worth one dollar. Make 100 dots representing the elements of the set "M." The set "C", the cost of production contains 20 fewer points than set "M." Represent the set "C" as a subset of set "M" and answer the following question: What is the cardinality of the set "P" of profits?

Teaching Math in 1980:
A logger sells a truckload of lumber for $100.
His cost of production is $80 and his profit is $20.
Your assignment: Underline the number 20.

Teaching Math in 1990:
By cutting down beautiful forest trees, the logger makes $20. What do you think of this way of making a living?

Topic for class participation after answering the question: How did the forest birds and squirrels feel as the logger cut down the trees? There are no wrong answers.

Teaching Math in 2000:
A logger sells a truckload of lumber for $100.
His cost of production is $120, paid to a partnership owned by his son-in-law. His accounting department tells him his profit is $60. This is

verified by his auditing firm, Arthur Andersen, blessed by his lawyers, Vinson, Elkins, and touted by assorted Wall Street investment bankers.

Question: How can Jesse Jackson share the spotlight on this deal?

This functions as both an Enron joke and as a timeline showing the decline of American education from dumbing down in the 1980s to choking on political correctness in the 1990s. There's an implicit connection: if Americans weren't so poorly educated, they might have noticed what Enron was up to and be less susceptible to chuckle-headed liberal ideas. Note the little kicker aimed at Jesse Jackson, here lampooned as an opportunistic publicity hound. The next item is rather long, but too well executed to paraphrase or cut.

Dear kind-hearted friends . . .

Now that the holiday season has passed, please look into your heart to help those in need. Enron executives in our very own country are living at, or just below the seven-figure salary level . . . right here in the land of plenty.

And, as if that weren't bad enough, they will be deprived of it as a result of the bankruptcy and current SEC investigation.

But now, you can help! For only $20,835 a month, about $694.50 a day (that's less than the cost of a large screen projection TV), you can help an Enron executive remain economically viable during his time of need.

This contribution by no means solves the problem, as it barely covers their per diem . . . but it's a start!

Almost $700 may not seem like a lot of money to you, but to an Enron exec it could mean the difference between a vacation spent in DC, golfing in Florida or a Mediterranean cruise. For you, seven hundred dollars is nothing more than rent, a car note or mortgage payments. But to an Enron exec $700 will almost replace his per diem.

Your commitment of less than $700 a day will enable an Enron exec to buy that home entertainment center, trade in the year-old Lexus for a new Ferrari, or enjoy a weekend in Rio.

HOW WILL I KNOW I'M HELPING?

Each month, you will receive a complete financial report on the exec you sponsor. Detailed information about his stocks, bonds, 401(k), real estate, and other investment holdings will be mailed to your home. You'll also get information on how he plans to invest his golden parachute. Imagine the joy as you watch your executive's portfolio double or triple! Plus upon signing up for this program, you will receive a photo of the exec (unsigned- for a signed photo, please include an additional $50.00). Put the photo on your refrigerator to remind you of other peoples' suffering.

HOW WILL HE KNOW I'M HELPING?

Your Enron exec will be told that he has a SPECIAL FRIEND who just wants to help in a time of need. Although the exec won't know your name, he will be able to make collect calls to your home via a special operator just in case additional funds are needed for unexpected expenses.

YES, I WANT TO HELP!

I would like to sponsor an Enron executive. My preference is checked below:

[ ] Mid-level Manager
[ ] Director
[ ] Vice President (Higher cost; please specify which department)
[ ] President (Even higher cost; please specify which department)
[ ] CEO (Contribution: Average Enron janitor monthly salary x 700)
[ ] Entire Company
[ ] I'll sponsor an Exec most in need. Please select one for me.

SPECIAL LIMITED TIME OFFER

Already an Enron supporter? Don't worry, in this troubled economy, there are many executives who need your help. Ford today is laying off 35,000. The NASDAQ is deflated. Now you can show your patriotism and do something about it. *The Invisible Hand* will allow supporters to substitute executives from any downtrodden company listed on ****edcompany.com.

You will never own a Bentley, wear hand-tailored silk shirts, or have a gentleman's gentleman; why deprive a worthy executive from ascending, and more importantly, from maintaining the lifestyle he so richly deserves? (pun not intended) Imagine the feeling of satisfaction, the pure joy of knowing that your sponsor ex-executive at the former spilt-milk.com will be able to have his caviar and eat it too.

It's just that easy - do it now!

Please charge the account listed below _____ per day and send me a picture of the Enron executive I have sponsored, along with my very own Enron "Keep America Strong Sponsor an Enron Exec: Ask Me How!" t-shirt to wear proudly.

Your Name: _____

Telephone Number:_____

Account Number: _____

Exp. Date:_____[ ] MasterCard [ ] Visa [ ] American Express [ ] Discover

Signature: _____

Mail completed form to *"The Invisible Hand"* or call 1-900-2MUCH now to enroll by phone.

Note: Sponsors are not permitted to contact the executive they have sponsored, either in person or by other means including, but not limited to, telephone calls, letters, e-mail, or third parties. Keep in mind that the executive you have sponsored will be much too busy enjoying his free time, thanks to your generous donations.

Contributions are not tax-deductible.

This is a splendid inversion of appeals to help children in the third world. It uncannily anticipates government bailouts of banks and automakers in 2008–9. But where Enron executives and their peers at other large corporations are seen to have emerged unscathed from their companies' financial woes, in jokes about the 2008–9 financial crisis, the execs get their comeuppance:

How do you define optimism?
A banker who irons five shirts on a Sunday.

What's the difference between an investment banker and a large pizza?
A large pizza can still feed a family of four.

The Enron–Arthur Andersen scandal lent itself to a joke cycle where an embarrassing revelation is used to mask an even more embarrassing revelation.

What Daddy Does for a Living

It's the first day of school in Houston and the teacher thought she'd get to know the kids by asking them their name and what their father does for a living.

The first little girl says: "My name is Mary and my daddy is a postman."

The next little boy says: "I'm Andy and my Dad is a mechanic."

Then one little boy says: "My name is Jimmy and my father is a strip-tease dancer in a cabaret for gay men."

The teacher gasps and quickly changes the subject, but later in the school yard the teacher approaches Jimmy privately and asks if it was really true that his Dad dances nude in a gay bar.

He blushed and said, "I'm sorry but my dad is an auditor for Arthur Andersen and I was just too embarrassed to say so."

There are football variations of this joke where what Dad really does is coach the Buffalo Bills, the team that lost four consecutive Super Bowls, or play for the worst team in the league. There are also political variations where Dad works for the Bush administration, for John Kerry, or "for the Democratic National Committee and is helping to secure the nomination of Hillary Clinton."[10] And there are fake "Dear Abby" letters in which the writer describes various disreputable members of his family and asks if he should tell his fiancée that his cousin works for Microsoft (see chapter 7) or in television. Among the indignities to befall bankers in the 2008–9 financial crisis is that a classic lawyer joke has been adapted to them:

What do you call 12 investment bankers at the bottom of the ocean?
A good start.

The next joke takes the unusual form of a transcript of a presidential press conference.

From the Desk of the President of the United States

PRESIDENT: "I DID NOT HAVE IMPROPER RELATIONS WITH THAT WOMAN: MISS ENRON"

Press Briefing by the President
THE PRESIDENT: Good morning. Alright, I want to get right down to business. It seems that a few of you liberal intellectuals in the press corps are doing your best to aid and abet terrorism by focusing the searing spotlight of truth on the sordid details of an alleged relationship between myself and a sexy little Houston debutante named Miss Enron.

So before this nonsense goes any further, I want to state a few things for the record:

1. I DID NOT HAVE IMPROPER RELATIONS WITH THAT WOMAN: MISS ENRON.

2. Over a seven year period, I DID NOT repeatedly moan in indescribable ecstasy as she slithered her agile and velvety tongue deep inside my campaign war chest, depositing $623,000 worth of hot political love juice.

3. In 1999, I DID NOT squirm with unimaginable delight as she lowered her exquisite self snugly around my mighty gubernatorial staff, gently coaxing me to deregulate the Texas energy markets ever further, further, *further!*

4. Early in 2001, I DID NOT shriek in superb pleasure as she slapped my inaugural balls with generous check after check after check, again and again and again, until each one was left utterly *spent and exhausted!*

5. Finally, just several months ago, as Miss Enron repeatedly arrived at the White House bearing her full complement of eco-political implements of gratification, I DID NOT feverishly satisfy myself upon learning of her energetic servicing of not only my partner Vice President Richard Cheney, but also *every last member* in his Energy Task Force club!

NO, not ONE of these grotesque assertions is accurate, and to even so much as imply that they are, during this, our nation's hour of peril, is tantamount to giving Osama bin Laden himself the greasy reacharound. And needless to say, any journalist who continues down this road will find himself in a whole world of traitor's trouble. I hope I make myself perfectly clear.

No questions. Thank you.

According to the Center for Responsive Politics, Enron made almost $5.8 million in campaign contributions from 1990 to 2000, with about 73 percent of the money going to Republicans. The company gave more than $100,000 to Bush's first presidential campaign and contributed close to that amount to the newly elected president's inaugural gala.[11] Of course, the language he uses in this phony press conference transcript to deny his Enron ties echoes President Clinton's denials of impropriety in his relations with Monica Lewinsky. It also chillingly alludes to pressure on journalists to toe the administration line lest their patriotism be impugned.

Finally, Laura Bush gets into the act with instructions on turning Enron stock into a craft project.

Reaching Out: The First Lady's Message
to Victims of the Enron Collapse

Gals, wondering what to do with your worthless Enron stock certificates? *Decoupage!* That's right, Decoupage - the French art of dressing
up surfaces with attractive scrap paper!

It seems like a whole mess of folks out there are sitting on Enron
Stock Certificates, wondering what to do with them. Well, as your First
Lady and Chairlady of the Washington chapter of Bringing Integrity To
Christian Homemakers, I feel as if it is my responsibility to reach out to
you all and help.

There are two tips that I have come up with to help people put their
Enron stock to good use. Now, if you didn't get a call from me back in
August (after I'd spent 30 minutes wide-eyed talking over cosmos with
Kenneth Lay) telling you: "Sell those suckers!" then you missed out on
my first tip. So, here I am with my second tip: Decoupage!

There are many dear, sweet people out there who aren't part of Bush-
ies' Pioneers and, therefore, not on Bushie's or my calling list. It just
breaks my heart that they are holding trunk-fulls of now worthless
Enron stock. If only you had used some of that stock when it was actually worth something to contribute to my husband, you would have
been one of the people we let know to get rid of the rest of it before the
bottom fell out! Golly, it's just like I told the officer after I ran my car
through a stop sign just as my boyfriend was driving through the same
intersection and I killed him: Doesn't everything in life just have the
cutest way of coming down to timing?

How to Decoupage Enron Stock:

As with any craft project, you should read through and understand
all directions before starting. Don't rely on your husband—or you'll end
up stuck to the kitchen counter for 2 days while he finds all the places
you hide your vodka!

If you have not prepared the surface of the item you plan to
decoupage on, do so now. Make sure it is clean and paint/seal it now. If
you didn't hold much Enron stock, you may wish to decoupage a wood-
en tool or tackle kit. If you are one of the many Enron employees who
had your entire life savings in stock, you will have enough to wallpaper
several rooms of your home. Just think! The little extra time you spend

giving your walls a novel, topical finish will really help your home sell after it is foreclosed on!

1. Cut out your Enron stock certificates. If you are a really bitter person, cut out letters and play smutty word games with Kenny Boy's last name.

2. Arrange the Enron stock before you add the glue so you know where you want everything. Personally, as homemaker who loves crafts, I prefer a theme! Try adding pictures of cars or colleges you can no longer afford! Use your imagination!

3. Completely coat the back of the picture with your glue. Make sure that the room is well-ventilated and that your husband is not hovering over the glue pot as, if memory serves, he will wind out passing out on the fumes and go head-first into your unfinished decoupage!

4. Stick the Enron stock on the glue. Use your finger to gently push down the stock (don't worry about tearing it—there is plenty more where that came from!) and push out any wrinkles and excess glue. You can also use a popsicle stick or brayer (which is what I also call my Mother-In-Law Bar).

5. Continue with the last 2 steps until all your stock is glued on (for some of you in Houston, this could take several weeks of 24-7 decoupaging, but like those cute kitties on the poster say: Hang in there baby!) Let the glue dry.

6. Now, coat your Enron stocks completely with diluted white glue (approximately 3 parts glue to 1 part water) or decoupage medium. Let this dry completely before you let your husband rest Corona bottles or pretzels on it—or they will wind up part of your decoupage!

7. Now, you can continue to add coats of the glue or decoupage medium or use another sealer (polyurethane, acrylic spray, etc.) until you get the desired results. You will, however, want to keep adding coats until the edges of the pictures are smooth—or until you are thrown out of your house for not meeting mortgage, whichever comes first.

    Mrs. George W. Bush ("Laura")

Several digs are folded into this fake news release. Its Suzy Homemaker theme and tone may be a dig at Laura Bush's reversion to First Lady as domestic duenna after her predecessor's forays into policy making. The piece also takes a shot at Mrs. Bush's causing a fatal accident when she ran a stop sign as a seventeen-year-old driver, and at President Bush's supposed ineptitude, clumsiness, and erstwhile substance-abuse problems, with specific reference to the time he choked on a pretzel while watching a football game on TV (see chapter 5). Above all, the suggested craft project underscores the worthlessness of Enron stock. By focusing on the victims of Enron's malfeasance rather than on the dastardly deeds of the Enron executives themselves, it bears some thematic similarities to a couple of one-liners about the 2008–9 crisis:

> I went to the ATM this morning and it said "insufficient funds."
> I'm wondering is it them or me?

Variations:

> I went to an ATM today, and it asked to borrow a twenty till next week.

> With the current market turmoil, what's the easiest way to make a small fortune? Start off with a large one.

7

Not-So-Heavenly Gates
Newslore of the Digital Age

GOING AFTER GATES

While others argue about the relative merits of Macs and PCs or complain that the machines could be a lot more user-friendly if the techies who designed them didn't behave like members of a priesthood (this is a recurring theme of Walter Mossberg's technology columns in the *Wall Street Journal*), I confess I'm more the carnival gawker type when it comes to computers. The first time I cut and pasted on my old Kaypro, I thought it was the greatest thing that had ever happened to writing. I still think so. When I went from the glowing green characters on gray background of the Kaypro to the black-on-white-on-blue of my Gateway, I found the screen as beautiful as a stained-glass window or an illuminated manuscript.

Perhaps because I had both a Mac and a PC on my desk when I was a newspaper editor, I don't much care which I use. And while I find both can be maddeningly obtuse at times (why don't they know what I'm trying to do?), I mostly appreciate that they, like air travel, work as well as they do. But while Steve Jobs of Apple and Bill Gates of Microsoft have both achieved a new kind of revenge-of-the-nerds celebrity, it is Gates who is the favorite target of computer jockeys. To the cognoscenti like Larry Brash, who describes himself as "an evangelically zealous Mac user," Microsoft is a monopolistic octopus that chokes innovation, stifles competition, and produces software that fails too often. Brash is the founder (in 1997) and keeper of the Microsoft and Bill Gates Joke Page, which is my principal source for the material in this chapter.[1] Entries include a fake news story, "Microsoft

Nearing Completion of Death Star," parodies of poems and songs, lightbulb jokes, top ten lists, anagrams and acronyms, and parodies of Microsoft error messages. Here is a sampling:

Now We Know

> After the Hugh Grant/Devine Brown incident that made the papers, Bill Gates called up Hugh Grant. Bill asked him "Was it really worth $50 to almost ruin your career?"
> Hugh replied "Bill, actually it was worth a million".
> So Bill called up Hughes' favorite prostitute, but since she became so famous, her prices had gone up quite a bit. So Bill paid $10,000 for a night with Divine.
> In the morning he said, "That was fantastic! Now I know why professionally you call yourself 'Divine'".
> She answered "Thank you, and now I know why you call your company Microsoft."

A variation, minus the topical reference to Hugh Grant's being charged with lewd conduct after being caught in a car with a prostitute in 1995:

> Q: What did Bill Gates' wife say to him on their wedding night?
> A: "Now I know why you named your company Microsoft!"

The implication seems to be that Bill Gates is the quintessential geek and that geeks are not famed for their virility.

Toddler Property Laws

> 1. If I like it, it's mine.
> 2. If it's in my hand, it's mine.
> 3. If I can take it from you, it's mine.
> 4. If I had it a little while ago, it's mine.
> 5. If it's mine, it must never appear to be yours in any way.
> 6. If I'm doing or building something, all the pieces are mine.
> 7. If it looks just like mine, it's mine.
> 8. If I think it's mine, it's mine.
> 9. If I . . . Oops! I'm sorry; I goofed! Instead of typing in the Toddler Property Laws, I've been typing in Bill Gates' primary Business Plan.

The Toddler Property Laws list is another bit of photocopier/faxlore with a Bill Gates punch line tacked on.

3. Acquisition

Microsoft Addresses Justice Department Accusations

REDMOND, Wash. - Oct. 23, 1997—In direct response to accusations made by the Department of Justice, the Microsoft Corp. announced today that it will be acquiring the federal government of the United States of America for an undisclosed sum.

"It's actually a logical extension of our planned growth", said Microsoft chairman Bill Gates, "It really is going to be a positive arrangement for everyone."

Absurd as it is, this fake news story reads pretty well—apart from the punctuation problems.

The World's Thinnest Books

This is a long list—it includes the aforementioned "The Wild Years" by Al Gore, "My Book of Morals" by Bill Clinton, "Things I Love About Bill" by Hillary Clinton, and "How to Find Osama Bin Laden" by George Bush—with three items pertaining to Microsoft. Classic entries from older lists that spring to mind are "The Wit and Wisdom of Jerry Ford [or Dan Quayle], " "Polish [or Italian] War Heroes," and my favorite, "Great Jewish Athletes." (My aunt gave me a book with a similar title when I was a kid that featured profiles of the bullfighter Sidney Franklin, the boxer Barney Ross, and the baseball stars Hank Greenberg and Sandy Koufax, among others.)

23. Microsoft's complete guide to virus protection.
22. Microsoft's complete guide to data security.
21. Bill Gates' guide to creating unique applications and PC operating systems.
20. Things I Can't Afford - by Bill Gates.

Spreading the Wealth

Gates is not afraid to spread his money around to realize his dream of world domination. Or so we may infer from this much-circulated chain letter:

Dear Friends,

Please do not take this for a junk letter. Bill Gates is sharing his fortune. If you ignore this you will repent later. Microsoft and AOL are now the largest Internet companies and in an effort to make sure that Internet Explorer remains the most widely used program, Microsoft and AOL are running an e-mail beta test.

When you forward this e-mail to friends, Microsoft can and will track it (if you are a Microsoft Windows user) for a two week time period. For every person that you forward this e-mail to, Microsoft will pay you $245.00, for every person that you sent it to that forwards it on, Microsoft will pay you $243.00 and for every third person that receives it, you will be paid $241.00. Within two weeks, Microsoft will contact you for your address and then send you a cheque.

I thought this was a scam myself, but two weeks after receiving this e-mail and forwarding it on, Microsoft contacted me for my address and within days, I received a cheque for US$24,800.00. You need to respond before the beta testing is over. If anyone can afford this Bill Gates is the man. It's all marketing expense to him. Please forward this to as many people as possible. You are bound to get at least US$10,000.00.

A related chain letter casts AOL and Intel in the role of e-mail testers. This letter gets the urban legend hat trick for attestations of authenticity. First, we have a lawyer's testimony ("I'm an attorney, and I know the law. This thing is for real. Rest assured AOL and Intel will follow through with their promises for fear of facing a multimillion dollar class action suit similar to the one filed by PepsiCo against General Electric not too long ago"). Then we have the narrator's brother's girlfriend who "got in on this" when the narrator visited them on the occasion of the Baylor–University of Texas football game ("It was for the sum of $4,324.44 and was stamped 'Paid In Full'"). Best of all, "a friend of my good friend's Aunt Patricia, who works at Intel, actually got a check of $4,543.23 by forwarding this e-mail." As the narrator says, "What have you got to lose?" These promises of payments to those who help the new titans of computing and computer-mediated communication are the flip side of an unkillable set of warnings that the days of free e-mail are about to end unless "you forward this to everyone you know" so that there is enough of an outcry to bring AOL or Congress, as the case may be, to its senses.

Is This a Diana Joke or a Microsoft Joke? Both.

Microsoft announced that they are to rename Windows 98 "Windows Diana". They expect that it too will be superficially attractive, consume lots of resources and crash horribly. [See Chapter 8 for Diana jokes.]

User Unfriendly

Each of the next set of items mocks the vaunted user-friendliness of personal computers by showing, à la Mossberg, how unreliable or nonsensical other machines and services would be if they worked the way Microsoft's products did. Note, too, that a couple of these items get in their digs at Microsoft by mentioning the ease of use of Apple's version of the product. The first item started as a joke and developed into an urban legend:

MS vs. GM

At a recent computer expo (COMDEX), Bill Gates reportedly compared the computer industry with the auto industry and stated, "If GM had kept up with technology like the computer industry has, we would all be driving $25.00 cars that got 1,000 miles to the gallon." In response to Bill's comments, General Motors issued a press release stating: If GM had developed technology like Microsoft, we would all be driving cars with the following characteristics (and I just love this part):
1. For no reason whatsoever, your car would crash twice a day.
2. Every time they repainted the lines in the road, you would have to buy a new car.
3. Occasionally your car would die on the street for no reason. You would have to pull to the side of the road, close all of the windows, shut off the car, restart it, and reopen the windows before you could continue. For some reason you would simply accept this.
4. Occasionally, executing a manoeuvre such as a left turn would cause your car to shut down and refuse to restart, in which case you would have to reinstall the engine.
5. Macintosh would make a car that was powered by the sun, was reliable, five times as fast and twice as easy to drive - but would run on only five percent of the roads.

6. The oil, water temperature, and alternator warning lights would all be replaced by a single "This Car Has Performed an Illegal Operation" warning light.

7. The airbag system would ask, "Are you sure?" before deploying.

8. Occasionally, for no reason whatsoever, your car would lock you out and refuse to let you in until you simultaneously lifted the door handle, turned the key and grabbed hold of the radio antenna.

9. Every time a new car was introduced car buyers would have to learn how to drive all over again because none of the controls would operate in the same manner as the old car.

10. You'd have to press the "Start" button to turn the engine off.

Gates gets his comeuppance when his new house proves to be as kludgy as his computers:

Bill Gates' New House

As many people have probably heard by now, Bill Gates built a new home, a VERY large home, 35 garages, several buildings and so on. However, the problems he's had with the house are much less known. The following is an excerpt from a conversation Bill had with his new home contracters:

Bill: There are a few issues we need to discuss.
Contractor: Ah, you have our basic support option. Calls are free for the first 90 days and a $75 call thereafter. Okay?
Bill: Uh, yeah. The first issue is the living room. We think it's a little smaller than we anticipated.
Contractor: Yeah, some compromises were made to have it out by the release date.
Bill: We won't be able to fit all our furniture in there.
Contractor: Well, you have two options. You can purchase a new, larger living room. Or you can use a stacker.
Bill: Stacker?
Contractor: Yeah, it allows you to fit twice as much furniture into the living room. By stacking it, of course, you put the entertainment center on the couch, the chairs on the table, etc. You leave an empty spot, so that when you want to use some furniture, you can unstack what you need and put it back when you're done.

Bill: Uh, I dunno . . . Issue two. The second issue is the light fixtures. The lightbulbs we brought with us from our old house don't fit. The threads run the wrong way.

Contractor: Oh, that's a feature! The bulbs you have aren't plug and play. You'll have to upgrade to new bulbs.

Bill: And the electrical outlets? The holes are round instead of rectangular. How do I fix that?

Contractor: That's another feature designed with the customer in mind. Just uninstall and reinstall the electrical system.

Bill: Your kidding!?!

Contractor: Nope, it's the only way.

Bill: (Sighing) Well, I have one last problem. Sometimes when I have guests, someone will flush the toilet and it won't stop. The water pressure drops so low that the showers don't work.

Contractor: That's a resource leakage problem. One fixture is failing to terminate and is hogging the resource, preventing other fixtures from accessing.

Bill: And how do I fix that?

Contractor: Well, after each flush, you all need to exit the house, turn off the water at the street, turn it back on, reenter the house. Then you can get back to work.

Bill: That's the last straw! What kind of product are you selling me?

Contractor: Hey, if you don't like it, nobody made you buy it.

Bill: And when will it be fixed?

Contractor: Oh, in the next house, which we'll be ready to release next year. Actually it was due out this year, but we've had some delays . . .

Sound familiar.....

If Microsoft were to branch out into kitchen appliances, consumers would face similar challenges:

Microsoft's New TV Dinner

You must first remove the plastic cover. By doing so you agree to accept and honor rights to all Microsoft TV dinners. You may not give anyone else a bite of your dinner (which would constitute an infringement of Microsoft's rights). You may, however, let others smell and look at your dinner and are encouraged to tell them how good it is.

If you have a PC microwave oven, insert the dinner into the oven. Set the oven using these keystrokes: <<\mstv.dinn.//08.5min@50%heat//

Then enter: ms//start.cook_dindin/yummy\| /yum~yum:-) gohot#cookme.

If you have a Mac oven, insert the dinner and press start. The oven will set itself and cook the dinner.

If you have a Unix oven, insert the dinner, enter the ingredients of the dinner (found on the package label), the weight of the dinner, and the desired level of cooking and press start. The oven will calculate the time and heat and cook the dinner exactly to your specification.

Be forewarned that Microsoft dinners may crash, in which case your oven must be restarted. This is a simple procedure. Remove the dinner from the oven and enter: <<ms.good/tryagain\again/again.please.

The conflation of Microsoft and microwave recalls the legend of the tanning-bed user who cooks her insides.[2] Where the one plays off both the Microsoft/microwave name similarity and the superficial resemblance between micro-wave ovens and computer monitors, the other plays off the lay inability to distinguish between different kinds of invisible radiation. The next item, a top ten list plus one, teleports Microsoft's glitchy technology back in time.

The Top 11 Differences in the Middle Ages if Microsoft Had Existed Then

11. Chastity belts require a password rather than a key.

10. Last year's pitchfork not compatible with this year's hay.

9. Lord Gates claims he has no memory of any memo describing his intention to "wipeth my arse with the Magna Carta."

8. The "Good Plague" hoax.

7. Horses routinely stop in mid-stride, and require a boot to the rear to start again.

6. The Microsoft Rack would work, but it would be 3 times larger than it should be and never completely kill anyone.

5. Forget about William Tell; William Gates shoots Apple off the head of Steve Jobs.

4. Use of a large, clumsy broadsword instead of yet-to-be- invented scis-sors helps explain Lord Bill's haircut.

3. Archbishop of Canterbury gets hit in the face with a pie.

2. Stained Glass Windows MCCCXXXXV actually not released until Spring of MCCCXXXXVI.
Number 1 Difference in the Middle Ages if Microsoft Had Existed Then ...
1. The Y1K bug threatens to cripple high-tech industries, like stone-masonry and weaving.

This brings us to our next set of computer jokes. But before closing out this section, it's worth considering what Bill Gates thinks about all the non-sense that his products have helped disseminate:

Wasting somebody else's time strikes me as the height of rudeness. We have only so many hours, and none to waste.

That's what makes electronic junk mail and e-mail hoaxes so mad-dening. The "free" distribution of unwelcome or misleading messages to thousands of people is an annoying and sometimes destructive use of the Internet's unprecedented efficiency.[3]

THE MILLENNIUM BUG

In a nutshell, it seemed not to have occurred to computer programmers that the year 2000 would ever come; thus, it was thought, when we rang out '99 and rang in the year '00, computers worldwide would fail, and chaos would ensue. An Associated Press story outlined the worst-case scenario: "chaos in the financial markets, electricity shutdowns, disrupted airline schedules and missed paychecks."[4] Another doomsayer predicted "loss of electricity and water, business failures, major infrastructure damage, lawsuits, and munici-pal bankruptcy."[5] Some worst cases were worse than others. The *Pittsburgh Post-Gazette* captured the mood in a story headlined "Preparing for the End of the World as We Know It." To the list of impending disasters it added "food riots, the declaration of martial law and the seizure of food stockpiles by the federal government" among the possibilities. One source invoked the tale of the lazy grasshopper and the industrious ants—best lay in the sorts of supplies we might need if we were going camping: nonperishable foodstuffs and devices that generate heat and light without electricity. Another source, a writer named Sandra Ghost, who was working on "a Christian thriller involving UFOs and the Second Coming," spoke of failed pacemakers and backed-up sewers at a meeting with her neighbors at a local motel. The apocalyptic vibe is unmistakable. If anything, the hard-core survivalist types claimed, the government was soft-peddling the dangers to avoid sowing panic among the populace.[6] The Y2K story connects to urban legends about harmful technology when it cites those who see the millennium bug as a punishment for our overdependence on technology.[7] Afterward, a *Seattle Post-Intelligencer* columnist acknowledged that the news media had blown things out of proportion.[8] But our friends the Internet jokesters knew that already. As far as they were concerned, the only appropriate course of action was parody.

Y2K Backup System

Enclosed with this memo is a "Y2K Backup System" device designed to meet short time emergency needs in case of a *computer* operations failure, or operational delay. This device is the company's Primary Emergency Network Computer Interface Liaison device (P.E.N.C.I.L.).

This device has been field tested extensively, including certification testing, as well as volume and stress testing. Properly maintained, the device meets all the requirements for coding and data input.

Prior to use, the (P.E.N.C.I.L.) will require preparation and testing. Tools and supplies required will be a sharpened knife or grinding device; and a supply of computer paper (with or without holes).

Gripping the device firmly in your hand, proceed to scrape or grind the wooded end until it has a cone-like appearance. The dark core area must be exposed to properly function. (Left-handed employees should read this sentence backwards, and then go to your supervisor for assistance.)

Place a single sheet of computer paper on a smooth, hard surface. Take the backup device, place the sharpened point against the paper, and pull it across the paper. If properly done, this will input a single line.

CAUTION: Excessive force may damage components of the device or damage the data reception device. If either the P.E.N.C.I.L. or the paper are damaged, go back to the preparation instructions above.

Proper use of the device will require data simulation input by the operator.

Placing the device against the computer page forming symbols as closely resembling the computer lettering system you normally use. At the completion of each of the simulated letters, lift the device off the page, move it slightly to the right, replace it against the page, and form the next symbol. This may appear tedious, and somewhat redundant, but, with practice, you should be able to increase your speed and accuracy. The P.E.N.C.I.L. is equipped with a manual deletion device. The device is located on the reverse end of the P.E.N.C.I.L. Error deletions operate similarly to the "backspace" key on your computer. Simply place the device against the erroneous data, and pull it backwards over the letters. This should remove the error, and enable you to resume data entries.

CAUTION: Excessive force may damage the data reception device. Insufficient force, however, may result in less than acceptable deletion, and may require re-initialization of action as above.

This device is designed with user maintenance in mind. However, if technical support is required, you can still call your local computer desk supervisor at (800)-YOU-DUMMY.

The memo recalls Horace Miner's little treatise on the "Nacirema," a classic of introductory courses in anthropology.[9] One is given various clues early on—"Nacirema" and "Notgnihsaw" in Miner's essay, "Primary Emergency Network Computer Interface Liaison" here—but the inattentive reader might not notice that these are "American" and "Washington" spelled backward or (less likely) an acronym for pencil, and could get fairly deep into the essay before realizing that familiar practices—tooth brushing in Miner, writing and erasing here—are being described in ways that make them seem strange and new. Another low-tech alternative in the event of computer failure is touted in this next bit of memo parody, predicated on the superficial similarities between the new notebook-sized computers and a classic children's toy:

Y2K SOLUTION
Corporate has determined that there is no longer any need for network or software applications support. The goal is to remove all computers from the desktop by Jan, 1999. Instead, everyone will be provided with an Etch-A-Sketch. There are many sound reasons for doing this:
1. No Y2K problems
2. No technical glitches keeping work from being done.
3. No more wasted time reading and writing emails.

The following FAQ parody, written in the same spirit, gives a good idea of how the Etch A Sketch works:

Etch-A-Sketch tech support

Date: Tue, 26 May 1998 14:56:16 -0500

Frequently Asked Questions for Etch-A-Sketch Technical Support

Q: My Etch-A-Sketch has all of these funny little lines all over the screen

A: Pick it up and shake it.

Q: How do I turn my Etch-A-Sketch off?

A: Pick it up and shake it.

Q: What's the shortcut for Undo?

A: Pick it up and shake it.

Q: How do I create a New Document window?

A: Pick it up and shake it.

Q: How do I set the background and foreground to the same color?

A: Pick it up and shake it.

Q: What is the proper procedure for rebooting my Etch-A-Sketch?

A: Pick it up and shake it.

Q: How do I delete a document on my Etch-A-Sketch?

A: Pick it up and shake it.

Q: How do I save my Etch-A-Sketch document?

A: Don't shake it.

The next parody, of a news release this time, is nothing more than an extended pun on the term "Y2K"—and loops us back to Microsoft:

REDMOND, WA (API)—MICROSOFT (MSFT) announced today that the official release date for the new operating system "Windows 2000" will be delayed until the second quarter of 1901.

"Our staff has completed the 18 months of work on time and on budget. We have gone through every line of code in every program in every system. We have analyzed all databases, all data files, including backups and historic archives, and modified all data to reflect the change. We are proud to report that we have completed the "Y-to-K" date change mission, and have now implemented all changes to all programs and all data to reflect your new standards:

Januark, Februark, March, April, Mak, June, Julk, August, September, October, November, December

As well as:

Sundak, Mondak, Tuesdak, Wednesdak, Thursdak, Fridak, Saturdak

I trust that this is satisfactory, because to be honest, none of this Y to K problem has made any sense to me. But I understand it is a global problem, and our team is glad to help in any way possible. And what does the year 2000 have to do with it? Speaking of which, what do you think we ought to do next year when the two digit year rolls over from 99 to 00?

We'll await your direction."

Finally, a couple of clever writers imagined that people living at the dawn of the first century and in the year 999 must have had millennial problems of their own. Note that the first is in the form of a letter; the second, a news story.

Translated from Latin scroll dated 2BC

Dear Cassius:

Are you still working on the Y zero K problem? This change from BC to AD is giving us a lot of headaches and we haven't much time left. I don't know how people will cope with working the wrong way around. Having been working happily downwards forever, now we have to start thinking upwards. You would think that someone would have thought of it earlier and not left it to us to sort it all out at this last minute.

I spoke to Caesar the other evening. He was livid that Julius hadn't done something about it when he was sorting out the calendar. He said he could see why Brutus turned nasty. We called in Consultus, but he simply said that continuing downwards using minus BC won't work and as usual charged a fortune for doing nothing useful. Surely, we will not have to throw out all our hardware and start again? Macrohard will make yet another fortune out of this I suppose.

The money lenders are paranoid of course! They have been told that all usury rates will invert and they will have to pay their clients to take out loans. Its an ill wind. . . .

As for myself, I just can't see the sand in an hourglass flowing upwards. We have heard that there are three wise men in the East who have been working on the problem, but unfortunately they won't arrive until it's all over.

I have heard that there are plans to stable all horses at midnight at the turn of the year as there are fears that they will stop and try to run backwards, causing immense damage to chariots and possible loss of life. Some say the world will cease to exist at the moment of transition. Anyway, we are still continuing to work on this blasted Y zero K problem. I will send a parchment to you if anything further develops.

If you have any ideas please let me know,

Plutonius

Year 1K Crisis

Canterbury, England. A.D. 999.

An atmosphere close to panic prevails today throughout Europe as the millennial year 1000 approaches, bringing with it the so-called "Y1K Bug," a menace which, until recently, hardly anyone had ever heard of. Prophets of doom are warning that the entire fabric of Western Civilization, based as it now is upon monastic computations, could collapse, and that there is simply not enough time left to fix the problem.

Just how did this disaster-in-the-making ever arise? Why did no one anticipate that a change from a three-digit to a four-digit year would throw into total disarray all liturgical chants and all metrical verse in which any date is mentioned? Every formulaic hymn, prayer, ceremony and incantation dealing with dated events will have to be re-written to accommodate three extra syllables. All tabular chronologies with three-space year columns, maintained for generations by scribes using carefully hand-ruled lines on vellum sheets, will now have to be converted to four-space columns, at enormous cost. In the meantime, the validity of every official event, from baptisms to burials, from confirmations to coronations, may be called into question.

"We should have seen it coming," says Brother Cedric of St. Michael Abbey, here in Canterbury. "What worries me most is that THOUSAND contains the word THOU, which occurs in nearly all our prayers, and of course always refers to God. Using it now in the name of the year will seem almost blasphemous, and is bound to cause terrible confusion. Of course, we could always use Latin, but that might be even worse - The Latin word for Thousand is Mille, which is the same as the Latin for mile. We won't know whether we are talking about time or distance!"

Stonemasons are already reported threatening to demand a proportional pay increase for having to carve an extra numeral in all dates on tombstones, cornerstones and monuments. Together with its inevitable ripple effects, this alone could plunge the hitherto-stable medieval economy into chaos. A conference of clerics has been called at Winchester to discuss the entire issue, but doomsayers are convinced that the matter is now one of personal survival. Many families, in expectation of the worst, are stocking up on holy water and indulgences.

So there we all were, late in the year 1999, being told to lay in food and water and cash and candles in the event that utilities and transportation and banking systems all failed. We felt foolish complying but knew we would feel even more foolish if the dire prophecies were fulfilled and we found ourselves without power or supplies or the means to acquire them. And then, of course, nothing happened.

8

Diana's Halo
Newslore as Folk Media Criticism

During the fall of 2006, a community group invited me to give a talk at their February meeting. The topic was up to me, but they needed a title right away. Little did I know when I came up with "Is Contemporary Journalism as Bad as Everyone Says It Is?" that I would end up making my defense of the news media during the very week that the big story was the death of Anna Nicole Smith. My strategy that night was preemptive: I brought up the Anna Nicole problem before anyone else could, then mounted my defense as planned. I even tried to include celebrity news in that defense. Rather than argue that the news media do a better job than they are given credit for *despite* excessive coverage of the lives (and deaths) of celebrities, I tried to make a case for celebrity coverage as a legitimate part of the mix.

I come at this position as a folklorist, arguing, unoriginally, that these stories are direct descendants of "Cinderella," "Snow White," "Sleeping Beauty," and the other fairy tales of tradition. Today's actors, singers, and athletes are our princes and princesses, our heroes and ogres.[1] The arc of news coverage of celebrities' lives, from their successes and fairy-tale weddings to their addictions, arrests, divorces, and deaths, reflects our age-old ambivalence. On the one hand, we admire the fame, wealth, and beauty of the demigods in our midst. On the other hand, we know that we can never attain such boons for ourselves and are therefore comforted to know that all that privilege does not protect them from the problems of life. If anything, it magnifies them: the bigger they are, the harder they fall. Trade places with Anna Nicole Smith? No, thanks. The price of fame is too high. Better to live a normal life.

Students in my journalism ethics class, where we discuss celebrity news as part of a larger consideration of privacy issues, deplore news media prying into the lives of the rich and famous while overlooking the paradox of their own fascination: more students try to sign up to give a presentation on this topic than on any other, and on the day when the lucky few do their stints in front of the class, discussions of whether Paris Hilton, Britney Spears, and their ilk are getting a fair shake from the news media are both vehement and knowledgeable.

The three quintessential celebrity stories of our time are the O. J. Simpson, Princess Diana, and Michael Jackson sagas. The OJ story touched on some of the most resonant themes in American life: A handsome black man with enormous physical prowess achieves wealth and fame, marries a beautiful white woman, and moves to Hollywood, where he achieves even more success as a pitchman and broadcaster. And then: divorce, jealous rage, murder, flight, capture, and trial. Who needs Othello? We've got this guy. Of course we're fascinated. Yet people clucked their tongues at the way the story became a national obsession, just as the audience at my talk in February 2007 clucked their tongues over the way Anna Nicole Smith's death became a national obsession.

As for Diana: A prince courts a beautiful woman. They have their fairytale wedding, two beautiful baby boys, and live lives of unimaginable splendor and glamour—with a social conscience. Then they stray, divorce, and she takes up with a dazzlingly wealthy Arabian paramour, with whom she winds up dead on a Parisian roadway, a victim, seemingly, of the very newshounds who made her the most photographed and therefore the most recognizable person in the world.

The fascination with Michael Jackson stemmed first from the way he transformed himself, almost before our eyes, from a black boy to an androgynous and racially ambiguous and ageless man by sculpting his features and whitening his skin. And then he stood accused of child molestation charges—twice—though the first case was settled out of court and he was acquitted in the second case. Like Diana, he died suddenly, in the prime of life.

I defend public and news media interest in these stories, but the measured complaint about them is not they should not be covered at all but that they are covered to excess.[2] When you have wall-to-wall coverage of the death of someone, who, however up-close-and-personal our mediated view of them has been, we did not know, the wise guys among us will rebel—and that rebellion will take the form of some very disrespectful jokes.

Studies of jokes about the *Challenger* disaster offer a paradigm.[3] Most of the jokes focused on the schoolteacher Christa McAuliffe. NASA's thinking seemed to be that the presence of a civilian on board would help the public feel more connected to the shuttle's mission. To cynics, the teacher in space was little more than a publicity stunt and celebrity par excellence—a person who is famous for being famous. Putting it another way, the gap between McAuliffe's prominence and her impact, that is, between her fame and her actual importance, could scarcely be larger. When people perceive that to be the case, their sense of proportion is violated. When McAuliffe, along with the six astronauts, died in the explosion and the news media milked the pathos of the story for all it was worth, with particular focus on the civilian, the cynics had a field day.

A modest amount of coverage of a celebrity's life would probably prompt an appropriately modest response to her death. Yes, the worshippers will be devastated;[4] the rest of us might feel a little bit sad. Disproportionate coverage exasperates us: we don't feel *that* sad (or if we do, it's because of the media's maudlin coverage). The jokes are a form of collective eye rolling over the news media's lack of restraint. They have less to do with the foibles of the celebrities themselves than with the unseemly level of news media—and public—interest in them. A Web site that invited visitors to weigh in on the question of whether jokes about the death of Anna Nicole Smith were inappropriate drew the following response: "About her, yes. About the media's insatiable, vulture-like coverage of her, no."[5]

The enormous volume of jokes about O. J. Simpson, Princess Diana, Michael Jackson, and other celebrities who have weathered lurid scandals or suffered lurid deaths suggests two corollaries to my hypothesis that the more newsworthy elements a story contains, the likelier it is to generate a folkloric response (see appendix B): First, a story that is strong on prominence and novelty but weak on impact is likelier to generate a folkloric response than a story that is strong on impact but weak on prominence and novelty. Second, a story that is strong on prominence and novelty is likelier to generate newslore that targets the news media than a story that is strong on impact but weak on prominence and novelty. Such newslore may be thought of as a form of folk media criticism—though an element of self-mockery may also be present here as well: we who get caught up in the mediathon and thereby make it possible (which is to say, profitable) ought to be ashamed of ourselves.

Let us begin our survey of dead celebrity jokes with Lady Di.

DIANA (AND MOTHER TERESA), 1997

Q: What does Princess Diana have in common with Hugh Grant?
A: They both bought it in the backseat of a car.

The actor Hugo Grant was arrested in a car with a prostitute in 1995, as we know from the Bill Gates joke in chapter 7. "Buying it" refers to sex in Grant's case and to dying ("buying the farm," the derivation of which is obscure) in Diana's.

Q: Why is Di like a mobile phone?
A: They both die in tunnels.

Prince Charles was out early the other day walking the dog. When a passer-by said "Morning", Charles said "No, just walking the dog."

To get this joke, you have to know that Prince Charles and Lady Di were estranged, and you have to catch the pun: Charles hears the greeting as a question, "Mourning?"

Mother Teresa, who appears on the AP Top Ten Stories list for 1997 but not on Richard Roeper's most-talked-about list (see appendix B), mostly surfaces in Diana-Teresa combo jokes, not so surprising when one considers that the two women died within a week of each other. In fact, that's the punch line, such as it is, of one of the jokes:

Q: What's the difference between Mother Theresa and Princess Diana?
A: 5 days.

The same joke was told about Michael Jackson and Farrah Fawcett in the summer of 2009:

Q: What's the difference between Michael Jackson and Farrah Fawcett?
A: About three hours.

And the same joke was told about Michael Kennedy and Sonny Bono, who, oddly enough, also died within five days of each other and were further linked by virtue of having died in the same freakish way—by skiing into a tree. Kennedy, the son of Robert F. Kennedy, died on the last day of

1997—too late to make Richard Roeper's list. Bono, who parlayed his fame as one half of the 1960s singing duo Sonny and Cher into a political career, died in January 1998. (We'll return to Kennedy and Bono [and Kennedy-and-Bono] jokes momentarily.)

A number of Diana jokes parodied the song "Candle in the Wind," which Elton John originally wrote about Marilyn Monroe and then reworked (opportunistically, some said) as a tribute to Diana. Here is the Mother Teresa version:

> Elton John is writing a tribute for Mother Teresa. He's calling it "Sandals in the Bin."

Then there's this sick joke:

> Mother Teresa is walking around Heaven one day as she notices Princess Diana passing by. "What a lovely woman," Mother Teresa thought, "doing all those wonderful things for the sick and starving of our world." As Princess Diana passes by, Mother Teresa notices that Diana's halo is much bigger than that of her own. "I had dedicated my entire life on earth to those sick and hungry, and her halo is bigger than mine?!" So, Mother Teresa decides to go find St. Peter and ask him about her problem.
>
> Upon hearing the problem, St. Peter smiles a little and reassures Mother Teresa that, "It's not a halo; that's the steering wheel."

This joke is one of several in which an accident victim's body is so fearfully rearranged that either parts of the vehicle become entangled with the body or parts of the body become entangled with the vehicle:

> Q: What was the last thing to go through Diana's mind?
> A: The dashboard.

> If Princess Diana's heart was in the right place, why was it found on the dashboard?

> Did you hear that Diana had Blue eyes? Yep, one blew out the left window and the other out the right window.

> Did you hear that Princess Di was on the radio a couple of weeks ago? Yep, and on the dashboard, and on the window, and on the hood. . . .

The radio joke goes back at least as far as the crash that killed Princess Grace of Monaco in 1982. The jokes about what went through Diana's mind and about her blue eyes were familiar to me from the studies of *Challenger* jokes ("Q: What was the last thing to go through Christa McAuliffe's mind? A: Sheet metal"). They have also been adapted in turn to more recent celebrity deaths:

Q: What was the last thing on JFK jr's mind before he died?
A: His plane's console.

(The son of the thirty-fifth president was piloting a plane that crashed in the Atlantic en route to a family wedding on Martha's Vineyard in 1999, killing Kennedy, his wife Carolyn Bessette, and his sister-in-law Lauren Bessette.)

Q: What was the last thing to go through Michael Kennedy's mind?
A: A branch.

Then there's this odd variation, which suggests that Sonny Bono, like a lot of sixties survivors, emerged drug-addled from the decade of sex and drugs and rock and roll. Or as the saying goes, if you remember the sixties, you probably weren't really there.

Q: What was the last thing that went through Sonny Bono's mind?
A: The 60's.

SONNY BONO AND MICHAEL KENNEDY, 1997–1998

These connections offer a segue into other Sonny Bono jokes. There were other Michael Kennedy jokes as well—many rely on weak puns on words having to do with trees and wood—but Bono was a better-known and more comical figure. Sonny's lack of success as a solo performer compared to Cher's led people to conclude that she had been the real talent in the duo all along, as these jokes suggest:

Q: What preceded Sonny Bono's senseless death?
A: Sonny Bono's senseless life.

Police reported it was a quick death. Just like his solo career.

A tree turns out to be Sonny's greatest hit.

The Kennedy and Bono skiing deaths even inspired an OJ joke: "Did you hear Goldman is trying to get OJ Simpson to take up skiing?"

GIANNI VERSACE, 1997

Though gays complained that coverage of Gianni Versace's murder in south Florida at the hands of Andrew Cunanan was riddled with stereotypes about gay life, the jokes are dominated by popular ideas about the fashion world, seen as populated with people who are obsessed with appearance, even in life-and-death situations.

Q: What is Versace's latest line?
A: Chalk.
[Versace's fashion lines are conflated with a police outline around a corpse.]

Q: Why was Versace killed?
A: He wanted Cunanan to model for him and asked for two head shots.
[Head shots could either be bullets to the brain or photos of models' faces.]

Q: How can you tell it's a genuine Gianni Versace blouse?
A: It has 6 holes but only 4 buttons.

Q: Why did Cunanan shoot Versace?
A: Because Gianni was wearing plaids and stripes together.

Q: How did Versace actually die?
A: He died of a heart attack when he saw that the red from his blood didn't go with the rest of his ensemble.

JOHN F. KENNEDY JR., 1999

Jokes about the death of John F. Kennedy Jr. borrow from other joke cycles about celebrities who went to watery graves. One even alludes to another such death, that of the actress Natalie Wood, who fell off a boat and drowned in 1981 ("Q: Who did JFK Jr. meet on his last flight? A: Natalie Wood"). Here are the others, both familiar to me from the *Challenger* studies:

Q: Why did JFK Jr. refuse to take a shower the day of the crash?
A: He figured that later on he'd wash up on shore.

Q: What was JFK Jr drinking at the time of the crash?
A: Ocean Spray.

The more interesting JFK Jr. jokes were more specific to the Kennedys. A surprising number of them worked in his Uncle Teddy and the infamous 1969 incident on Martha's Vineyard, where he drove a car off a bridge, resulting in the death of a campaign staffer named Mary Jo Kopechne:[6]

Q: Why was JFK Jr flying that night?
A: Teddy Kennedy offered him a lift.

Everyone keeps saying how good looking and popular JFK jr was. It just goes to show that he was twice the lady killer as his uncle Ted.

Q: Why in the world did JFK Jr. let his plane nosedive into the water like that?
A: He was hunting up Mary Jo Kopechne souvenirs for Uncle Teddy.

Other jokes brought his cousins, Michael Kennedy and William Kennedy Smith, into the mix. Smith is the son of Jean Ann Kennedy, the sister of the late president and his famous brothers, and he is notorious for being accused of rape (he was acquitted in 1991).

The Kennedy Family was so upset they called off the Sunday wedding. And William Kennedy Smith was so upset, he postponed his Sunday night rape.

I have to end the section on JFK Jr. with this bad metajoke:

Q: Why aren't there more JFK Jr jokes out there?
A: They just haven't surfaced yet.

MICHAEL JACKSON, 2009

Along with the Clintons and George W. Bush, Michael Jackson is near the top of the leader board of most-joked-about public figures. As with jokes about the Clintons, Michael Jackson jokes have had remarkable staying power. The oldest ones date to the first set of child molestation charges against him, filed in 1993. Just when the joking might have died down, Jackson faced another round of accusations ten years later. Given the volume of jokes, if we limit the discussion here to the latest and presumably last round of jokes coined after Jackson's death in 2009, we'll have a fair idea of the tenor of the jokes, most of which deploy bad puns to comment on Jackson's supposed pedophilia. The list of double entendre words: rode, nuts, wiener, touch, dates, meat, buns, come, stroke. First, the "touch" jokes:

I dont feel any emotion after MJ's death . . . He never really touched me when I was younger . . .

Q: What's the difference between Michael Jackson and Disney films?
A: Disney films can still touch kids.

Michael Jacksons death is so tragic, he touched so many children in so many special ways.

The next few are creepier, which is to say, more explicit:

Jockeys at tomorrow's race meetings will wear black armbands out of respect for Michael Jackson, who successfully rode more three yr olds than anyone in living memory.

Michael Jackson actually died of food poisoning.
He ate some 12 year old nuts.
. . . Er or was it a five-year old wiener?

What's the difference between Michael Jackson and acne?
Acne doesn't come on your face until you're about 13 . . .

Out of respect, McDonalds has released the McJackson burger, 50 year old meat between 10 year old buns.

The milder jokes are slightly more clever:

Michael Jackson had to cancel all of his up coming dates.
They were named James (aged 9) and Thomas (aged 11).

Say what you like about Jackson, at least he drove past schools slowly.

There were also a few one-liners that we might think of as cause-of-death jokes:

Michael Jackson suffered his heart attack while racing to a Los Angeles department store. Someone told him boys trousers were half off.

Michael Jackson died of shock after finding out Boyz II Men was a band not a delivery service.

Reports of Michael Jackson having a heart attack are incorrect. He was found in the children's ward having a stroke.

That last joke leads us to the other hospital ward jokes:

Michael Jackson was taken to the hospital. The maternity ward was immediately put on lockdown.

Michael Jackson did manage to whisper a brief message to paramedics on his way to the hospital . . . "Put me in the children's ward."

Perhaps the cleverest pedophilia jokes invoke the language of addiction:

At the autopsy they found children's underwear strapped to Michael Jackson's upper arm. According to his doctors it is just a patch, he's been trying to quit for a while.

At the time of Jacko's death he was trying to quit the Cub Scouts . . . he was down to ONE pack a day!

Also clever are the jokes that allude to the rumors of Jackson's multiple plastic surgeries:

Since Michael Jackson is 99% plastic, they are going to melt him down and turn him into lego blocks so that little kids can play with him for a change.

It has been reported on the "Angels News" Michael Jackson was refused entry to heaven due to the fact they don't accept plastic.

On the bright side, Michael Jackson had so much plastic surgery, he can be recycled!

Early reports are that the hospital does not know what to do with the body, as plastic recycling is not collected until next Thursday.

Several jokes paired the coincident deaths of Jackson and Farrah Fawcett, some of which address head-on what made Jackson such a fascinating figure:

Today's mourners break into two camps: Farrah Fawcett Majors and Michael Jackson minors.
[Fawcett married the actor Lee Majors and was known, for a time, as Farrah Fawcett Majors.]

When Farrah Fawcett arrived in Heaven, God was such a big fan he decided to grant her one wish. She asked that all the children in the world could be safe. So God killed Michael Jackson.

First Farrah, now MJ. Yesterday was a horrible day to be a white woman.

Q: Why did Michael Jackson die on the same day as Farrah Fawcett?
A: He didn't want her to be the only white woman grabbing all the headlines.

Michael is the only person I know who was born a black man and died a white woman.

A little boy was asking his mom about god. "Is god man or woman?" he asked. His mom said, "honey, god is both man and woman." the boy asked, "Well is god black or white?" Mom replied: "god is both black and white." Boy: "but is god gay or straight??" Mom, flustered: "Both, honey." The boy thought for a second, and then asked, "Mom, is god michael jackson?"

Clearly, to the jokesters, God is not Michael Jackson. Given the steady metamorphosis of his appearance, the molestation charges, and the all-around weirdness of his life, I suspect many of the jokesters, like me, were simply mystified, even dismayed, by the outpouring of grief over his death. Each joke is like a face slap aimed at curbing the hysteria.

BACKLASH

The abundance of celebrity jokes on the Internet suggests that whatever the compunctions of newspaper people about offending the delicate sensibilities of their readers, in the online world, anything goes. Not so. In keeping with the cyberspace mania for interactivity, many of the jokelore Web sites invite visitor comments. Arguments between defenders of the harmlessness of the jokes and those who are censorious of them are inevitable. The Suburbarazzi Web site is typical. In February 2007 the site asked visitors to weigh in on the appropriateness of jokes about the death of Anna Nicole Smith. More than half of the three hundred respondents disapproved of the jokes—a surprising number, given that it is not a random sampling of the population but the people who choose to visit Web sites devoted to jokes. Another site, Answerbag.com, included the following responses to the same question:

Yes. Defaming the dead is detestable.

I think it would be distasteful to make jokes about anyones death whether it was expected or not. Regardless of their opinion towards Anna Nicole I think that people should keep their snide comments and jokes to themselves for a while, you never know who is still grieving the loss.

I don't care who you are, death jokes are NOT funny. As much as I hate Paris Hilton, I'd never make or laugh at any jokes made about her if she died in the near future. As annoying (or whatever other word I can't write here lol) as someone is, they're still human and in death it should be treated with nothing but respect. When that comedian/talk show guy, whoever he was, went to a Halloween costume as Steve Irwin with a barb in his bloody chest for a costume I was fuming what a *%#@$%$!!! That was SICK! And yes in Anna's case, that poor woman was a misunderstood soul no matter how outrageous or gold digging or inappropriately flamboyant, she just made some mistakes in looking for love/acceptance. Just think about being in their shoes, would you want people making fun or you or making jokes/bad taste comments, etc, about you after you die, even if it is tragically?

She made a ridiculous, pathetic laughingstock of herself when she was alive. No reason she should be able to get out of that just by dying.

Yes..it is always distasteful to make jokes about the misfortunes of others.[7]

Answerbank asked the same question about jokes about Steve Irwin, the Australian host of a television show about wildlife who died in 2006 from a freak stingray attack. The responses were rather more sophisticated (apart from their orthography and sentence structure):

Maybe it is because we dont know the person and can feel shocked amd ammused at the same time.

It's a trait of human nature that people's reaction to death is humour - almost a psychological re-balancing. People who deal with death on a daily basis cope with the trauma by indulging in the very blackest humour, again it's simply a way of dealing with death, which we in western society have never learned to deal with properly.

Although sometimes in bad taste, I don't believe they are malicious, just a way of dealing with bad or shocking news. Sometimes they are very, very funny, and you feel you shouldn't be laughing.

I'm always up for a joke but this is way too soon.

i think sometimes they are 'technically' very clever and funny - as such if you were a professional joke writer who had done some sort of course . . . sometimes these jokes are well crafted and fit all the criterior of what a joke should be - its just unfortunate that they happen to be about a sad subject and that makes us a bit uncomfortable about recognising it as just a joke.

Gallows humour has been around as long as people have been coming to unfortunate ends and others have found themselves being glad it was someone else and not them.
    I think with technology as it is, it is just a bit more noticable as the jokes spread further, quicker and sometimes to people who might not appreciate them.[8]

Along the same lines were the shocked and outraged responses to jokes about Terri Schiavo, the Florida woman who had been in a coma for fifteen years until her husband, despite much grandstanding by conservative politicians, was able to have her feeding tube removed in 2005. First, the jokes. I was in the library on campus when I decided to Google Terri Schiavo jokes.

There wasn't anyone around, but I caught myself turning my laptop away from public view, because I didn't want anyone to think I was the sort of person who hid himself in an obscure corner of the library to visit garish Web sites (though that was exactly what I was doing). There were sixty Schiavo jokes on the Web site www.laughline.com. By comparison, the site featured 244 Michael Jackson jokes, 43 George W. Bush jokes, 23 Bill Clinton jokes, and 19 Iraq jokes. It goes without saying that all the Terri Schiavo jokes were in poor taste; most were guilty of the worse sin of being insufferably lame. Picture people with too much time on their hands straining—and failing—to come up with a really nasty zinger. Here are the ones I found interesting for one reason or another:

Did you hear Teri Schiavo is coming out with a new album?
Schiavo—unplugged.
[In recent years, a number of musicians who normally play or are backed by electric instruments have recorded albums on which they play stripped-down arrangements of their songs on mostly acoustic instruments.]

What is Jeb Bush's favorite vegetable?
Terry Schiavo.

What is the Florida state vegetable?
Terry Schiavo.
[Governor Bush, who had taken a lead role in efforts to keep Schiavo alive, made a last-ditch effort to take her into the custody of the state of Florida to keep her feeding tube from being removed. Jokes about human "vegetables" are nothing new.]

What is the worst part about eating a vegetable?
Putting Terri Schiavo's diaper back on.
[This is by far the sickest joke of the bunch. It relies on the slang meaning of "eating" as performing cunnilingus.]

What does Terry Schiavo have in common with the CIA?
Dubya thought they both had intelligence.
[This joke connects conservatives' arguments that Schiavo was misdiagnosed as being in a "persistent vegetative state" and was in fact aware of, and reacting to, what was going on around her with erroneous

intelligence—used to justify invading Iraq—about Saddam Hussein's ability to manufacture and deploy weapons of mass destruction and his ties to the al-Qaeda terrorist organization.]

Here is a response to the jokes:

What the freak do y'all think you are doing making jokes about Terry Schiavo. It's wrong. It was a serious matter and there should be no jokes. She was a human being and her and her family went through hell and every one of you who wrote a joke should be ashamed of yourselves. This is NOT RIGHT!!!

To bring the discussion back to Princess Diana, one can also find a good bit of commentary on the propriety of Diana jokes. A story on the London Net Web site (headline: "Pub Brawl Over Di Joke") described a fight in a pub precipitated by the telling of a Diana joke ("Q: What's the difference between a Mercedes and a Skoda? A: Diana wouldn't be seen dead in a Skoda"), and noted that psychologists see jokes as "an effective means for coming to terms with grief."[9]

A story in the *Indian Express* about the phenomenon quoted a stand-up comic named Timandra Harkness, who said she joked about "the way we were expected to be very upset."[10] Similarly, the Web site Mindspring.com took issue with "the massive drenching of the English speaking world in syrup as the masses shed tears for a woman they never met, and the papers took her death as a news event on the order of the first moon landing, or a major war."[11] I even found a metajoke expressing exasperation with those who disapprove of Diana jokes:

Q: What's the difference between those who get offended by Princess Diana jokes and a puppy?
A: Eventually, a puppy will stop whining.

CELEBRITY DEATHS—NOT!

True stories of celebrities cut down in their prime, which we savor perhaps more than we would care to admit—knowing that it often ends badly for the rich and famous keeps our envy in check—make us susceptible to celebrity death hoaxes, much as real computer viruses or product recalls bolster the credibility of computer virus hoaxes and legends of contaminated goods.[12] Who can be surprised to learn that yet another actor/singer/athlete/politician has died in a freak accident? All it takes is a writer with sufficient command of journalistic conventions (and time on his or her hands) to craft a plausible-sounding news story. I find it helpful to think of these stories in terms of x and y axes, where the x axis represents the plausibility of the content, and the y axis represents the plausibility of the mechanics, by which I mean spelling, grammar, punctuation, story and sentence structure, and word choice. If the story is improbable yet not preposterous and reads like a polished piece of journalism, it is going to be pretty believable. If it is improbable yet not preposterous but deviates from journalistic standards, it's going to fool only the more credulous readers. And if it's preposterous but adheres to journalistic standards, it will probably be a pretty good joke, with the humor arising from the disconnect between its serious tone and silly content. Some examples:

> (CNN)—Former L. A. Laker Earvin "Magic" Johnson is in a coma tonight at Cedars-Sinai Medical Center in Los Angeles and is not expected to live. Johnson, 44, is suffering from complications related to HIV, and internal bleeding, a spokesman for Johnson's attorney told CNN. "His eyes are open, but it's just a dead stare. He could go any day now," said the spokesman, who asked that his name not be used. Johnson was last seen publicly on July 27 in Los Angeles when he hosted "A Midsummer Night's Magic", a charity basketball event at the Staples center. The 6ft - 9in. Johnson, three-times voted the NBA's most valuable player, was admitted to the intensive care unit last weekend under another name. A hospital spokeswoman refused to confirm reports Johnson was a patient there.
>
> A press release submitted to media outlets on Sept. 17 announced Johnson's new production company had signed a multimillion-dollar Hollywood movie deal with Warner Bros. Pictures. Johnson, the NBA star-turned-entrepreneur, co-founded Magic Hallway Pictures in July with producer Paul Hall, whose credits include "Higher Learning" and the 2000 remake of "Shaft." Hall could not be reached for comment.
>
> On November 7, 1991, Johnson stunned the sports world when he announced he had tested positive for HIV, the virus that causes AIDS, during a routine physical exam. Johnson also announced his retirement from basketball but returned in 1992 and again in 1996. He turned his enthusiasm and leadership skills to business. Among his successes, he

developed movie theaters and shopping malls in poor and neglected sections of large cities where no one else would invest.

In September 1991, just before he learned he had HIV, Johnson wed longtime friend Earletha "Cookie" Kelly. The couple had a son in 1993 and adopted a daughter in 1995. Johnson also has a son from a previous relationship who lives near his estate. Ever optimistic, Johnson believed that the right combination of medicine, diet, and exercise would help him to survive until a cure for AIDS was found.

Johnson's physicians announced in early 1997 that the AIDS virus in his body had been reduced to undetectable levels. They attributed the improvement to the use of powerful drugs, including protease inhibitors. His wife Cookie gave the credit to God stating, "The Lord has definitely healed Earvin. Doctors think it's the medicine. We claim it in the name of Jesus." The Johnsons attended the West Angles Church of God in Christ, to which he donated $5 million in 1995. Calls to the Lakers front office were not returned.

Journalistically speaking, this story is almost flawless, from the formal rendering of Johnson's full name on first reference to the end-of-sentence attribution, the judicious use of a quote, and the inclusion of relevant background. In fact, I could detect only one deviation from standard practice—the paragraphs are too long—and four minor errors: the style in which Johnson's height is listed is incorrect, and there's one misplaced comma and one missing comma. The story is entirely plausible primarily because Johnson does, in fact, have AIDS, but also because the news media feed us a steady diet of stories of celebrities dying young. If dead celebrity jokes give voice to the grim satisfaction we may take in knowing that wealth and fame offer no protection from disease and disaster, fake celebrity death news reports seem to express folk exasperation with our culture's obsession with celebrity. Phony grief for dead celebrities deserves to be met with phony stories about dead celebrities. But the story has to be journalistically sound. On a scale of 1 to 5 from least to most plausible, and 1 to 5 from least to most journalistically sound, I'd give the Magic Johnson a 5 for content and a 4 for mechanics. Compare another dead celebrity story:

Los Angeles—Actor Will Ferrell accidentally died in a freak para-gliding accident yesterday in Torey Pines, Southern California. The accident apparently happened somewhere near the famed paragliding site after a freak wind gush basically blew Ferrell and his companion towards a wooded area where they lost control before crashing into the dense foilage.

Ferrell and his professional guide, Horacio Gomez of Airtek Paragliding Center attempted the jump at around 2 in the afternoon. According to witnesses, the conditions were basically ideal for paragliding and the weather did'nt pose a problem at all.

The jump started normally as Ferrell and Gomez glided carefully across the vast area and were seemed headed into the righ direction just before what witnesses said a freak wind somehow blew them off course, causing the paragliding professional Gomez to somehow lose control.

As horrified witnesses looked on, the duo headed straight for the dense woods near the jump off point and crashed at an estimated 60 mph hitting the trees as they hurtled to the ground.

Some friends of the actor who witnessed the accident immediately called up 911. The paramedics vainly attempted to revive the two on their way to the nearby UCSD Thornton Hospital in nearby La Jolla.

The duo suffered major injuries to the head and broken bones that caused the death of the two.

In an interview with Will's parents who was John W. Ferrell in real life, Mary and Hubert Ferrell said their sonn died while doing one of the things he loved the most.

Will was a graduate of the University of California where he finished his Sports Information Degree. Will was born on July 16, 1968. He was 36.

In the world of celebrity deaths, this story is plausible enough—let's give it a 4 on my 5-point scale—but for mechanics, it probably doesn't deserve any higher than a 2.

- The lead: "Torrey," "gust," and "foliage" are misspelled. The time element, which is the most indispensable of the five Ws in a hard news lead, is missing. The two adverbs, "basically" (which is repeated in paragraph 2) and "apparently," are glaring examples of the sort of clutter journalists are trained to eschew. Instead of saying what "apparently" happened, a real story would attribute that information to the police.
- Paragraph 2: The comma is missing after "Paragliding Center." The apostrophe in "didn't" is misplaced.

- Paragraph 3: The first sentence is poorly written and includes a typo in the word "right." Neither use of the word "somehow" belongs.
- Paragraph 4: The sentence needs a comma.
- Paragraph 5: The second "nearby" is superfluous, as is the word "up" in "called up."
- Paragraph 6: The phrase "the two" is awkward the first time it is used. Its repetition is even more so. By now, surely some of the details of Ferrell's death would be attributed to the police.
- Paragraph 7: This sentence begins with a number of unnecessary words and awkward writing. "Son" is misspelled. And again, Ferrell would be referred to by his last name, not his first.

Despite all the errors, the story was apparently posted on the i-newswire. com press release distribution site, according to About.com's urban legends site. Here is a third celebrity tragedy story:

> Multi-platinum artist Marshall Mathers, known by the stage name "Eminem", was killed at 2:30 AM EST while driving a rental car on his way to a late-night party.
>
> Mathers, who authorities believe was under the influence of alcohol or drugs, was behind the wheel of a Saturn coupe that witnesses say swerved to avoid a slow moving vehicle, then lost control and slammed into a grove of trees.
>
> The car was crumpled by the impact, making extraction of Mather's body very difficult. He was declared dead on the scene by paramedics who arriced a short time later.
>
> Authorities would not comment on details surrounding the accident other than to confirm the identity of the victim.
>
> Mathers was 26.

This is a much cleaner piece of writing than the Will Ferrell piece (I count one typo, one misplaced comma, and a lack of conformity to Associated Press style on the time of the accident), but it has one glaring weakness: it's missing two of the five Ws. It tells us neither when the crash took place nor where. The omission of the day might be understandable if we were to assume the accident happened on the day the story was posted. The omission of the name of the city or town (or the law enforcement agency with which "the authorities" are affiliated) where the accident occurred is simply unheard of. That knocks the story's content plausibility rating down to about a 2, while its mechanics rating is probably good for a 4. The next one is a little different from the others:

Colts kicker Vanderjagt attempts life
By CLIFF BRUNT, Associated Press Writer
January 17, 2006
INDIANAPOLIS (AP)—Colts kicker Mike Vanderjagt attempted to
take his own life yesterday at his Indianapolis home.

Carmel 911 received a frantic call from Janalyn Vanderjagt at
about 4:35 Monday evening. Apparently, Janalyn had just arrived
home along with the couples son Jay Michael. Janalyn found her
husband Mike attempting to hang himself in the couples bedroom.
Janalyn tried to persuade Mike to rethink what he was about to do.
Mike repeatedly attempted to kick the chair out from under him but
was unsuccessful.

That's when Janalyn called 911. Police along with fire and rescue
were dispatched to the suburban Indianapolis home. Rescue personnel
were able to talk Vanderjagt down after about 10 minutes. Vanderjagt
remained in an area hospital today in stable condition.

Colts fans couldn't believe that the normally dependable Vanderjagt
missed a 46-yard field goal with 21 seconds left that could have sent
the game into overtime. They were equally shocked that the Colts, who
started the season with 13 straight wins and had the league's best record,
trailed 21-3 heading into the fourth quarter.

The result was all too familiar, as Indianapolis has qualified for the
playoffs the last four seasons but hasn't reached the Super Bowl.

James Dungy, the 18-year-old son of Indianapolis Colts coach Tony
Dungy, was found dead in a Tampa-area apartment last month.

Dungy said that Vanderjagt did a great job for the Indianapolis Colts,
but the bottom line is he came up short—again.

Initially, this story is even more convincing than our first example. It has
a headline, a dateline, a byline and a solid, no-nonsense lead. But in the
second paragraph it begins to break down in a number of significant ways.
A real news story would not assume everyone knows who Janalyn is. She
would be identified as Vanderjagt's wife. The failure to deploy an apostrophe when needed—twice—though all too common among amateur writers,
amounts to a dead giveaway that we are not in the hands of a professional
journalist. Yes, journalists are notoriously sloppy, and it's possible that there
are reporters out there who are apostrophe challenged, but it's less likely that
no one on the copy desk caught the mistakes.

A story about two people with the same last name wreaks havoc with the journalistic practice of identifying people by last name only after the first reference, but in this story, standard procedure would be to consistently refer to the kicker by his last name.

Finally, the story lacks attribution. The bit about Janalyn trying to talk her husband out of his suicide attempt, in particular, would certainly be attributed to the police instead of stated as something that "apparently" happened.

The third paragraph contains an inconsistency: Carmel 911 is a specifically local reference, which might be familiar to local readers. But then we learn that Vanderjagt is being treated in an unnamed "area hospital."

But these are the kinds of things a journalism professor would notice. Here is how some posters responded on a Web site called Sportsgamer.com:

> holy ****, thats unbeleivable!....im guessing that will be all over the news in a few minutes.

> Thank god he missed the chair. You never want to see anyone take away their own life. It's ironic that Vanderjagt tried to kill himself the same way James Dungy reportedly took his life.

> Why would you do that over a football game? I mean comeon there is always next year!

But not everyone was so gullible:

> This is one of the oldest jokes. "Hey, the kicker that messed up the game tried to kill himself . . . but he couldn't kick the chair out from under him".

> LMAO @ people believing this could be a real story. There are some AHOTW nominees here for sure.

> Anyone in here who believed it should be banned immediately. These kinds of threads can be used as a good "member weed out" process.

> Don't believe it but the guy who wrote it is a pretty good writer.

This last comment is telling: false though the story is, it looks and reads like a real news story, at least to the untrained eye, though the last couple of paragraphs reveal the fan disgruntlement that gave rise to the false report. I'd give the story a 3 on both content and mechanics.

The back-and-forth comments between those who believe the story, those who are astonished at the gullibility of those who believe such an obvious fake, and those who are appalled that anyone would fabricate such macabre tales, play out again and again on Web sites like Museumofhoaxes.com, which has debunked stories of the demise of Paris Hilton, Britney Spears, Michael Jackson, John Goodman, Eminem, Lou Reed, Justin Timberlake, and Carl Lewis, among others.[13] In some cases, the hoaxers go so far as to duplicate the design of legitimate news sites like CNN or ABC News.

At the other extreme was a phony story about the death of the *Napoleon Dynamite* star Jon Heder on the Web site Ninjahpirate.com. The writing is atrocious, and the cheesy photo features a ghostly Heder floating out of the wrecked car with a halo above his head and two cartoon deer cavorting in the background (Heder's car supposedly hit a deer). Nevertheless the story elicited four pages of hand-wringing comments from fans, along with skeptics who noted that Ninjahpirate didn't even get Heder's name right in the headline ("John" instead of "Jon") and that the mainstream news media would certainly have reported Heder's death. There were several jibes along the lines of "You guys are retarded," one writer who asked, on page 3, "Why is this conversation still going on?" and one who offered the following spoof:

> Jon Heder is certainly dead. He died in a five-way car crash among Paul Mcartney, the ghost Elvis, John Goodman, and Louie Anderson. Next time check the facts, it's all there.

The conversation might have gone on longer had Museumofhoaxes founder Alex Boese not called a halt: "I'm turning comments off on this thread, because I think that just about everything interesting that could be said about this topic has now been said."[14] Responses to news of the alleged suicide of Jaleel White, who played the nerdy character Steve Urkel on the TV show *Family Matters*, went on for twelve pages. Some offer insight into the peculiar relationship between actors and their fans:

> I rec'd an email last week stating that Jaleel committed suicide. I sat at my desk and cried. I so love this young man and was grieving over the news.

> O my word. I thought he was dead and I didn't know what to do. I don't know him personally but i grew up watching him on t.v. and had me a

little crush on some Steve. I kind of panicked and had to do a search for him, thank God it's not true.

I am so glad that he is alive. I have had the biggest crush on Jaleel White. As Urkel, he was beautiful, I was totally into him.

My mom told me..and my heart started to race like you were a relative of mine...

Other commentators had so little patience for celebrity worship, one wonders why they were reading the posts at all:

I think it's sad and pathetic that so many people even CARE. I mean, he's a kid on a tv show, not Mother Teresa! It's one thing if you actually KNOW him (and I'm betting that 100% of you don't!), but it's another to put so much time and energy into worrying about someone you'll never even meet.
    Stand up, walk away from the computer, and go do something productive with your lives! Feed the poor! Protest an unjust war! Teach someone to read! DO SOMETHING!

Remarkably, Jaleel White himself weighed in, unless it was someone who was claiming to be Jaleel White:

I'm heartened to hear that so many people still love me all these years after *Family Matters* aired. I'm encourage by your love and support, but sadly I have retired from acting and just want to live a quiet life with my wife and daughter now. But who knows, maybe someday when my daughter is grown and I'm looking for something to replace my full-time parenthood I'll try my hand at acting once again. Look for Urkel: The Next Generation in about 15 years!

That broke at least one reader's heart, or so she claimed:

WIFE AND KIDS???!!! NNooooo!!! Somebody stole my man!!!! She bedda not slip up. I'ma be at your door with a roast and potatoes. This is Wifey material right hur!![15]

CONCLUSION
Attention Must Be Paid, but for How Much Longer?

THE FUTURE OF NEWSLORE

When I started working on this book in the winter of 2006, I was surprised at how much old newslore was still kicking around. Bill and Hillary Clinton jokes, in particular, remained popular although his presidency was long past and her campaign for president had not yet begun. Jokes about the 2004 presidential candidates had not entirely supplanted jokes about the 2000 presidential candidates. Even jokes about many of the biggest newsmakers of the 1990s—O. J. Simpson, Michael Jackson, Princess Diana, and others—persisted.

Before I finished the first draft of this book in 2008, I felt obliged to make one final tour of cyberspace in search of the most up-to-date newslore. I did so with trepidation, expecting to have to incorporate a substantial body of new material pertaining to the 2008 presidential campaign. But there was much less new material than I expected. Much of the Hillary Clinton lore was recycled from her years as First Lady. One new set of related jokes, at least to me, centered on her supposed lack of personal warmth:

Hillary Clinton is very concerned with the threat of global warming. She's afraid of melting.

There has been a cold front moving across the country during Hillary's presidential campaign. It was coinciding with her campaign stops.

Hillary Clinton won't commission a Presidential portrait if she's elected. She'll commission an ice sculpture instead.

"However this campaign turns out," Stanley Fish predicted in early 2008, "Hillary-hating, like rock 'n' roll, is here to stay."[1] Barack Obama lore was limited to a handful of rumors: he is a Muslim who used the Koran when he was sworn into office and refuses to recite the Pledge of Allegiance; he was endorsed by the Ku Klux Klan (!);Venezuelan president Hugo Chavez provided financial backing; he's the anti-Christ; he was not born in the United States; he is a socialist/communist/fascist; and his health care reform proposal (really, it was Congress's health care reform proposal) would establish government "death panels" charged with deciding which lives were worth saving. Rumors, though related to folklore, particularly legends, lack an artistic dimension; they're not clever. They are more fake news than commentary on the real news—which makes them more dangerous.[2]

A "How to Tell Barack Obama Jokes" entry on the eHow.com Web site ("How to Do Just About Everything") noted that Obama jokes were in short supply and cautioned would-be jokers that "he's on the road to sainthood and mocking him in front of his faithful followers might lead to you being stoned for blasphemy."[3] A Barack Obama Jokes Web site alluded to the "small handful" of Obama jokes on the Web and claimed to be "the REAL Barack Obama Jokes Website," but most of the jokes turned out to be recycled lawyer jokes, and one was a joke about the lack of Obama jokes:

Q: Why are there so few real Barack Obama jokes?
A: Most of them are true stories.[4]

At least as surprising was the paucity of jokes about New York governor Eliot Spitzer's sudden fall from grace when it was reported that he was consorting with high-priced hookers. On March 10, 2008, the Web site freerepublic.com put out the call: "The Eliot Spitzer prostitution ring scandal is the PERFECT situation for jokes. I am sure there will be a plethora of such jokes. Therefore please post on this thread all Eliot Spitzer jokes that you hear. Let this be the Eliot Spitzer Joke Resource Center."[5] The last post, number 136, is dated March 16, 2008. Neither that one nor any of the previous 135 is especially funny.

Closer to the date when I put the manuscript to bed once and for all, I searched for jokes about Sarah Palin, Wall Street swindler Bernie Madoff, disgraced Illinois governor Rod Blagojevich, and the latest sex-crazed politicians, South Carolina governor Mark Sanford and Nevada senator John Ensign (and, while I was at it, former North Carolina senator John Edwards and former Idaho senator Larry Craig, in case I had missed anything on any of my earlier tours)—and was again surprised at the slimness of the pickings. Most of the Sarah Palin material, for example, was either recycled numbskull-politician jokes (which is to say that most of them had already been applied to Dan Quayle and then George W. Bush) or photoshopped images of her head on a scantily clad body.[6]

Most of the jokes about John Edwards centered on his perfect blow-dried hair, especially when news broke in 2007 that he had paid $400 for a haircut. A parody of a classic soft-focus ad for Breck hair-care products photoshopped Edwards's face onto the head of a model with flowing locks. YouTube has a clip of Edwards combing his hair, then being hair-sprayed by an aide, then checking his hair and making adjustments in a mirror, set to the song "I Feel Pretty" from *West Side Story*.[7] Then, the *National Enquirer* reported that Edwards had fathered a child with a campaign worker with whom he had an adulterous affair. Edwards eventually admitted to the affair but denied he was the father of Rielle Hunter's child. But the scandal inspired this joke:

How do you get John Edwards to play with his illegitimate child?
Put it in front of a mirror.

Is it possible that the period around the turn of the twenty-first century was the golden age of newslore? Possibly. I think back to when telephone answering machines were new. The first users felt obliged to instruct callers in their use: Leave your name and number at the beep. As the recorders became more commonplace and their use spread from the office to the home, owners began to assume that callers knew what to do. The announcement could be more personal and more playful. Some were so clever that people who had called them before would urge their friends to call for their sheer entertainment value, the way we might be eager to show a friend a new YouTube clip today. Eventually, though, the clever answering machine announcement became a cliché. In deference to frequent callers who would tire of even the wittiest song or patter after a while, one would have to continually update one's announcement, and it began to feel like one ought to have better things to do.

I bought my first computer in the mid-1980s. I had my first experience with e-mail around the same time: I was working at my first newspaper job, and I was able to exchange messages with my newsroom colleagues (when I complained, in response to an e-mail announcing that there were chocolate chip cookies in Sports, that it was cruel to tantalize us bureau reporters with treats that we couldn't get our hands on, someone photocopied the plate of cookies and faxed the image to me). I had my first computer with a graphic capability beyond glowing text on a dark background in the early 1990s.

My second such computer, bought in the late 1990s, provided a new thrill: the ability to look at video clips. Each computer I've used since has been faster than the previous one, but not appreciably different. The little thrill of anticipation triggered by AOL's "You've got mail" prompt is long gone. These days I feel about e-mail the same way I feel about snail mail: Sorting through the junk has become another chore. I keep threatening to switch from being alerted whenever new e-mail arrives to a system where I only check a couple of times a day, but I haven't done it yet. I use a computer so much for work that I'm less inclined to use it for play. If a lot of people are experiencing this kind of e-mail fatigue—in 2001 the Pew Internet and American Life Project registered a shift in the Internet's status from "dazzling new thing" to "purposeful tool"[8]—it might explain a decline in the amount of new e-mail jokes and photoshops in circulation. In a similar vein, a 2005 survey of two hundred e-mail users found that long-term users were less likely to forward e-mailed folklore than new users.

I also notice a decline in the quality of the newer material, which, if true, suggests that the early adopters, like the early answering machine wags, have moved on and the Johnny-come-latelies simply aren't as clever. The Pew report found that "newcomers tend to have lower levels of educational attainment and lower incomes than the long-wired."[9] One of the things people may have moved on to is the development of audio jokes—either song parodies or remixes that combine audio clips from more than one source (if you search for jokes about Howard Dean, the former governor of Vermont who ran for president in 2004, what you mostly find are multiple versions of his famous scream speech after the Iowa caucuses, set to music)—and video jokes, whether homemade animations or recuts, defined by the *New York Times* reporter Virginia Heffernan as "videos that take existing photography and film and use music and new juxtapositions to create a story that's at odds with a master narrative."[10] Writing in 2005, William Gibson declared that "the remix is the very nature of the digital."[11] In 2006 most of the MasterCard "Priceless" parodies were send-ups of print ads. By 2008 many more of them were mock TV commercials. There is more humor on YouTube pertaining to Madoff, Blagojevich, and the other recent additions to the national rogues' gallery than there is on the countless Web sites devoted to jokes, but most of the material consists of song parodies. Many of the old joke Web sites, meanwhile, seem to have scarcely been updated since the turn of the millennium.

The other thing I've noticed about the humor Web sites is that many of them are dominated by the latest bons mots of the late-night comedians.

Before the Internet, if Johnny Carson got off a particularly snappy one-liner, people might retell it around the water cooler the next day, but all but the absolute classics would quickly fade away. Now, though, more people probably "hear" the jokes from a secondary source than from the television broadcast. As a result, perhaps, the output of the professional gag writers may be crowding out the amateurs' witticisms. Why wrack your brains trying to come up with an apt response to the day's news when the pros are right on top of it? For that matter, when you've got a guy like Vice President Joe Biden routinely putting his foot in his mouth, why do anything at all beyond posting footage of his latest gaffe on YouTube?

Netlore will be around as long as we use computers, just as face-to-face folklore will be around as long as we continue to communicate face-to-face, but now that the novelty has worn off, perhaps the mania for netlore has peaked. Or at least that's what I thought until my in-box began filling with Michael Jackson jokes in July 2009. It is interesting to note that I didn't receive a single e-mailed joke in 2010 pertaining to the succession of women who claimed to have had affairs with Tiger Woods after news broke that he crashed his car near his home in the wee hours of the morning, but they're out there:

Q: What's the difference between a car and a golf ball?
A: Tiger Woods can drive a ball 400 yards.

Q: What should Tiger Woods change his name to?
A: Cheetah Woods.

Obviously 19 holes wasn't enough for Tiger Woods.

Q: What's the difference between Tiger Woods and Santa Claus?
A: Santa stops at three hos.

And here is a late-breaking variation on the joke with which I started this book:

It is near the Christmas break of the school year. The students have turned in all their work and there is really nothing more to do. All the children are restless and the teacher decides to have an early dismissal.

Teacher: "Whoever answers the questions I ask, first and correctly can leave early today."

Little Johnny says to himself "Good, I want to get outta here. I'm smart and will answer the question."

Teacher: "Who said 'Four Score and Seven Years Ago'?"

Before Johnny can open his mouth, Susie says, "Abraham Lincoln."

Teacher: "That's right Susie, you can go home."

Johnny is mad that Susie answered the question first.

Teacher: "Who said 'I Have a Dream'?"

Before Johnny can open his mouth, Mary says, "Martin Luther King."

Teacher: "That's right Mary, you can go."

Johnny is even madder than before.

Teacher: "Who said 'Ask not, what your country can do for you'?"

Before Johnny can open his mouth, Nancy says, "John F. Kennedy."

Teacher: "That's right Nancy, you may also leave."

Johnny is boiling mad that he has not been able to answer to any of the questions.

When the teacher turns her back Johnny says, "I wish these bitches would keep their mouths shut!"

The teacher turns around: "NOW WHO SAID THAT?"

Johnny: "TIGER WOODS. CAN I GO NOW?"

Before we take it entirely for granted, it is worth remarking on how much our ability to instantaneously communicate with each other at a distance has expanded in just a few decades. The change from telling stories and jokes face-to-face and, in the twentieth century, by telephone to sharing them by e-mail and Web site is a relatively small one, at least as far as content is concerned. The ability to tell stories and jokes visually and aurally, through the long-distance exchange of still and animated photographs and cartoons, and through short audio and video clips, has launched what amounts to a whole new branch of folklore that has few antecedents. For folklorists, myself included, it will never be as much fun to study virtual storytelling and joke telling as it is to observe the face-to-face variety, however rich the material, but the one will never entirely supplant the other.

And the material is rich. Or, to put it more precisely, the phenomenon is rich. That is, even if much of the material is utterly sophomoric, it is giving the public a voice it never had before. The exchange of newslore may be more slacktivist than activist, but it puts the politicians and the celebrities and the news media on notice: the public is wise to them. People know when they're being deceived and when they're being manipulated. By the time George W. Bush left the White House, he was virtually naked. The same may be said of all the media giants and media creations whose claims to authority or stature are stripped away in the material that fills this book.

Yet here's a paradox: while much newslore is grounded in skepticism, if not cynicism, much of it feeds on credulousness. It is because we disbelieve the noble version of President Bush offered to us by his handlers and the respectful version offered by the news media that we are susceptible to the most preposterous caricatures of President Bush. The explanation lies in the steady erosion of trust in the mainstream news media. A July 2009 survey of attitudes toward the press by the Pew Research Center for the People and the Press found that the number of people who think the press is "influenced by powerful people/organizations" or "tends to favor one side" had reached all-time highs of 74 percent for each of those propositions. The number who said the press was politically biased matched the all-time high of 60 percent reached in 2005.[12] Suggest to a person who swallows the "Got Fish?" photo hook, line, and sinker (so to speak) that if the photo were authentic, we would have seen it in the *New York Times*, and you will either be pitied or scorned. The *Times* wouldn't print that. They're in bed with the powers that be. If you want the real story, you have to go to www.wackadoo.com. (Of course, when the *Times* prints something that one thinks it should not have printed, it did so "just to sell papers" or because it has a bias that is opposite to one's own.)

A curious state of affairs, to be sure. I don't profess to understand it. But I hope I have at least convinced you of this: if you want to know who and what Americans found ludicrous and dangerous around the beginning of the third millennium, all you need to do is look at the newslore.

APPENDIX A
A Week in the Life of My In-Box: A Newslore Miscellany

On Sunday afternoon, February 12, 2006, I check the *New York Times* Web site, as has been my custom since 9/11, to see if anything horrendous has happened since the morning papers arrived on my doorstep. The breaking news is that Vice President Dick Cheney has accidentally shot a quail-hunting buddy in Texas. What strikes me immediately about the story is not just that the vice president had shot somebody, but how he and the White House staff seemed to be handling it. The accident happened on Saturday night. The story wasn't made public until Sunday afternoon, and it came out in an odd manner: not from any announcement by Cheney or the White House but from a story on the Web site of the *Corpus Christi Caller Times*, the result of a call Cheney's host made to the local paper. Then, while the vice president remained out of view, members of the hunting party blamed the victim, Harry Whittington, for failing to observe hunting protocol. My reaction, which turned out to be the typical one, was that the incident perfectly illustrated the modus operandi of the Bush administration: when things go wrong, try to suppress the news; then, if you can't, try to blame somebody else.

The timing of the story was remarkable for me personally. I had asked my friend Michael Yonchenko to help me collect e-mailed folklore from his friends on the day before the shooting. The column in which I asked my readers to help me with this project appeared on the day after the shooting. Here is what poured into my in-box in the days that followed:

SUNDAY, FEBRUARY 12

- Two photoshops under the helpful subject line "German Pope Makes Changes in Mass." The first shows Pope Benedict XVI raising a glass of beer instead of a chalice of wine. The second shows him bearing a pretzel where the Eucharist would be.
- A talking parrot joke.
- A set of attorney-witness exchanges supposedly taken from transcripts of real trials. The exchanges were preceded by a friendly warning to me: "You may get more e-mail than you really want."
- A joke about a psychiatrist and a proctologist.
- A joke letter to the IRS:

Dear IRS:

Enclosed is my 2005 tax return showing that I owe $3,407.00 in taxes. Please note the attached article from USA Today, wherein you will see that the Pentagon is paying $171.50 for hammers and NASA has paid $600.00 for a toilet seat.

I am enclosing four toilet seats (value $2,400) and six hammers (value $1,029), bringing my total remitted to $3,429.00.

Please apply the overpayment of $22.00 to the "Presidential Election Fund," as noted on my return. You can do this inexpensively by sending them one 1.5" Phillips Head screw (article from USA Today detailing how HUD pays $22.00 each for 1.5" Phillips Head Screws is enclosed for your convenience.)

It has been a pleasure to pay my tax bill this year, and I look forward to paying it again next year.

Sincerely,

A Satisfied Taxpayer

- Subject line: "E-junk," followed by a series of amusing and, presumably, real, road signs. (My favorite: A yellow, diamond-shaped sign says "Open Range." Next to the sign is an oven with its door open.)

MONDAY, FEBRUARY 13

- An outsourcing joke, in which the photoshop shows a man pedaling a stationary bicycle-like generator that he is using to power up his laptop, the lid of which is labeled "Microsoft Tech Support Center #25 Bombay."
- Two Bush jokes (see chapter 5).

TUESDAY, FEBRUARY 14

I, along with a hundred or so other people, received an extraordinary response to a rather innocuous message that I and the same hundred or so other recipients had received the day before. Here, in its entirety, is the first message (I've changed the names and withheld the common denominator of this group of addressees to spare those involved any embarrassment):

Everyone,
Hopefully, we've solved my e-mail problems . . . you can go back to using my original e-mail address. Thanks for your patience.
Dave

And here was the response:

Dave,
I've asked you twice in private (once last year and once recently - both with no response) so now I'll try asking in public and see if that gets any results...

Please....please, please, PLEASE stop listing everyone on the 'To' line of your emails! There is something called a 'BCC' line that will still deliver the email to everyone, but will hide the addresses from the recipients. [The URL for an online tutorial followed.]

Why should you do this?

1) My email address is now vulnerable to every email worm that may infect the computer of anyone on this list.

2) It violates the privacy of everyone on this list. What if my email address was "venereal@disease.com"? Maybe I don't want it splashed all over the place after I submitted it to you in confidence.

3) My email address is now free for anyone on the list to grab and use for spam.

4) Everyone has to scroll through the whole thing in order to get to the meat of the email. The headers of the email I'm replying to were longer than the email itself!

While I'm at it, may I suggest you clean up your list? I took the liberty of sorting it all out for you. Here is a list of duplicate addresses and the number of times they appear on your 'To' line: [The list followed.]

As I said, Dave, I've asked you to stop doing this twice before in private emails - - you did not respond and did not stop. I'm sure you're a nice guy and all but please be more considerate and cautious when it comes to other peoples private information!

That message was followed, inevitably, by a succinct e-mail from another member of that interminable list of addressees: "I think you're nuts. In the future, kindly spare me your rantings." And finally, a "mea culpa" message from the ranter:

To all (and particularly to Dave),

Rash actions are flattering to no one, nor is there any honor in refusing to admit to mistakes. My mistake was including you all in my message to Dave who . . . does not deserve public flogging.

Thus, in response to my public diatribe, I offer a public apology in its place.

I also offer a subscription-based email list which I can host for free. This would allow users to add and remove themselves and provide moderation control if desired. I will leave it up to Dave and the rest of you to decide if you want it.

Again . . . my apologies.

Aaron

There's much to be learned from this little exchange. First, as Aaron's message makes clear, people handle their mass e-mailing chores in ways that reveal not only their technical expertise but their familiarity with what has come to be called "netiquette." Aaron obviously finds it rude of Dave to make him scroll past all those addresses when they could all be suppressed. As one who, for the purposes of this book, is interested in getting some idea of how many generations of forwards preceded an item of newslore's arrival in my in-box, I'm disappointed when the addresses have been deleted or suppressed, but generally, I see Aaron's point. What's surprising about his diatribe is that in berating Dave about his breach of netiquette he committed two more egregious breaches himself: he sent a message that was meant only for one person to an entire list of people, which compounds the second sin of "flaming." All this hints at our growing impatience with the sheer volume of e-mail pouring into our in-boxes, and our inexperience at presenting our social selves in this strange new world of communication. Both issues, volume and netiquette, underscore the risks of forwarding newslore.

Here is what else arrived on Tuesday:

- Lyrics to "The Kennebunkport Hillbilly," sung to the tune of the *Beverly Hillbillies* theme song.
- Another Bush joke (see chapter 5).
- A Bill and Hillary joke dated February 7, 2001 (see chapter 2).
- A Bill Clinton–George W. Bush joke dated February 9, 2001 (see chapter 5).

Then came the Cheney jokes:

- A fake news story from the *Onion*, not attributed.
- A list of Cheney's Top Ten Excuses from the Letterman show, not attributed.
- An exchange between host Jon Stewart and "correspondent" Rob Corddry from *The Daily Show*.
- A triple one-liner, the humor of which depends on one's knowing that Cheney has a heart problem, that the Bush administration was fending off charges that it was engaging in illegal domestic surveillance, and that the United States has been accused of torturing suspected terrorists in Iraq and through proxies in other countries:

After Cheney shot the guy he called out to the Secret Service: "Save his heart!" [Leno]
  And then: "OK, anyone else have a problem with domestic wiretaps?!"
  Before he shot him he reportedly tortured him for 30 minutes.

- Two editorial cartoons and a photo collage of Cheney making a number of hand gestures, with the caption "Ten Ways Dick Cheney Can Kill You."

WEDNESDAY, FEBRUARY 15

- A transcript from "Ye Olde Briefing Room," in which a presidential spokesman stonewalls questions about Vice President Aaron Burr's role in the death of Alexander Hamilton, attributed to salon.com.
- "Actual SAT answers from Arkansas."

THURSDAY, FEBRUARY 16

There were the usuals: "Russell Frank, I am calling from Benin republic West Africa" and "Congratulations, You Have Won US$500,000.00." Funny that we don't even bat an eyelash anymore when we see such tidings. Then came a poem consisting of verbatim quotes from

George W. Bush, attributed to a *Washington Post* writer, a fake news story from *Salon*, and still more Bush jokes (see chapter 5).

While I'm getting all this e-mail, and the late-night comedians are doing their thing, the newspapers are printing sidebars to the hunting accident story about the jokes. The key to this departure from standard operating procedure is that the shooting victim was not considered to be in any danger. On Wednesday, Cheney comes out from behind various administration spokespersons and takes responsibility for the accident. This does not stem the tide of e-mailed jokes about the incident.

"How about this one?" a colleague asks. It's an animated game. Cheney raises his shotgun. A covey of quail flies up from the trees. Click your mouse when you want Cheney to shoot. I do so. Cheney spins and shoots one of the three people standing off to the side.

FRIDAY, FEBRUARY 17

• Unconfirmed Urban Myth (1/19/02): Hard Laughter:

A female news anchor in Michigan, the day after it was supposed to have snowed and didn't, turned to the weatherman and asked, "So Bob, where's that eight inches you promised me last night?"

Not only did the weatherman have to leave the set, but half the crew did too, because they were laughing so hard.

• Five Enron/Arthur Andersen jokes (see chapter 6).
• Two unattributed political jokes (one of which is a metajoke):

I don't approve of political jokes . . . I've seen too many of them get elected.

How come we choose from just two people for President and 50 for Miss America?

• A Social Security joke:

Kathy and Suzy are having a conversation during their lunch break.
    Kathy asks, "So, Suzy, how's your sex life these days?"
    Suzy replies, "Oh, you know. It's the usual, Social Security kind."
    "Social Security?" Kathy asked quizzically.
    "Yeah, you get a little each month, but it's not really enough to live on."

• A couple of Bill Clinton jokes, one of which is in chapter 2. Here is the other:

Clinton is in the supermarket picking up some things for the new office in New York when a stock boy accidentally bumps into him.

"Pardon me," the stock boy says.

"Sure," Clinton replies, "but it'll cost you."

• An oversexed and hypocritical pastor joke:

Jesse Jackson, Jim Baker, and Jimmy Swaggert have written an impressive new book. . . . It's called: "*Ministers Do More Than Lay People*."

• A George W. Bush joke (see chapter 5).

The Cheney joke of the day is a two-panel photo cartoon. In the first panel, Dick Cheney is on the phone; in the second, Bill Clinton is on the phone. Cheney is saying, "Bill—interested in doing a little quail hunting next weekend?? Bring the wife!"

SATURDAY, FEBRUARY 18

• An Arthur Andersen joke (see the introduction).
• Three Bush jokes, two of which are in chapter 5. Here's the other:

Q: How many members of the Bush administration does it take to change a light bulb?
A: Ten.
1. One to deny that a light bulb needs to be changed;
2. One to attack the patriotism of anyone who says the light bulb needs to be changed;
3. One to blame Clinton for burning out the light bulb;
4. One to tell the nations of the world that they are either for changing the light bulb or for eternal darkness;
5. One to give a billion dollar no-bid contract to Halliburton for the new light bulb;
6. One to arrange a photograph of Bush, dressed as a janitor, standing on a step ladder under the banner 'Bulb Accomplished';
7. One administration insider to resign and in detail reveal how Bush was literally 'in the dark' the whole time;
8. One to viciously smear No. 7;
9. One surrogate to campaign on TV and at rallies on how George Bush has had a strong light-bulb-changing policy all along;
10. And finally, one to confuse Americans about the difference between screwing a light bulb and screwing the country.

• A newspaper joke:

Five cannibals get jobs at a newspaper. During the welcoming ceremony the managing editor says, "You're all part of our team now. You can earn good money here, and you can go to the cafeteria for something to eat. So please don't trouble any of the other employees." The cannibals promised.

Four weeks later the boss returns and says, "You're all working very hard, and I'm very satisfied with all of you. However, one of our janitors has disappeared. Do any of you know what happened to him?"

The cannibals all shake their heads no.

After the boss has left, the leader of the cannibals says to the others, "Which of you idiots ate the janitor?"

A hand raises hesitantly, to which the leader of the cannibals replies, "You fool! For four weeks we've been eating copy editors and supervisors and no one noticed anything, and you have to go and eat the janitor!"

• 25 Rules for Being a Loyal Republican

1) You have to believe that the nation's recent and sorrowfully-missed 8-year prosperity was due to the work of Ronald Reagan and George Bush, but that yesterday's gas prices are all Clinton's fault.

2) You have to believe that those privileged from birth achieve success all on their own.

3) You have to be against government programs, but expect your Social Security and farm subsidy checks on time.

4) You have to believe that government should stay out of people's lives, yet you want government to ban same-sex marriages and determine what your official language should be.

5) You have to believe that pollution is ok, so long as it makes a profit.

6) You have to believe in prayer in schools, as long as you don't pray to Allah or Buddha.

7) You have to believe that only your own teenagers are still virgins.

8) You have to believe that a woman cannot be trusted with decisions about her own body, but that large multinational corporations should have no regulation or interference whatsoever.

9) You believe Jesus loves you, and by the way, Jesus shares your hatred of AIDS victims, homosexuals, and President Clinton.

10) You have to believe that society is colorblind and growing up black in America doesn't diminish your opportunities, but you still won't vote for Alan Keyes.

11) You have to believe that it was wise to allow Ken Starr to spend $50 million dollars to attack Clinton because no other U.S. presidents have ever been unfaithful to their wives.

12) You have to believe that a waiting period for purchasing a handgun is bad because quick access to a new firearm is an important concern for all Americans.

13) You have to believe it is wise to keep condoms out of schools, because we all know if teenagers don't have condoms they won't have sex.

14) You have to believe that the ACLU is bad because they defend the Constitution, while the NRA is good because they defend the Constitution.

15) You have to believe that socialism hasn't worked anywhere, and that Europe doesn't exist.

16) You have to believe the AIDS virus is not important enough to deserve federal funding proportionate to the resulting death rate and that the public doesn't need to be educated about it, because if we just ignore it, it will go away.

17) You have to believe that biology teachers are corrupting the morals of 6th graders if they teach them the basics of human sexuality, but the Bible, which is full of sex and violence, is good reading.

18) You have to believe that Chinese communist missiles have killed more Americans than handguns, alcohol, and tobacco.

19) You have to believe that even though governments have supported the arts for 5000 years and that most of the great works of art were paid for by governments, our government should shun any such support. After all, the rich can afford to buy their own and the poor don't need any.

20) You have to believe that the lumber from the last one percent of old-growth U.S. forests is well worth the destruction of those forests and the extinction of the several species of plants and animals that live there.

21) You have to believe that we should forgive and pray for Newt Gingrich, Henry Hyde, and Bob Livingston for their marital infidelities, but that bastard Clinton should have been convicted.

22) You have to believe that 50,456,169 is a higher number than 50,996,116.

23) You have to believe that "having a mandate" is defined as "losing the popular vote".

24) You have to believe a woman should be "pretty and in her place", unless she is a right-wing spokesperson or radio advice show hostess, in which case she should be "petty and in your face".

25) You have to believe that even though you attack scientists and the "intellectual elite" as godless, and try to prevent their discoveries and theories from being discussed in the public schools, you should take advantage of their labors to extend your life and improve its quality.

A week later, my friend Michael and I exchange the following e-mails:

Michael: Are my sources coming through for you?
Me: Loud & clear—it's a big help.
Michael: Your sources? I don't understand.
Me: YOU wrote "Are my sources coming through for you?" ya nimrod.
Michael: Let me try to explain again. You see the highlighted part below? So I thought you wrote that back to me, not realizing that it was the attachment of my email to you. So you see....oh, nevermind.

Michael, later the same day:

OK...it's been a very crazy day. Let me set the record straight on the email exchange we had today. But first, let me sound off. I love to sound off.

I hate all digital means of communications. Yes! Commander Buttons wants to resign his commission. I can't take it anymore. I had to replace my cell phone/Palm Pilot this week. I wanted the same model as the one I lost on a fishing expedition on Kauai (the second time I've done this in 2 years....a personal best). It is no longer made. So I get the new Treo 650 (which has already been replaced by the Treo 700). Because I need a phone that is Mac compatible, the only other choice was a Blackberry and for too many reasons to explain right now I definitely didn't want one. So I'm saddled with the Treo 650.

This thing can do everything but make an espresso. It may be able to, but I haven't figured out how to make it work. It can do so many things that I will never use. But in order for all of these things to work I will need an engineering degree. I don't want a "memo pad" that is different from a "task" application which is different from a "graffiti pad" which is different from a "graffiti-2 pad". I don't need 3 different email applications. I don't need the camera or camcorder. I suspect I can launch a missile attack with this thing....or maybe I'm looking at one of the many games I can play. ALL I WANT IS A CELL PHONE, CONTACT LIST, CALENDAR AND EMAIL!!! I can even live without the email!!!

The buttons are tiny. And given that Arthur Itis is beginning to set up housekeeping in my body, this presents problems. (If the body is the temple of my soul, then mine is the Temple of Doom). I make too many wrong mistakes...as Yogi would say (he's the Zen Master of my temple).

I have spent a week trying to eliminate all the applications I call "the fluff stuff"...too much fluff stuff on this damn thing. I have been on the phone with tech support several times this week. Not because I'm making too many wrong mistakes, but because this thing is full of bugs. Although they insist it is Mac compatible, they did not thoroughly test or debug the applications. They are doing this in the marketplace using customers as test subjects. I am their beta-test site. And at the risk of sounding intolerant, I don't like talking to the support people in India because their accents are impossible to understand on bad phone lines. I have had to apologize and ask politely to speak to someone else because I can't understand what is being said. And these people are so wonderfully patient and polite that I can't even consider getting frustrated or annoyed! So instead I snarl at Pinky and he doesn't understand that he didn't do anything wrong. So then he runs to Lea and she knows that I am having a problem with the Treo and she yells at me. I hide under my desk. I'm a bad dog.

And don't get me started on email. It is as primitive a form of modern communications as can be. It is fast, but it leaves you without enough information or understanding. There is no tone of voice. There is no body language. And on top of it all nobody writes good (I know....I'm just making a point). The language is clipped, cryptic and full of acronyms, abbreviations and is written without punctuation. "I went to the store to do my grocery shopping", becomes: "went to store. groceries." I find out that people are feeling insulted by my emails because they can't "hear" that I am joking about the subject of our "discussion". Puns are pointless. Sarcasm can't be understood. The laughter in my voice can't be heard. So now I have to "say" something with "(a joke)" typed next to what I have written.

Just look at the simple email exchange we had today.

I wrote:

Are my sources coming through for you?

This is the response I got from you:

Loud & clear—it's a big help.

Are my sources coming through for you?

I responded:

Your sources? I don't understand.

You responded:

YOU wrote "Are my sources coming through for you?" ya nimrod.

Your sources? I don't understand.

The previous sentence is the very core of our misunderstanding each other. As is usually the case, your email listed my original question without the date and time "quotation" of my original email. Therefore, I thought you were also asking me "Are my sources coming through for you?" Get it?

Me neither.

Huh? I'm thinking "Why are Russ's resources talking to me, who are they and what did I need from them or what does Russ think I need? Am I really being a Nimrod? Or is Russ making a joke? Or is he angry that I'm confused and taking up too much of his time? Is he really that busy? How can folklore be busy work? You can't rush folklore. There's no rushing in folklore. Perfessers don't ever rush. That's what makes Russ a good folklore perfesser. Am I being insulted? Should I tell him to 'go to hell?'" So now we are no longer addressing the simple subject at hand. We are now talking about what we THOUGHT we were talking about and what the intent of our words may or may not, have or have not, will or will not be or been.

And I'm trying to do this on Treo 650 that doesn't work in American English, that has tiny buttons. I'm trying to do this while I'm driving and listening to the NPR report on the copyright infringement lawsuit brought against the makers of the Blackberry.

You know how much I love the buttons. But they don't love me anymore. I could make them sing in the past, but now their tune seems like an aria from a Wagner (pronounced VAHGNUH) opera. Just give me a crayon, a piece of paper and a stamped envelope and I'm cool.

Murray Gotz,

Cmdr. Buttons (ret.)

Here are the totals for the week: 12 Bush jokes, 9 Cheney jokes, 6 Enron jokes, 3 Bill and/
or Hillary Clinton jokes, and 14 miscellaneous jokes, half of which I would consider newslore in the sense that you have to have been paying attention to the news to understand the
jokes.

One other postscript. On March 1, 2006, I received an e-mail with the following subject line, misspelling and all: "FWD: Chenney shot a lawyer." Oh good, I thought, another
Cheney joke. Here is what was in the body of the message: "It's time to save on medicines!
More than 900 meds"—including Cialis, Viagra, and Levitra. "Discreet package to your
door! Shipped from Canada!" I must salute whoever sent this e-mail. Such stuff pours into
my in-box every day, and it's usually obvious enough that I can route it right into the trash
without opening it. This one fooled me, and the way it fooled me is a measure of the mania
for Cheney hunting jokes in the winter of 2006.

APPENDIX B
Collecting and Analyzing Newslore

HOT TOPICS

The idea that there was a book to be written about newslore began to take shape as I contemplated the growing body of e-mailed jokes and urban legends forwarded by friends or family. I would have been happy to limit my study to this material if I thought I could get enough of it, because I like the way e-mailed newslore, unlike many humor Web sites, is subjected to the quality control standards of this peculiar marketplace.

As the volume of e-mail has grown and the percentage of it that could be considered junk mail has risen, most of us have become reluctant to forward netlore to our friends unless we believe it will be worth their time to look at. In a review of *Send: The Essential Guide to Email for Home and Office*,[1] Dave Barry, in his hyperbolic style, gives us a good idea of the widespread scorn for "Internet sludge"—and the people who forward it:

> You received a message addressed to many recipients—often a much-recycled joke, story, list, urban myth, etc. There are millions of these floating around; many of us simply delete them unread. But you, the "Reply All" abuser, read it and decide to respond with some clever comment of your own (such as "LOL"). And instead of hitting "Reply," which would inflict your reply only on the sender, you hit "Reply All," thereby forcing everybody on the recipient list to receive, and delete, yet another useless piece of e-mail. Please do not take this personally, "Reply All" people, but: everybody hates you. We hate you almost as much as we hate the people who mass-mail this Internet sludge in the first place.[2]

In other words, the same considerations that govern our decision to seize the floor in face-to-face conversations apply in cyberspace. Though we are not the creators of the material, our judgment is under scrutiny. We get mildly irritated at those who waste our time; we appreciate those who offer welcome diversion from our labors—and give us something good to pass along in turn, to our own credit. I am struck, in this regard, by the various ways forwarders vouch for the quality of their material. Common subject lines include:

- "This is interesting"
- "Thought-provoking"
- "This is VERY important"
- "AMAZING"

- "Please read this!!!"
- "This you have to SEE!!!!!"
- "ABSOLUTELY a MUST READ"

And so on. Within the body of the e-mail, one sees apologia like these:

- "Please do not take this for a junk letter."
- "I thought this was a scam myself, but . . ."
- "To all of my friends, I do not usually forward messages, but . . ."
- "I know everyone receives jokes and junk mail and tends to forward nonsense through their mailing lists" [but . . .]

Though forwarding tells us nothing specific about any given recipient's response to an item of netlore, it tells us one important thing: that the forwarders had enough confidence in their audience's response to believe that forwarding would enhance their prestige or at least do it no harm. The risks of forwarding may be slight compared to the risks of live performance[3]—but forwarding is a choice. One makes it with the awareness that addressees might be either grateful or annoyed to receive the item in question. (On the other hand, notes Brad Templeton, founder of the Rec.funny.net site, the forwarders of written humor have none of the advantages at the disposal of the oral joke teller: "You don't get the advantage of delivery, surprise or a funny face. You don't get a drunk audience [usually] or a chance to use your great German accent. You must prepare a joke that stands on its own."[4])

A fair question at this point is, why be concerned with quality at all? If the ethnographer's job is to offer a representative, if not complete, accounting of a given cultural phenomenon, why not present the lead balloons as well as the zingers? Here it must be admitted that folklore studies have long been driven by researchers' aesthetic appreciation of the material. Appreciation has driven advocacy: we exhibit or write about what we collect in the field not just to help complete the record of human culture but to expose the beauty or power of the work to a wider audience and thereby engender respect for the makers of the work.[5] In folklore as in journalism, documentation and advocacy often go hand in hand. Conversely, "inferior" items of folklore, which include objects that exhibit shoddy workmanship, unfunny jokes, dull stories, or musically or lyrically insipid songs, would only reinforce notions that nothing but the output of professional or elite artists or performers is worthy of our attention and respect. As it is, the discipline of folklore has had to struggle to overcome a sense that the arts it champions possess, at best, a crude or simple charm, which pales in comparison with the canonical works of fine literary, musical, or visual art. A similar hierarchical view obtains even in the world of humor: as we have seen, the jokes of the professionals who write material for Jay Leno, David Letterman, and the other mainstays of late-night television are accorded a privileged place on Web sites devoted to humor.

So yes, if I'm writing a book about jokes, I do so conscious that critical and market reception of the book will depend, in part, on whether readers agree with my assessment of the cleverness of the material. But we mustn't overlook the *functional* dimension of aesthetics.

Items of folklore circulate and remain in circulation because they're good. We might even say that the circulation of jokes and stories is what makes them folklore. What's useful about this formulation is that it solves one of the thorniest problems of dealing with Internet humor, the problem of professionalism and copyright. As broad as the definition of folklore has become, we stop short of saying that the jokes Jay Leno tells on *The Tonight Show* or the parodies that appear on the *Onion* Web site are folklore, at least initially. But netizens are notoriously casual when it comes to attribution. If people see or hear a joke they like, they pass it on, usually without bothering to say where they got it. So one of the things that has troubled me as I grappled with the material that fit the theme of this book is what would happen if I traced an oft-e-mailed joke back to a professional source.

The day after the news broke that Vice President Cheney had accidentally shot a hunting companion in February 2006, for example, I received a list of Top Ten Cheney Excuses, unattributed to any source (see appendix A for a detailed accounting of the Cheney lore that circulated that week). Top Ten lists are a regular feature of the Letterman show, but they also inspire people to compose their own. Was this a Letterman list or a Letterman-like "folk" list? It was easy to find out it was from Letterman. Does this disqualify it from consideration as folklore though it may closely resemble a joke whose provenance cannot be determined? Is known authorship or payment for services rendered a meaningful disqualifier? Tracing a joke to its source is a practical matter. It's silly to make the success or failure of this sort of detective work determinative of whether the joke is folklore or something else. If we make circulation a criterion, provenance ceases to matter. Whatever its source, a joke retold (and retold and retold) becomes folklore by virtue of the retelling. Its creator, even if he or she wants to sue for copyright infringement, should be flattered.

Thus my preference for forwarded e-mail, or forwards (or "forwardables").[6] But knowing that all the items that came my way were popular was not the same as knowing that all the popular items were coming my way. I had to consider the possibility that I was out of the loop, relatively speaking. My network of acquaintances may not be as large as that of, say, my friend Michael Yonchenko, who travels often on business and, as an independent video producer, works with many clients and freelancers. I suspect he also has geekier friends—techie types who spend more time on the Internet than my friends do. To augment my certainly incomplete and possibly even woefully incomplete trove of newslore, I did several things. First I asked Yonchenko to ask his e-mail cohort to add me to the group of addressees to whom they usually send items that tickle their fancy, and I took shameless advantage of my position as a columnist with my local newspaper to let my readers know what I was looking for. Those pleas bore fruit, but I still felt obliged to augment the e-mailed material with the overwhelmingly vast collections on various Web sites.

There are a lot of them, especially for jokes. The folklorist Elliott Oring pinpoints the problem with this kind of Web site: often it's "more like an archive than a repertoire."[7] Putting it another way, the Web masters don't see themselves as gatekeepers, deciding which material deserves a wider audience. In keeping with the democratic spirit that informs much of the Web, they would rather let site visitors rate the jokes than do it for them. Some of the sites keep lists of the most frequently e-mailed items; others tout their most popular categories. In January 2006, for example, About.com's political humor page guided visitors to "funny pictures, political cartoons, doctored photos, and parodies" mocking President Bush, Saddam Hussein, Osama bin Laden, John Kerry, Bill Clinton, Hillary Clinton, Arnold Schwarzenegger, Jenna and Barbara Bush, and the 2004 presidential election. By August 2010 an updated version of the list replaced doctored photos and parodies with "dumbest quotes" and "late-night jokes." Saddam Hussein, Osama bin Laden, John Kerry, Bill Clinton, Arnold Schwarzenegger, Jenna and Barbara Bush, and the 2004 election were subtracted; Barack Obama, Sarah Palin, and Joe Biden were added.[8] Thus do the public world of the Web sites and the private world of personal e-mail recipient lists overlap: a surfer can find a good joke on a Web site, copy and paste it into an e-mail, and let the forwarding begin. Web sites such as Jokesgallery.com make it easier for us. The site enables one to compose a message and send a joke to as many as ten friends, or post it to one's social network. One can also subscribe to the JokesGallery online newsletter and "receive hundreds of jokes each week" via e-mail.[9]

Much of the material on the humor Web sites, I was relieved to discover, was pretty lame, from which I inferred that it had not circulated as much as the material I received via e-mail or material that made the lists of most e-mailed. The most useful humor site for my purposes was Rec.funny.net, which subjects all submissions to the site moderator's own critical eye, with a view toward keeping the archive a manageable size. Since keeping the data set to a manageable size was an important consideration for me also, I wound up relying on Rec.funny.net as my guide to the best jokes. But first I had to decide which joke *topics* to include. For that I went to the Associated Press annual lists of the top ten stories of the year. If newslore is folk commentary on the news, I reasoned, the most newsworthy stories of the year would generate the most jokes. But what makes a story newsworthy? Pick up any news-writing textbook, and somewhere near the beginning the authors will offer a list of the elements of newsworthiness that usually looks something like this:

- Impact: occurrences that affect large numbers of people in significant ways are more newsworthy than either occurrences that affect small numbers of people in significant ways or occurrences that affect large numbers of people in insignificant ways.
- Prominence: the doings of prominent people—office holders, captains of industry, celebrity actors, athletes, artists and intellectuals—are of greater interest than the doings of ordinary citizens.
- Proximity: people are more interested in the nearby than the faraway. For a national press organization like the AP, that means stories that directly affect America or Americans are of greater interest than stories that do not. The same would turn out to be true when it came to folklore: I found much less material pertaining to foreign disasters and political upheavals than to domestic ones.
- Novelty: we are more interested in unusual occurrences than we are in usual ones.
- Conflict: clashes of ideas, nations, constituencies, and individuals are inherently dramatic.
- Timeliness: obviously the news concerns itself with what's new. World War II contained all the elements listed earlier in ample measure, but it isn't newsworthy now unless there's a timely hook such as an anniversary, publication of a book, release of a film, or death of someone who played a prominent role.
- Death and destruction: though death and destruction are inherently high-impact events and may be a result of conflict or unusual occurrences, like the 2004 tsunami in the Indian Ocean, some textbook

writers break them out into their own category in acknowledgment of our interest in fatal car accidents or structure fires that might not involve large numbers of people or any prominent people but are still considered worthy of notice, perhaps because they remind us of the transient nature of life and material goods.

It stands to reason that the more of these elements that come into play, the more newsworthy an occurrence becomes. Though coverage of the 1994 case in which O. J. Simpson was accused of murdering his wife Nicole Brown Simpson and her friend Ronald Goldman was widely criticized for being excessive, which is to say, out of all proportion to its impact, if we look at how many other newsworthy elements were involved, it's easy to see why it got the coverage it did, and why, despite many people's protestations to the contrary, they followed it so avidly. A corollary hypothesis might be that the more elements of newsworthiness involved in a story, the more we are likely to see a folkloric response. (The OJ story was a huge folklore generator.)

The AP lists, it turns out, are a mixed bag. On one hand, they tend to include stories that were big on impact, but short on the other elements. Stories about the economy, taxes, or rising oil prices are hardy perennials—they appeared on the AP list six times in ten years—but they aren't about events or people so much as they are about ongoing trends. As such, I did not expect to find much newslore in response to these kinds of stories, and, in fact, I did not.

The AP lists are also partial to stories about the deaths of well-known personages: Princess Diana, Mother Teresa, John F. Kennedy Jr., Ronald Reagan, Yasir Arafat, Michael Jackson, and Ted Kennedy all made the lists. These seemed more promising. In a column about AP's top ten for 1997, which included both Diana and Mother Teresa, Richard Roeper had no quarrel with the sensational and unexpected death of Diana but took exception to the unsurprising death of Mother Teresa at eighty-seven.[10] Roeper invoked the "water cooler" standard in crafting his own alternative top ten list for 1997: he didn't deny that the AP's top

AP	Roeper
1. The death of Princess Diana	**1. Princess Diana**
2. The conviction and sentencing of Oklahoma City bomber Timothy McVeigh	2. The [Andrew] Cunanan saga
3. The death of Mother Teresa	3. Au pair trial
4. Bullish U.S. stock markets	4. The Iowa septuplets
5. The cloning of a Scottish sheep	5. Tiger Woods
6. Birth of McCaughey septuplets	**6. Heaven's Gate cult suicide**
7. Tobacco settlement	7. The JonBenet Ramsey investigation
8. *Pathfinder* explores Mars	8. O. J. Simpson's civil trial
9. Fund-raising scandals dog the Democrats	9. Marv Albert scandal
10. Suicide of Heaven's Gate cult members	10. Ellen DeGeneres leaps out of the closet

stories were important, but he argued that other stories were more talked about.[11] Here are AP's list and Roeper's list side by side (items that appear on both lists are in bold):

"Newsworthiness aside," Roeper wrote, "that's what people were talking about in 1997."[12] What people were talking about, what captured people's imaginations, would probably be as good a predictor of newslore as one might find. No one, to my knowledge, has followed Roeper's lead in compiling an annual alternative most-talked-about stories list, but the Center for Media and Public Affairs compiles a list of the most-joked-about topics by television's late-night comedians year in and year out, and it stands to reason that what those guys find joke-worthy is fodder for amateur jokesters as well, especially when we factor in the likelihood that the late-night comedians set the joking agenda for the country.[13] (When Dan Quayle's name surfaced as a possible presidential candidate in 2000, a joke suggested that the late-night comedians would be glad to have him back in public life: "I recently saw a poll on the news showing that Dan Quale had 7% of the Republican support. I found this very disturbing - I had not realized that such a large majority of our nations comedians were Republicans.") So I also relied on CMPA's lists to point me toward my subject matter. Here, for example, is the CMPA list for 1997:

1. Bill Clinton
2. O. J. Simpson
3. Al Gore
4. Janet Reno
5. Hillary Clinton
6. Newt Gingrich
7. Boris Yeltsin
8. Bob Dole
9. Paula Jones
10. Rudy Giuliani

Looking at a dozen years' worth of CMPA lists reveals several distinct patterns. First, the joke targets are all people, not topics like the economy or oil prices. Second, most of the people are politicians. (They are also mostly men, but that follows from their being mostly politicians.) Third, Bill Clinton has had remarkable staying power as a joke target, remaining at or near the top of the list even after he left the White House. Here is my own composite list of top joke targets based on years on the CMPA list from 1997 to 2008 (numbers for 2007 are missing from the CMPA Web site):

1. Bill Clinton (11 for 11)
2. George W. Bush, Hillary Clinton (9 for 11)
3. Dick Cheney, Al Gore (8 for 11)
4. Saddam Hussein, Arnold Schwarzenegger (4 for 10)
5. O. J. Simpson, Janet Reno, Monica Lewinsky, Martha Stewart, Osama bin Laden (3 for 10)

The only other surprise on this list apart from Bill Clinton's dominance is former U.S. attorney general Janet Reno. My suspicion, soon confirmed, was that most of the jokes had to do with her central role in the protracted battle over custody of the six-year-old Cuban refugee Elian Gonzalez in 2000. But I was also reminded that she ran (unsuccessfully) for governor of Florida in 2002 and took some of the blame for the FBI's disastrous raid on the Branch Davidian compound in Waco, Texas, in 1993 (the raid itself proved to be fertile ground for jokes).[14] The crucial limitation of the CMPA list as a guide to joking in general is that sick jokes are underrepresented. Specifically, the late-night comedians are much more circumspect about celebrity deaths than they are about celebrity sex scandals. Note the absence of Princess Diana.

As for the AP's annual top ten list, these are the stories that generated the most newslore over the past ten years and that I therefore examined or at least mentioned in this book, along with most of the names in my top five CMPA list earlier:

- Princess Diana (no. 1 in 1997)
- The Clinton-Lewinsky scandal (no. 1 in 1998)
- Y2K and the millennium (no. 4 in 1999)
- John F. Kennedy Jr. dies (no. 5 in 1999)
- Presidential elections (no. 1 in 2000, 2004, and 2008)
- Elian Gonzalez custody dispute (no. 2 in 2000)
- Microsoft breakup ordered (no. 6 in 2000)
- September 11 attacks (no. 1 in 2001)
- Corporate scandals (no. 4 in 2002) / economic meltdown (no. 2 in 2008)
- Hurricane Katrina (no. 1 in 2005)
- Michael Jackson dies (no. 7 in 2009)

HOT GENRES

Every new communication medium becomes a new way to transmit folklore. Jokes and stories told face-to-face can easily be told and quickly spread over the telephone, and though jokes and stories may arise that involve the phone itself—the urban legend about the babysitter who takes a call from a murderer on the premises comes to mind[15]—it is hard to see how the medium has given rise to new *forms* of folklore. Fax machines and computers, on the other hand, have not only served as media for the communication of folklore but provided the tools for the creation and transmission of new forms of folklore. Forms of expression like the composite photograph, the phony document, or the video production may not be new, but computer applications have so reduced the cost and labor-intensiveness of producing them that they are available to amateurs and may be disseminated by amateurs on a scale that was simply not possible before. Here I will discuss in greater detail the forms of newslore we have encountered in this book.

The Fake Photograph: Beyond the Jackalope

There is nothing new about the doctored photograph.[16] The apparent verisimilitude of the photographic image drew pranksters right from the start. Photos could be faked before the film was exposed, by arranging a tableau, and after, by cutting out one image and pasting it onto another. Folklorists have been interested in two types of hoax photograph: spirit photographs, which purport to capture ghosts and other otherworldly manifestations on film,[17] and tall-tale photographs, which typically show a gigantic fruit or vegetable on a farm wagon or railroad flatcar, or a chimerical beast like the jackalope—half jackrabbit, half antelope.[18] As the name implies, the tall-tale postcard is offered as real; gullible souls like I was at age twelve when I saw my first jackalope card might even believe it.

The best of these images are pretty seamless; if you disbelieve them, it isn't because the cutting and pasting were poorly executed but because you know enough about the world to doubt the existence of super-sized potatoes or antlered rabbits. But when the cutting and pasting involved real scissors or knives and real paste, the task took considerable skill. And still there was the problem of the slightly raised surface of the superimposed image, resolved only by taking a photograph of the photograph. At that point, the project became not just labor-intensive but costly.[19] Computers, then, don't allow us to do what could not be done before as much as they allow us to do it better, more easily, and, aside from the initial outlay for hardware or software—presumably purchased for purposes other than doctoring photographs—less expensively. This, logically, makes it more likely that people with a modicum of skill will doctor photographs just for the fun of it. As a result, digitally altered photographs, or photoshops, as they are called by aficionados, have become part of that "virtual Niagara of lore flowing over the electronic grapevine."[20]

In his survey of what he refers to as World Trade Center humor, Bill Ellis expresses his surprise at "the proliferation of 'computer-generated cybercartoons' . . . a phenomenon that will need much closer study in the future."[21] "Cybercartoon" is a good term to the extent that the closest analogue for most of this material is the political cartoon, but I prefer the term "photoshop" to "cybercartoon" or "computer-generated art"[22] for two reasons. First, most of the images I examined in this book are digitally altered photographs rather than cartoons, which I think of as drawings, whether they are drawn by hand or with the aid of the computer. Second, "photoshops" is the preferred (emic) term among people who create, upload, and archive the images.[23]

Evidence of the robustness of the culture of photoshopping is found on Web sites like Worth1000.com, where veteran photoshoppers offer step-by-step instruction in how to achieve effects such as "zombifying, gender bending, face swapping, fattening and aging." Also included are guides for making a specific image:

- How I turned a stack of pancakes into something you probably wouldn't want to find on your plate.
- How to turn Tom Cruise into an Alien.
- How I chocolatized a skull.
- How I puppetized Charlize [Theron].[24]

Worth1000 hosts what it calls a "daily manipulation contest." Those who would enter photoshopped images involving Britney Spears, President Bush, "scantily clad women (i.e. in bikinis) for no practical reason," "Star Wars references," the Statue of Liberty, the World Trade Center, and Hitler "or Nazi references" are advised that these are "annoying overused entries (clichés)" and therefore unlikely to win.[25]

Digitally altered photographs circulate among friends via e-mail and turn up on a host of netlore sites, just as jokes and urban legends do. (And less innocuously, they turn up on Web sites run by pranksters and propagandists.) In fact, jokes and urban legends have their photographic counterparts. Joke photographs are the obvious fakes, intended to amuse; photographic urban legends are the subtle fakes, intended to amaze. And, as with verbal jokes and legends, there are hybrid forms: the subtle fakes intended to amuse and the parodies of the subtle fakes. There are also various kinds of verbal-photographic compounds: legends consisting of both photo and text, true photographs with false back stories,[26] and legends that claim a true photograph is a hoax.

The Photographic Urban Legend

In light of several decades of scholarship on the urban legend, a photograph would have to meet three criteria to be given serious consideration as a visual manifestation of the genre:

1. It must tell a story.
2. It must be extraordinary, yet believable.
3. It must express, at least obliquely, anxiety about threats to our health, safety, and psychic equilibrium.

1. *It must tell a story.* Urban legends are narratives. A picture may be worth a thousand words, but all those words do not necessarily add up to a story. One could use a thousand words to describe an Edward Weston photo of a nautilus or a pepper, but the description is not likely to include narrative elements. A photo of an occurrence, however—whether it shows something that has already happened, or something that is happening or about to happen—implies a plot as defined by one of my folklore mentors, Robert Georges: "a series of incidents set in a specific locale and presented in a logical time sequence that builds to a kind of climax."[27] The idea of a photographic urban legend is predicated on the notion that there can be such a thing as a narrative photograph.

2. *It must be extraordinary, yet believable.* It is difficult to imagine how the urban legend could exist independently of the documentary tradition. Though fiction (usually), it "hitchhikes," as John McPhee might put it, on the credibility of nonfiction.[28] Like news stories, urban legends are third-person accounts that derive much of their credibility from the attribution of information to supposedly reliable sources. Whether a State Department official or the narrator's aunt's hairdresser, the source is implicitly someone who possesses firsthand knowledge. The reporter's credibility, additionally, is implicitly buttressed by the institutional integrity of the newspaper. Lacking that institutional support, the legend narrator can only attest to the truthfulness of the tale. Listeners believe it, or are at least willing

to entertain the possibility of it, because the documentary tradition offers ample evidence that truth is stranger than fiction and men will occasionally bite dogs. In the case of the photographic urban legend, credibility rests on the credibility of the documentary photo tradition.

A photographic urban legend, then, is a narrative photo that, like many a news photo, appears to be strange but true but, unlike the news photo, is ultimately false.

3. It must express, at least obliquely, anxiety about threats to our health, safety, and psychic equilibrium. Urban legends are a reliable guide to what keeps us up nights. They reflect doubt about the competence and integrity of the institutions that dominate our lives, namely, the government and big business, including big media, big health care, and big education. We worry whether these institutions can protect us from harm, and we worry whether they are themselves agents of harm. Specifically, we worry about:

- Our health and safety, especially the threat of sexually transmitted diseases, contaminated food and drink, insufficiently tested technologies, transportation accidents caused by incompetent operators or designers, and natural disasters such as earthquakes, hurricanes, tidal waves, and meteorites.
- Life in a multiracial, multiethnic society bound to a global economy.
- Monsters, large and small, human and inhuman, real and imaginary, including insects, spiders, snakes, rats, sharks, attack dogs, rapists, murderers, extraterrestrials, despots, and terrorists.

Thus while the news brings us word of product recalls, photoshoppers offer us a tiny frog in a can of peas or a snake in a computer. The news alarms us with tales of illegal immigration, while a photoshop regales us with an image of an undocumented worker smuggled over the Mexican border behind a car's dashboard. From the news we learn that many of the goods that were once manufactured in the United States are now produced overseas; a photoshop of a larvae-infested breast shows us the dangers of wearing imported clothing without washing it first. A news photo shows a single waterspout; a photoshopped version of the image shows three waterspouts. And so on. Most of the photoshops we looked at might be thought of as folk editorial cartoons: they combine or manipulate news photographs to offer biting commentary on the news and the newsmakers.

To summarize the discussion, a photographic urban legend is a narrative photo that circulates on the Internet, appears to be strange but true (but isn't), and compels our attention by depicting contemporary fears and anxieties.

News Jokes

"There is nothing of which we are more communicative than of a good jest," wrote the eighteenth-century philosopher Francis Hutcheson. Whether one is sitting down to compose a poem or song or joke, the easiest way to go about it is to find a tried-and-true form and fill it with (slightly) new content. Most jokes are either riddles or stories with punch lines. Riddles are questions with unexpected answers. Look at enough of them and you see variations on several questions. Examples will be jokes I did not use elsewhere in this book.

What's the difference between X and Y?

Q: What is the difference between Rush Limbaugh and the Hindenburg?

A: One is a flaming Nazi gasbag, while the other is just a dirigible.

A subtype of the "what's the difference" riddle involves a bawdy spoonerism:

Q: What's the difference between a cross-eyed hunter and a constipated owl?

A: One shoots and can't hit.

What do X and Y have in common? (or, How is an X like a Y?)

Q: What do the state of California and Taco Bell have in common?

A: Both can give O.J. gas.

What does/did X say to Y?

Q: What did the Zen Buddhist say to the hot dog vendor?

A: "Make me one with everything."

What's the first/last thing X saw/said?

Q: What's the last thing Christa McAuliffe said?

A: "What's this button for?"

What does X (if it were an acronym) stand for?

Q: What does WACO stand for?

A: We aren't coming out/We all cremated ourselves, etc.

Other perennial riddle jokes include "What do you get when you cross an X with a Y?"; "How many Xs does it take to screw in a lightbulb?"; and "Why did the X cross the road?"

The story jokes are more various. One persistent motif is the presence of three or more characters who engage in some form of one-upsmanship. In a common subtype, the three characters have arrived at the pearly gates. Another story joke type involves a magic lamp, a genie, and three wishes.

A third joke type, inspired by a staple of the David Letterman show, is the Top Ten list. A fourth type is the parody, with a wide assortment of subtypes—parodies of "Dear Abby" letters, newspaper stories and television news reports, press releases, chain letters, commercials, movie posters, office memorandums, and instruction manuals in general and frequently asked questions (FAQs) in particular.

Legends That Sound Like News Stories, Press Releases, or Interoffice Memorandums

I tell students in my news-writing classes that reporters obtain information in three ways: via observation, interviews, and documentary research. If they hear on the scanner that there's a house fire at the corner of Maple and Elm, they'll race over so they can describe the charred belongings on the lawn and the residents weeping as they watch their house being consumed by the flames. Then they'll ask the firefighters how the fire started and ask the residents about discovering the fire and getting out of the house. When they get back to the newsroom, they might look at back issues of their own paper or fire department records to find out how many house fires there have been in the past year, or how many have been caused by faulty furnaces, and so on.

This three-pronged approach to information gathering has served journalists—and the public—well for the past century. Other witnesses can challenge the accuracy of the reporter's observations. Interviewees can complain if they believe they were misquoted or misrepresented. Anyone with a mind to can consult the same public records the reporter consulted. Thus even today, despite reporters' getting caught inventing the news or being accused of bias, when Noam Chomsky reads that Ted Kennedy has a brain tumor, he believes it.

Urban legends have their own authenticating conventions. By setting the tales in specific locations, attributing them to a supposedly reliable source (a friend of a friend), and attesting to their veracity, narrators attempt to convince their audiences and possibly themselves that these improbable events really happened or could have happened. Flimsy as these devices are, they seem to give legends an air of what Stephen Colbert calls "truthiness." Though journalism has tightened the rules governing the use of anonymous sources—there had better be a good reason for withholding the name, and the information the source is providing had better be important—the use of such sources is par for the course in conversational storytelling. When a storyteller has the floor, the clock is ticking. The pressure is on. Clutter up your narrative with irrelevant information, and you might lose your audience. If I'm telling you about people you don't know and you'll probably never meet, I might not bother telling you their names. It's enough that it happened to my mechanic's sister.

Now, though, in the age of electronic reproduction, when legends have become as much, if not more, of a written phenomenon than an oral one, some legends are deriving their authority by assuming the guise of supposedly authoritative written genres, such as the news story, the business memorandum, and the press release, and visual genres, specifically the news photograph. Where the typical written legend aggressively asserts its factuality through the use of exclamation points, the sender's expression of disdain for junk e-mail, or even claims that the story has been verified by Snopes, the stories that parody official forms of communication rely on the rhetorical trappings of those forms. The result is what Rob Rosenberger, who writes about computer virus hoaxes, calls "false authority syndrome."[29] We can debate whether these parodies are subgenres of the contemporary legend, but they certainly possess some of the essential features of legends: they are narratives (implicitly so in the case of the phony news photo), they are fictions presented as matters of fact, and their subject matter tends, broadly, to engage with one modern bedevilment or another.

The News Story

Our first example riffs on the academic study story, a longtime newsroom staple. So routinely are readers exposed to the arcane researches of academics, they are unlikely to be surprised by *what* scholars study, only the results.

70% OF EXISTING MARRIAGES MAY ALREADY BE GAY

New Study Jolts White House

The Bush White House's plan to push for a constitutional amendment banning gay marriages suffered a surprising setback today as a new study revealed that well over seventy percent of existing marriages may already be gay.

The study, conducted by Dr. Charles Cranborn of the University of Minnesota, confirmed what many social scientists have long suspected: that within the first five years of marriages, most men become, for all intents and purposes, gay.

"Soon after marrying, most men stop hitting on women and start shopping for furniture," Dr. Cranborn said. "Scientifically speaking, how gay is that?"

Within ten years of marriage, Dr. Cranborn added, a significant number of married men stop having sex with women altogether.

"There's only one way to describe someone who does not have sex with women, does not hit on women, and spends his free time shopping for furniture," Dr. Cranborn added. "That word, to be scientific about it, is gay."

When news of the University of Minnesota study hit Washington, the White House immediately abandoned its plans for a constitutional amendment banning gay marriage for fear of alienating the seventy percent of married voters who are already in a gay marriage "whether they know it or not," to quote Dr. Cranborn.

Instead, the Administration will ask Congress for over 1.2 billion dollars in funds to promote gay divorces.

According to those familiar with the Bush proposal, gay couples who come forward and ask for a divorce will be granted total amnesty, a dividend tax cut, and a major reconstruction project in Iraq.

Note all the news-writing conventions this story invokes:

- Headline: The story has not only a headline but also what's known as a deck-head—a smaller headline below the main headline. Note the command of headlinese: the headline is written in the present tense with no articles.
- Lead: The first sentence includes the time element, "today." It uses the conventional synecdoche "The White House" to stand in for "members of the Bush administration." The writer withholds details about the provenance of the study under the assumption that such information would clutter up the lead and is less important than the study's findings and its conclusion. "Suffered a surprising setback" is an apt bit of "journalese," which is to say, a formulation that one only sees in a news story.
- Second paragraph: the second "graf" elaborates on the lead while revealing the provenance of the study parenthetically, between commas.
- Third graf: The attribution of the quotation is placed in the middle of the quote rather than at the end so that readers will know quickly who is being quoted. On second reference, the first name of the author of the study is omitted.
- Fourth graf: here we switch to an indirect quote (reporters do not like to stack quotes), again with attribution in the middle.

- Fifth graf: The first little slip-up. A good reporter wouldn't write, "Dr. Cranborn added" in back-to-back paragraphs.
- Sixth graf: Another slip. Reporters are likelier to write, "as Dr. Cranborn put it" rather than "to quote."
- Eighth graf: the phrase "according to those familiar with the Bush proposal" is a deft way of introducing information given to the reporter "on background."

The story, though obviously absurd, maintains a deadpan tone apart from the quotes from Dr. Cranborn, which seem a bit too colloquial or flip for the context. But if the quotes didn't arouse your suspicions, the last six words, which throw in the Iraq reconstruction project, function as the punch line. If you didn't know your leg was being pulled before, you know it now. Silly as it is, the story has much to tell us about contemporary male attitudes or folk beliefs about the emasculating effects of marriage. "Real men," we may infer, are both promiscuous and lustful, and have little interest in "female" pursuits such as shopping for home furnishings.

Our second example is also a sex study story, legitimated by its touting of the health benefits of a sexual practice.

Study: Fellatio may significantly decrease the risk of breast cancer in women

(AP)—Women who perform the act of fellatio and swallow semen on a regular basis, one to two times a week, may reduce their risk of breast cancer by up to 40 percent, a North Carolina State University study found.

Doctors had never suspected a link between the act of fellatio and breast cancer, but new research being performed at North Carolina State University is starting to suggest that there could be an important link between the two.

In a study of over 15,000 women suspected of having performed regular fellatio and swallowed the ejaculatory fluid, over the past ten years, the researchers found that those actually having performed the act regularly, one to two times a week, had a lower occurance of breast cancer than those who had not. There was no increased risk, however, for those who did not regularly perform.

"I think it removes the last shade of doubt that fellatio is actually a healthy act," said Dr. A.J. Kramer of Johns Hopkins School of Medicine, who was not involved in the research. "I am surprised by these findings, but am also excited that the researchers may have discovered a relatively easy way to lower the occurance of breast cancer in women."

The University researchers stressed that, though breast cancer is relatively uncommon, any steps taken to reduce the risk would be a wise decision.

"Only with regular occurance will your chances be reduced, so I encourage all women out there to make fellatio an important part of their daily routine," said Dr. Helena Shifteer, one of the researchers at the University. "Since the emergence of the research, I try to fellate at least once every other night to reduce my chances."

The study is reported in Friday's Journal of Medical Research.

In 1991, 43,582 women died of breast cancer, as reported by the National Cancer Institute.

Dr. Len Lictepeen, deputy chief medical officer for the American Cancer Society, said women should not overlook or "play down" these findings.

"This will hopefully change women's practice and patterns, resulting in a severe drop in the future number of cases," Lictepeen said.

Sooner said the research shows no increase in the risk of breast cancer in those who are, for whatever reason, not able to fellate regularly.

"There's definitely fertile ground for more research. Many have stepped forward to volunteer for related research now in the planning stages," he said.

Almost every woman is, at some point, going to perform the act of fellatio, but it is the frequency at which this event occurs that makes the difference, say researchers. Also key seems to be the protein and enzyme count in the semen, but researchers are again waiting for more test data.

The reasearch consisted of two groups, 6,246 women ages 25 to 45 who had performed fellatio and swallowed on a regular basis over the past five to ten years, and 9,728 women who had not or did not swallow. The group of women who had performed and swallowed had a breast cancer rate of 1.9 percent and the group who had not had a breast cancer rate of 10.4 percent.

"The findings do suggest that there are other causes for breast cancer besides the absence of regular fellatio," Shafteer said. "It's a cause, not THE cause."

Copyright 2003 The Associated Press. All rights reserved. This material may not be published, broadcast, rewritten, or redistributed.

Absurd as it is, this news story is particularly deft in its use of statistics, technical-sounding terms like "ejaculatory fluid," and the bogus AP copyright at the end to create an aura of trustworthiness.[30] The only errors are the repeated misspelling of "occurrence," a word that appears on everyone's list of frequently misspelled words, and of "research," and the inconsistent spelling of Shifteer/Shafteer. Bafflingly, a source identified only as Sooner is quoted. The mystery is resolved by consulting other versions of the story in which Dr. A. J. Kramer of Johns Hopkins is called Dr. B. J.—blowjob, presumably—Sooner.

Assuming we accept the just barely plausible premise that academic researchers had hypothesized a link between fellatio and breast-cancer reduction and were able to recruit subjects to test the hypothesis, the only elements of the story that would strain our credulity would be the female researcher who volunteers the rather titillating information about her own oral sex regimen, the vaguely salacious-sounding names, and the rather insistent promotion of frequent fellatio, which reveals the story to be a fairly transparent male fantasy.

Like the fake news story, the fake press release and fake memo employ the rhetorical conventions of their genres, though their tone and their liberal use of exclamation points and capital letters make many of them seem a good deal less formal or bureaucratic sounding than one would expect such documents to be. Consider these three warnings:

Identity Theft

Department of Public Safety and Corrections
Public Safety Services

July 26, 2007

To All Employees:

DO NOT write checks at any Wal-Mart. There is a multi-city fraud and theft ring currently operating in Wal-Mart involving numerous employees. When you pay by check the clerk takes a picture of your check using the camera on their cell phone. This information is then downloaded, fraudulent checks made from your account, and then "let the fun begin" for the thieves. One individual that this was done to had two checks totaling over $4000.00 posted against their checking account.

Some of you are thinking "well there is no way this will affect me because I don't keep that kind of money in my account." WRONG!!!! As stated, this involves numerous employees. The picture is taken and after the data is downloaded the checks are printed. Later, this fake check is given to same or another cashier. The cashier DOES NOT run the check through the check fax inquiry to verify the funds. The check is placed in the drawer for deposit and no one is the wiser until some days later when the check hits your account. One of the main things being purchased by the fraudulent checks are gift cards. How nice. With a gift card from Wal-Mart, any member of the theft ring can purchase items from any Wal-Mart or Sam's Club in the nation. No identification is required to purchase with a gift card, so Sally or Sam in Shreveport can be buying that fabulous plasma TV they have always wanted with the gift card bought by a fraudulent check drawn on YOUR account and no one is any the wise until you get your bank statement or you begin to get NSF notices in the mail.

This activity has become so widespread and so numerous have been the occurrences that not only is local law enforcement authorities involved in the case, i.e. City, Sheriff, and LSP, but the FBI and the Secret Service is now investigation as well.

So, you have been warned. Protect yourself and your money. It's 2007 and the criminals only seem to get smarter.

Spb/Rjp

Sergeant Rick Martinez
9105 Northwest 25th Street
Doral, FL 33172-1500 USA

There is much to admire about this item. The scam sounds devilishly clever and plays on media-hyped fears that no digital communication is safe from cyber-outlaws. Then there is all the verisimilitude offered by the monograms of the typist and writer and an address that includes a nine-digit zip code. The address, by the way, checks out as a Miami-Dade County law enforcement building; the warning, however, does not. In fact, according to Snopes, the warning came from the Louisiana Department of Safety and Corrections, which claimed that the message was not supposed to have been made public, but did not address the accuracy of the allegations—or why the department would be warning only its own employees.[31] Incidentally, the item is one of about twenty-five mostly fraudulent stories Snopes has chronicled about dangerous products, reprehensible policies, abductions, and other criminal acts at Wal-Mart stores. Yes, the stories seem to suggest, the prices are low, but you don't get something for nothing in this world, so here are the hidden risks and costs. At least this one spells "occurrences" correctly (though it is not exactly error free: "the Secret Service is now *investigation* as well").

The next example, inspired by post-9/11 fears of terrorism, includes the injunction to forward that is characteristic of other Internet chains:

Terrorists in Disguise

Subject: UPS Uniforms - Be Aware

UPS Uniforms

Government Warning regarding purchase of UPS uniforms:

There has been a huge purchase, $32,000 worth, of United Parcel Service (UPS) uniforms on eBay over the last 30 days. This could represent a serious threat as bogus drivers (terrorists) can drop off anything to anyone with deadly consequences! If you have ANY questions when a UPS driver appears at your door they should be able to furnish VALID I.D.

Additionally, if someone in a UPS uniform comes to make a drop off or pick up, make absolutely sure they are driving a UPS truck. UPS doesn't make deliveries or pickups in anything, except a company vehicle. If you have a problem, call your local law enforcement agency right away!

TAKE THIS SERIOUSLY! Tell everyone in your office, your family, your friends, etc. Make people aware so that we can prepare and/or avoid terrorist attacks on our people! Thank you for your time in reviewing this and PLEASE send to EVERYONE on your list, even if they are friend or foe. We should all be aware!

Kimberly Bush-Carr
Management Program Specialist
U.S. Department of Homeland Security
Bureau Customs and Border Protection
Washington, DC 20229

The key to this warning, I think, is the role of a rented truck in the bombing of the Alfred P. Murrah Federal Building in Oklahoma City in 1995. The ease with which Timothy McVeigh and Terry Nichols were able to fill a Ryder truck with fertilizer and explosives and crash it into a public building with horrific results made it easy to imagine similar deployments of any of the delivery trucks we routinely see on city streets.[32] The curious allure of the "men in brown" who drive the UPS trucks[33] would seem to make their uniforms perfect protective coloration for terrorists.

The last example plays on public fear and ignorance about AIDS.

Dangerous Gas Pumps

Please read and forward to anyone you know who drives.
My name is Captain Abraham Sands of the Jacksonville, Florida Police Department.
I have been asked by state and local authorities to write this email in order to get the word out to car drivers of a very dangerous prank that is occurring in numerous states.

Some person or persons have been affixing hypodermic needles to the underside of gas pump handles. These needles appear to be infected with HIV positive blood. In the Jacksonville area alone there have been 17 cases of people being stuck by these needles over the past five months.

We have verified reports of at least 12 others in various states around the country. It is believed that these may be copycat incidents due to someone reading about the crimes or seeing them reported on the television. At this point no one has been arrested and catching the perpetrator(s) has become our top priority.

Shockingly, of the 17 people who where stuck, eight have tested HIV positive and because of the nature of the disease, the others could test positive in a couple years.

Evidently the consumers go to fill their car with gas, and when picking up the pump handle get stuck with the infected needle. IT IS IMPERATIVE TO CAREFULLY CHECK THE HANDLE of the gas pump each time you use one. LOOK AT EVERY SURFACE YOUR HAND MAY TOUCH, INCLUDING UNDER THE HANDLE.

If you do find a needle affixed to one, immediately contact your local police department so they can collect the evidence.

******* PLEASE HELP US BY MAINTAINING A VIGILANCE AND BY FORWARD-ING THIS EMAIL TO ANYONE YOU KNOW WHO DRIVES. THE MORE PEOPLE WHO KNOW OF THIS THE BETTER PROTECTED WE CAN ALL BE. *******

A Freudian interpretation of this warning is irresistible: just think of the male gas pump nozzle's insertion into the female gas tank.[34] In variations, the needle is secreted in a movie theater seat or a public phone booth coin slot.[35] It all rests on the curious notion that people with AIDS avenge themselves against the world by deliberating infecting others.

Chains and Chain Parodies

Back when I was doing my dissertation research on the history and lore of gold mining, I read J. S. Holliday's magnum opus about the Gold Rush, *The World Rushed In*.[36] Holliday argues convincingly that the Gold Rush changed America's psyche by introducing the idea of not just making a living but making a killing—of striking it rich. Mining turned out to be—surprise—backbreaking work. Most forty-niners returned to the States no better off, and in many cases worse off, than when they left, though glad they had "seen the elephant." But the dream of getting rich (or fit or sexually adept) quick persists—as do all fantasies of accomplishment without effort, gain without pain. Now we are told of all the good we can do or the harm we can prevent or the boons we can obtain just by clicking a mouse.

Some folk beliefs tapped into by the culture of Internet forwarding:

- There are evildoers out there who intend to do us harm, and the people charged with keeping us safe from harm are either inattentive, incompetent, or intent on keeping us in the dark so as not to alarm us.
- Like prayer, good wishes are a form of action: they can heal the sick.
- People come into money not by working hard but by being in the right place at the right time when opportunity knocks.

Urbanlegends.com helpfully divides chains into freebie, charity, and fearmongering chains.[37] As with urban legends, the chains are rife with attestations of legitimacy and insistence on the importance of forwarding:

- This is for real. This was on the news.
- Please pass this on.
- Please do not take this as a junk letter.
- If you ignore this you will repent later.
- Please forward this to as many people as possible.
- I thought this was a scam myself, but . . .
- I do not usually forward messages, but . . .
- After all, what have you got to lose?
- I am asking you all, begging you to please, forward this email onto anyone and everyone you know, PLEASE.
- This isn't a chain letter, but a choice for all of us to save a little girl that's dying of a serious and fatal form of cancer.

The last example in the list is particularly interesting. The item in question clearly *is* a chain letter. The disclaimer suggests that "chain letter" has become synonymous with some sort of bogus appeal. The writer means that this is not a bogus chain letter but a legitimate one. Folklorists will recognize the attestations of legitimacy as the hallmarks of urban legends.

On the off chance that the money really will flow in or the child will be cured of cancer or suspicious packages will come in the mail, why not forward? Better be safe than sorry. What will it cost you? Yet forwarding is a public act. As with telling a joke, it's an implicit endorsement. Skeptical recipients of the appeal will impugn your judgment. "If it sounds too good to be true," we say, "it probably is." And so the chains have, inevitably, inspired parody (and YouTube rants). Here are several meta–chain letters that serve as concise guides to the world of chains and urban legends. You will note that there are several references to the warnings we have just seen or saw earlier in this book.

To all my friends, thanks to you sending me chain letters in 2003:

I stopped drinking Coca Cola after I found out that it's good for *removing toilet stains.*

I stopped going to the movies for fear of sitting on a *needle infected with AIDS.*

I smell like a wet dog since I stopped using deodorants because they *cause cancer* or Alzheimer.

I don't leave my car in the parking lot or any other place and sometimes I even have to walk about 7 blocks for fear that someone will *drug me with a perfume sample* and try to rob me.

I also stopped answering the phone for fear that they ask me to *dial a stupid number* and then I get a phone bill from hell with calls to Uganda, Singapore and Tokyo.

I stopped consuming several foods for fear that the estrogens they contain may turn me gay.

I also stopped eating chicken and hamburgers because they are nothing other than *horrible mutant freaks* with no eyes or feathers that are bred in a lab.

I also stopped drinking anything out of a can for fear that I will get sick from the *rat feces and urine.*

I think I'm turning gay because when I go to parties, I don't look at any girl no matter how hot she is, for fear that she will *take my kidneys* and leave me taking a nap in a bathtub full of ice.

I also donated all my savings to the *Amy Bruce* account, a sick girl that was about to die in the hospital about 7,000 times. Funny that girl, she's been 7 since 1993 . . .

I went bankrupt from bounced checks that I made expecting the $15,000 that *Microsoft and AOL* were supposed to send me when participated in their special e-mail program. My Erickson phone never arrived and neither did the passes for a paid vacation to Disney land.

But I am positive that all this is the cause of a stinking chain that I broke or forgot to follow and I got a curse from hell.

IMPORTANT NOTE: If you send this e-mail to at least 1200 people in the next 10 seconds, a bird will crap on you today at 7pm.

Here is another version, included because of the scourges it adds to the previous list.

I want to thank all of you who have taken the time and trouble to send me your damn chain letters over the past few years. Yes, thank you, thank you, thank you from the bottom of what's left of my heart for making me feel safe, secure, blessed, and wealthy.

Because of your concern . . . I no longer can drink Coca Cola because it can remove toilet stains.

I no longer drink anything out of a can because I will get sick from the rat feces and urine.

I no longer use Saran wrap in the microwave because it causes cancer.

I no longer check the coin return on pay phones because I could be pricked with a needle infected with AIDS.

I no longer use cancer-causing deodorants even though I smell like a water buffalo on a hot day

I no longer use margarine because it's one molecule away from being plastic.

I no longer go to shopping malls because someone will drug me with a perfume sample and rob me.

I no longer receive packages from UPS or FedEx since they are actually Al Qaeda in disguise.

I no longer answer the phone because someone will ask me to dial a stupid number for which I will get the phone bill from hell with calls to Jamaica, Uganda, Singapore, and Zebekistan.

I no longer eat KFC because their chickens are actually horrible mutant freaks with no eyes or feathers.

I no longer date the opposite sex because they will take my kidneys and leave me taking a nap in a bathtub full of ice.

I no longer buy expensive cookies from Neiman Marcus since I now have their recipe.

I no longer worry about my soul because I have 363,214 angels looking out for me and St. Theresa's novena has granted my every wish.

Thanks to you, I have learned that God only answers my prayers if I forward an email to seven of my friends and make a wish within five minutes. (Geez, the BIBLE did not mention it works that way!)

I no longer have any savings because I gave it to a sick girl who is about to die in the hospital (for the 1,387,258th time).

I no longer have any money at all, but that will change once I receive the $15,000 that Microsoft and AOL are sending me for participating in their special e-mail program.

Yes, I want to thank all of you soooooooooo much for looking out for me!

I will now return the favor.

If you don't send this e-mail to at least 1200 people in the next 60 seconds, a large bird with diarrhea will crap on your head at 5:00 PM this afternoon and the fleas of a thousand camels will infest your armpits.

I know this will occur because it actually happened to a friend of a friend of a friend of a friend of a friend of a friend of a friend of my next door neighbor's ex-mother-in-law's 8th husband's 2nd cousin's 3rd husband's ex-wife's mother's beautician! Ain't spam great?!?!?

The final compendium is written as a first-person urban legend rather than as a thank-you note.

I know this guy whose neighbor, a young man, was home recovering from having been served a rat in his bucket of Kentucky Fried Chicken.

So anyway, one day he went to sleep and when he awoke he was in his bathtub and it was full of ice and he was sore all over. When he got out of the tub he realized that HIS KIDNEYS HAD BEEN STOLEN and he saw a note on his mirror that said, "Call 911!" But he was afraid to use his phone because it was connected to his computer, and there was a virus on his computer that would destroy his hard drive if he opened an e-mail entitled, "Join the crew!"

He knew it wasn't a hoax because he himself was a computer programmer who was working on software to save us from Armageddon when the year 2000 rolls around. And it's a little-known fact that the Y1K problem caused the Dark Ages.

His program will prevent a global disaster in which all the computers get together and distribute the $600 Neiman-Marcus cookie recipe under the leadership of Bill Gates. (It's true, I read it all last week in a mass e-mail from BILL GATES HIMSELF, who was also promising me a free Disney World vacation and $5,000 if I would forward the e-mail to everyone I know.)

The poor man then tried to call 911 from a pay phone to report his missing kidneys, but reaching into the coin-return slot he got jabbed with an HIV-infected needle around which was wrapped a note that said, "Welcome to the world of AIDS."

Luckily he was only a few blocks from the hospital-the one where that little boy who is dying of cancer is, the one whose last wish is for everyone in the world to send him an e-mail and the American Cancer Society has agreed to pay him a nickel for every e-mail he receives.

I sent him two e-mails and one of them was a bunch of x's and o's in the shape of an angel (if you get it and forward it to 20 people you will have good luck but 10 people you will only have OK luck and if you send it to less than 10 people you will have BAD LUCK FOR SEVEN YEARS).

So anyway the poor guy tried to drive himself to the hospital, but on the way he noticed another car driving along without its lights on. To be helpful, he flashed his lights at him and was promptly shot as part of a gang initiation.
STOP THE INSANITY! NO URBAN LEGEND EMAIL STRINGS IN 1999!

Needless, to say, the e-mail strings continue unabated—as do the fears of AIDS, cancer, homosexuality, food contamination, scams, computer viruses, terrorists, and gangs that inspire them.

NOTES

PREFACE

1. Rheingold (2000, 350) cites J. McClellan's term "mouse potatoes" for "people who hide from real life and spend their whole life goofing off in cyberspace." I steel myself for charges that I share Oring's "apparent allergy to fieldwork" (Fine 2004, 225) and thus am offering little more than "denatured collactanea" (Ellis 1991, 123).

INTRODUCTION

1. Apte (1985, 16–17) is among the many scholars who stress the culture-boundedness of humor. "Familiarity with a cultural code," he writes, "is a requisite for the spontaneous mental restructuring of elements that results in amusement or laughter."

2. The Arthur Andersen version may be found at http://politicalhumor.about.com/library/jokes/bljokehistory101.htm, among other places.

3. I confess to having given short shrift to video and audio newslore in this book because they have come later than texts and still images and were not part of what I will argue was a golden age of newslore that lasted from the 1990s to the early 2000s.

4. Oddly, my own experience as a newspaperman and a folklorist recapitulated this orientation toward male-dominated occupational groups. As a reporter, I covered my fair share of local government meetings and court trials, but the Sierra Nevada mountains and foothills are prone to winter floods and summer fires, and they attract skiers and hikers who get lost in the woods, so I also spent a lot of time tagging along with firefighters, loggers, and search-and-rescue teams. During this same period, I was occasionally hired as a freelance folklorist to conduct fieldwork with fishermen, longshoremen, ranchers, coal miners, and steelworkers. Little wonder, then, that the profession as a whole, and I, as one of its foot soldiers, have a sort of macho view of fieldwork: real folklorists (and reporters) get dirty, get seasick, crawl on their hands and knees, and wear hardhats and goggles. I handled plenty of dirty material in the writing of this book, but none of it was the kind that washes off.

5. Mullen 1978.

6. McCarl 1984.

7. Santino 1989.

8. Nader 1974.

9. Green 1978.

10. Reuss 1974.

11. Dundes 1980, 7.

12. Dundes and Pagter 1975/1992, xxii.

13. Ibid., xxiii.

14. Dundes and Pagter 1987, 11.

15. Dundes and Pagter 1991b, 17.

16. Dundes and Pagter 1996, xiv.

17. Dundes and Pagter 2000, xvii.

18. See Dorst 1990, 185.

19. For a detailed discussion of how I obtained the material in this book, see appendix B.

20. Baym 1993, 1.

21. Pew Internet and American Life Project 2008.

22. Some support appears in the scholarly literature for drawing on one's own experience as a cyberspace traveler: "An ethnographer of the Internet cannot hope to understand the practices of *all* users, but through their own practices can develop an understanding of what it is to be *a* user" (Hine 2000, 52).

23. Dundes 1987, vii.

24. Oring 1992, 17.

25. Douglas 1991, 297.

26. Quoted in Powell and Paton 1988, 40.

27. Fine (2005, 5) calls it an expression of "apathy and powerlessness." Rheingold (2000, 351) writes of critics who believe that "online discussion disempowers citizens who would otherwise be engaged in authentic civic involvement."

28. The quote is originally from James Russell Lowell, according to the World of Quotes Web site, http://www.worldofquotes.com/topic/Sarcasm/index.html.

29. http://www.snopes.com/info/glossary.asp.

30. Benton 1988, 540.

31. Jones 1997, n.p. See also Hathaway (2005, 52), who describes netlore as "light-hearted resistance to media domination, a way of seizing the master's tools to construct one's own response." Then there's Freud (1928/1987, 113): "Humor is not resigned; it is rebellious. It signifies the triumph not only of the ego, but of the pleasure principle."

32. Jones cites a *Times-Mirror* survey that found that "computer users tend to read more newspapers, books and magazines than others" (1997).

33. Gamson 1994, 10. Gamson also cites Neil Postman's (1985, 160–61) call for a "demystification of media" whereby citizens become aware of how they are being manipulated.

34. Dundes and Pagter 1975/1992.

35. Brunvand 2001, 64.

36. This isn't true only of netlore. In general, David Weinberger (2002, 10) observed, "for all the overheated, exaggerated, manic-depressive coverage of the Web, we'd have to conclude that the Web has not yet been hyped enough."

37. Dorst 1990. The term comes from Redfield 1947.

38. Dorst 1990, 180.

39. Ibid., 183.

40. Ellis 2002, 1.

41. Ibid.

42. Baym 1993.

43. Fernback 2003.

44. Mason 1996. The term is also the title of a book by Christine Hine (2000).

45. Hine (2000, 15) notes that e-mail has "stripped out social context cues (features such as gender, age, race, social status, facial expression and intonation) routinely used in understanding face-to-face communication."

46. "Media technology," write Drucker and Cathcart (1994, 264), "has emancipated social interaction from place and redistributed it through space."

47. Joke scholars still know little about joke authorship. Christie Davies (1999, 254) proposes that jokes begin as spontaneous witticisms, then get "polished" in subsequent tellings, but he doesn't actually observe the process.

48. Weinberger 2002, 139.

49. Dundes 1987, 38. See chapter 1 for a longer defense of looking at offensive jokes.

50. Jokes and other "popular arts," writes Lawrence E. Mintz (1983, 130), "are collectively, at the very least, as important as any other social institution (e.g., church, school, family) in determining and revealing who and what we are."

51. Horrigan and Rainie 2002, 3, 16, 20.

52. Joel Best (2005, 181) writes that topical jokes "achieve very broad circulation remarkably quickly, and with minimal support from the mass media."

53. Lowney and Best (1996, 78) make the same point in their study of Waco jokes: "Ordinary people's constructions of particular issues . . . largely go unexamined; we hear the voices of the committed few, but too often ignore the reactions of the many who are less directly involved."

54. See Schudson 1978; Gans 1980.

55. University of Missouri School of Journalism 1998, 4.

56. Sims 1984, 3.

57. See, for example, Knowlton 1997.

58. Boorstin 1962.

59. Langellier 1989, 243.

60. The latest iteration of the code was adopted in 1995. http://www.spj.org/ethicscode .asp.

61. See Bird and Dardenne 1990.

62. Sims 1984, 3.

63. Myerhoff and Ruby 1982, 13.

64. See Frank 2003b.

65. See Brunvand 1981, 62–65.

66. For details, see Snopes, http://www.snopes.com/horrors/food/chili.asp.

67. DeFao 1995.

68. Rivers 2000.

69. Bridges 2001.

70. Boule 2004.

71. Benedetti 2001.

72. Ibid.

73. Beatty 2002.

74. Benedetti 2001.

75. "Never distort the content of news photos or video," says the code. "Image enhancement for technical clarity is always permissible. Label montages and photo illustrations. http://www.spj.org/ethicscode.asp.

76. Irby 2003.

77. *Los Angeles Times* 2003.

78. Quoted in Knowlton 1997, 189.

79. Frank 2003c.

80. McClain 2002. Another version of the accompanying text differs in only two respects. The "photo of the year" nomination is attributed to *Geo* magazine, and there is a teaser headline: "And you think you're having a bad day at work!!" The headline echoes the captions that accompany the cartoons exchanged by beleaguered office workers: instead of faxing the joke to a friend and then tacking it to the wall of one's cubicle, as soldiers of the paperwork empire might have done in the 1970s and 1980s, the computer jockeys of today commiserate with each other by sharing the photo via e-mail. Selachophobia, or fear of sharks, would seem to make shark attacks an inevitable theme for urban legends. Every summer, millions of people head for the shore, and every summer brings a smattering of encounters with these creatures, whose nightmarish teeth and hydrodynamics make them the closest things to living monsters on earth. The news media, driven, as ever, by the conflicting imperatives of sensationalism and responsibility, provide overblown coverage of the attacks, even as they drum up experts to reassure their audience that the threat of shark attacks is statistically insignificant.

Surprisingly, then, Brunvand finds few examples of shark attack stories to include in his collections of urban legends. One is an "animal's revenge" story about a fisherman who feeds an explosive to a shark that then swims under the boat and blows it up (Brunvand 1986, 39). The other, a variation on the "small pet devoured by a larger animal" theme, tells of a dog that jumps into the Marineland shark tank at feeding time, with disastrous results (130). It may be that the quantity of news accounts of shark attacks obviates the need to invent them.

81. Barringer 2001.

82. Ibid.

83. Degh and Vazsonyi 1976.

84. Gibson 2001.

85. Irby 2001.

86. John Stevens (1985) notes that people who complain about sensationalism in the news have always buttressed their arguments by fretting about the tender sensibilities of younger readers.

87. Soloski 1999, 151.

88. Siegal and Connolly 1999.

89. Ibid.

90. Holley 1981, 157.

91. Lippman 1989, 7.

92. Ibid., 6.

93. See Snopes, http://www.snopes.com/quotes/starr.asp.

94. Maykuth 2006.

95. Heffernan 2006.

96. Oldenburg 2006.

97. Horowitz 2008.

98. Pitts 2001.

99. Benjamin 1935/1969.

100. Quoted in University of Missouri School of Journalism 1998.

101. Douglas 1991, 292. As Arthur Asa Berger (1976, 115) writes, "Dissecting a joke is a very complicated operation, one in which the patient almost always 'dies.'" Or the eighteenth-century writer Francis Hutcheson (1750/1987, 35): "To treat this subject of laughter gravely may subject the author to a censure like to that which Longinus makes upon a prior treatise of the Sublime, because wrote in a manner very unsuitable to the subject."

1. WHERE IS THE HUMOR?

1. "Some insults aimed at women (*dyke, bulldyke, butch, lesbian*) may be based on the notion that women are supposed to be passive and feminine. These terms may be used when the woman in question acted assertively, aggressively or with 'masculine behavior'" (Jay 1992, 80).

2. See Davies 1996, 301: "This image of the unfit woman may have emerged in response to her early, visible involvement in health care reform, which is a departure from the traditional, more passive role of first lady."

3. Alan Dundes (1989, 49) argues that "the rash of Gary Hart jokes helped seal this particular politician's fate."

4. Dundes 1987, 29, 38. I might also have invoked Goodwin (1995, 161), who wrote: "Such material must be documented and analyzed to be understood; it must be understood to be challenged and to promote social change. . . . Ignoring—or denouncing—a subject will not make it go away."

5. Frank 2006b.

6. Frank 2007.

7. See Thomas 1997, 302. This joke recalls a *Spy* magazine cover photoshop of Hillary with her dress billowing à la Marilyn Monroe, revealing a masculine bulge in Hillary's drawers.

8. Fish 2008.

9. Horowitz 2008.

2. I COULD THROW ALL OF YOU OUT THE WINDOW

1. Oring 2003, 129.

2. For a detailed discussion of lightbulb jokes, see Dundes 1987.

3. Meyrowitz 1994, 73.

4. For a good discussion of this story, see Rosenberg 2000.

5. It may be found at http://www.snopes.com/photos/politics/kerry2.asp.

6. Light 2004. One of the better journalistic discussions of the Kerry-Fonda photo and of photoshopping generally may be found at Hafner 2004. "Playing with and circulating digital images," Hafner writes, "has become something of a national pastime, the visual equivalent of e-mailed jokes."

3. WHEN THE GOING GETS TOUGH

1. For the full text of Sinclair's column, see http://www.snopes.com/politics/quotes/sinclair.asp.

2. Pitts 2001. The column earned Pitts the Pulitzer Prize for commentary the following year.

3. Kurtzman 2001.

4. Malinowski 1948/1954.

5. The jokes began flowing into the in-box of the *Washington Post* columnist Gene Weingarten (2001) a little sooner: "The time, for all those keeping score, was 5 days 2 hours 8 minutes and 1 second. That was the hiatus between the arrival of the first plane at the North Tower of the World Trade Center, and the arrival of the first known attempt at Internet humor on the subject." The jokes were anagrams of the name Osama bin Laden: "Is a banal demon." "I am a bland nose." "No! A mad lesbian." "Animals on a bed." Weingarten was unimpressed. Christie Davies (1999, 253) reports receiving his first two Princess Diana jokes within forty-eight hours of her death.

6. Kuipers (2005, 78) and Ellis (2002, 4) include this image in their studies of the humor of 9/11.

7. Goodwin 2001; Ellis 2001.

8. Ellis 2001.

9. Much of the newslore of September 11 echoed the folkloric responses to the Iranian hostage crisis in 1979 and the Gulf War in 1991. See Dundes and Pagter 1991a.

10. Ibid., 303.

11. See Snopes for further discussion of the Klingerman virus: http://www.snopes.com/medical/disease/klingerman.asp.

12. Harmon 2001.

13. For a discussion of the Halloween warning, see http://americanhistory.about.com/cs/blmall-terror.htm.

14. Anderson and Mihalopoulos 2001.

15. Bronner 1995, 173–76.

16. See http://www.snopes.com/racial/business/hilfiger.asp and http://www.snopes .com/racial/business/claiborne.asp.

17. See Fine 1992.

18. Klebnikov 2003.

19. http://www.coca-colabottling.co.id/eng/ourcompany/index.php?act=faq.

20. Roeper 2001.

21. Ibid.

22. See Gibes 2001.

23. Hathaway (2005, 42) aptly compares Tourist Guy's wanderings to the phenomenon of the traveling garden gnome.

24. Connor 2002.

25. *Wall Street Journal* 2001.

26. Tomsho, Carton, and Guidera 2001. Similar headlines appeared in San Francisco Bay Area newspapers in the immediate aftermath of the 1989 Loma Prieta earthquake.

27. "In many ways, we are all 'Tourist Guy' to the events of 9/11," writes Hathaway (2005, 43).

28. Lule 2001, 282.

29. For further discussions of Tourist Guy, see http://www.touristofdeath.com; http://urbanlegends.about.com/od/mishapsdisasters/ig/Tourist-Guy/touristguy.htm; http://www.snopes.com/rumors/photos/tourist.asp.

30. Dundes and Pagter 1991a, 303.

31. See Jay 1992, 2.

32. Oring 1987.

33. Dorst 1990.

34. Ellis 2002, 2.

35. Ibid., 5.

36. Kuipers (2005, 78) mentions these "degrading pictures" in her study.

37. Dundes and Pagter 1991a.

38. Dundes 1997, 27.

39. Ellis 2002, 8.

40. Ibid., 5.

41. Oring 1987.

42. Ellis 2002.

43. Ibid., 4.

44. Perkins 2001.

45. Bearak 2001.

46. Morse 2001.

47. Hinckley 2001. Kuipers (2005) and Ellis (2002) cite the lake maps.

48. Dundes and Pagter 1991a, 316.

49. Ellis 2002, 8.

50. Quoted in deSousa 1987, 234.

51. Tierney 2008.

52. Kuipers 2005, 81.

53. Peterson 2001.

54. Caldwell 2001.

55. Harden 2001.

56. Tierney 2001.

57. *New York Times* 2001.

58. Oring 1987; Smyth 1986.

59. See, for example, Gans 1980; Fishman 1980; Schudson 1989; Bird and Dardenne 1997.

60. Goodwin 2001.

61. Oring 1987; see also Smyth 1986.

62. Kornblum 2001.

63. Smith 2001.

64. Davies 1999, 254.

65. Rainie et al. 2002, 4.

66. Ibid., 31.

67. Ibid., 48.

68. Found at http://politicalhumor.about.com/library/images/blbushtwofaces.htm (and credited to politicalstrikes.com).

4. GOT FISH?

1. *New York Times* 2005.

2. Nichols 2005.

3. http://politicalhumor.about.com/library/images/blbusheatcake.htm.

4. http://politicalhumor.about.com/library/images/blbushenduringvacation.htm.

5. Christensen 2005.

6. http://www.snopes.com/katrina/photos/recreate.asp.

7. Silva and Tackett 2005.

8. According to the rec.humor.funny Web site, Julian Bond originally made a similar joke about Vice President Quayle during a speech at the University of Colorado in 1989. The site says Bond was quoted in the *Boulder Daily Camera* as having said, "He thinks Roe v. Wade are options for crossing the Potomac."

9. Weeks 2006.

10. http://www.snopes.com/katrina/humor/churches.asp.

11. Carr 2005.

12. Dao, Treaster, and Barringer 2005.

13. Duncan 2005.

14. Dwyer and Drew 2005.

15. Haygood and Tyson 2005.

16. Dwyer and Drew 2005.

17. Carr 2005.

18. Dwyer and Drew 2005.

19. Britt 2005.

20. Carr 2005.

21. Thevenot and Russell 2005.

22. See Frank 2003a.

23. Carr 2005.

24. Britt 2005.

25. The photos may seen at Snopes, among other places: http://www.snopes.com/katrina/photos/looters.asp.

26. Azine (Asian American Movement Ezine), http://www.aamovement.net/news/2005/katrinacoverage.html.

27. I owe my knowledge of this phenomenon to Diane Goldstein, who presented a paper about it at the conference of the International Society for Contemporary Legend Research in July 2008 in Dublin.

28. http://politicalhumor.about.com/od/currentevents/a/katrinaquotes.htm.

29. http://www.snopes.com/photos/tsunami/tsunami2.asp.

30. Baer 1982.

5. IT TAKES A VILLAGE IDIOT

1. Dundes 1987, vii.

2. Ibid.

3. http://www.idealog.us/2004/03/correction_on_p.html.

4. http://www.anvari.org/fun/Political/Bush_Reading_Upside_Down.html.

5. http://www.snopes.com/photos/politics/binoculars.asp.

6. See http://www.snopes.com/quotes/bush.asp and http://www.snopes.com/inboxer/outrage/bushwave.asp.

7. This version is attributed to one Michael Dare by Philip Greenspun at http://philip.greenspun.com/humor/bush-nigerian-spam.html.

8. http://academic.evergreen.edu/g/grossmaz/nyt.html.

9. This letter is attributed to Barrett Brown by the Daily Kos, http://www.dailykos.com/story/2004/9/22/13121/2893.

10. Boule 2004.

11. Vlach (1971) coined the term "anti-legend" to refer to jokes that masquerade as legends.

12. Center for Media and Public Affairs 2006.

13. Lévi-Strauss 1966, 19.

14. See Brunvand 1984, 18–28.

6. YOU CAN'T RAFFLE OFF A DEAD DONKEY

1. Fine 1992.
2. Turner 1993.
3. http://www.snopes.com/photos/signs/bombus.asp.
4. Goodman 2004.
5. Cooper 2004.
6. http://www.snopes.com/photos/military/crossed.asp.
7. Ivanovich 2006.
8. See Dundes and Pagter 1975/1992, 40–41. An updated version: "I'm not pregnant, I'm not engaged, I don't have syphilis and there is no boyfriend of another race or religion in my life; however, I DID vote for Gov. Bush, and I just wanted you both to see this in its proper perspective. Your loving daughter, Chelsea."
9. Ibid., 37–38.
10. Ibid., 15–16.
11. http://www.opensecrets.org/alerts/v6/alertv6_31.asp.

7. NOT-SO-HEAVENLY GATES

1. http://members.ozemail.com.au/~lbrash/msjokes/msjokes.html.
2. Brunvand 1989, 29–36.
3. Gates 1998.
4. Allbritton 1999.
5. Hinkle 1999.
6. Logan 1999.
7. The classic technology-as-menace tale is the story of the panicked pet owner who puts her wet and shivering poodle in the microwave oven. See Brunvand 1989.
8. Ramsey 2000.
9. Miner 1956.

8. DIANA'S HALO

1. See Lule 2001.
2. In an age of hype and sensationalism, Kovach and Rosenstiel (2001) argue persuasively for a journalism that is proportional to the impact of events.
3. Oring 1987; Smyth 1986.
4. Scornful and skeptical as we may be of the outpourings of grief at the death of Michael Jackson or Princess Diana, Joshua Meyrowitz reminds us that among the mourners, the sense of connection is real, and the emotions are genuine. Such relationships,

he writes, "compensate for the impermanence of many real-life relationships." Moreover, unlike real-life relationships, they demand nothing of us (Meyrowitz 1994, 66).

5. http://www.answerbag.com/q_view/138725.

6. The death of Ted Kennedy in August 2009 occasioned a number of jokes that alluded either to Chappaquiddick, to the senator's supposed drinking problem, or to both:

Q: How did people find out Ted was dead?
A: He didn't show up at the bar this morning.

Saint Peter: I don't care how drunk you were, Ted, it's still murder.

Much like his brother, Ted Kennedy will also have an eternal flame in Arlington Cemetery, but for his they are just going to strike a match to his liver.

7. http://www.answerbag.com/q_view/138725.

8. http://www.theanswerbank.co.uk/News/Question287167.html.

9. LondonNet n.d.

10. Indian Express 1998.

11. http://www.mindspring.com/~squicker/di.html. Davies (1999, 258–59) calls the Diana jokes a rebellion against "the torrent of sentimentality that poured out of the media's treacle well."

12. See Kibby 2005, 775–77.

13. http://www.museumofhoaxes.com/hoax/Hoaxipedia/Celebrity_Death_Hoaxes.

14. http://www.museumofhoaxes.com/hoax/weblog/comments/2489.

15. http://www.museumofhoaxes.com/hoax/weblog/comments/4180.

CONCLUSION

1. Fish 2008.

2. Fine 2005.

3. http://www.ehow.com/how_2224292_tell-barack-obama-jokes.html.

4. http://barackobamajokes.googlepages.com.

5. http://www.freerepublic.com/focus/f-chat/1983609/posts.

6. Mitchell (1992, 209) refers to this process as "recapitation."

7. http://www.youtube.com/watch?v=7kCAFkfFLQQ.

8. Horrigan and Rainie 2002, 2.

9. Ibid., 7.

10. Heffernan 2008.

11. Gibson 2005.

12. Pew 2009.

APPENDIX B

1. Shipley and Schwalbe 2007.

2. Barry 2007.

3. Hine notes that the lack of "social context cues" in computer-mediated communication has a "disinhibiting effect" (2000, 15). See also Kibby 2005, 3. Joel Best (2005, 181) suggests that the "lack of performance dimension allows not very good jokes to survive longer."

4. Templeton n.d.

5. Henry Glassie has made this argument more passionately and consistently than most. See, for example, his *Passing the Time in Ballymenone* (1982).

6. Kibby 2005.

7. Oring 2003, 139.

8. http://politicalhumor.about.com.

9. http://www.jokesgallery.com/joke.php?joke=676&id=1.

10. Roeper 1997.

11. Rheingold (2000, xvi) refers to computer-mediated communication as taking place around an "electronic water cooler."

12. Roeper 1997.

13. The CMPA lists may be found at http://www.cmpa.com/media_monitor.html. Its more recent surveys of the late-night comedians include Jay Leno, David Letterman, Conan O'Brien, Jon Stewart, and Stephen Colbert.

14. See Lowney and Best 1996.

15. Brunvand 1981, 53–62.

16. Remarkably, Horace anticipated these kinds of shenanigans by about two thousand years: "If a painter chose to join a human head to a horse's neck, and to spread feathers of many colors over limbs brought together from everywhere, so that what was at the top a beautiful woman ended below as an ugly black fish, would you, my friend, allowed to see such a picture, be able to hold back your laughter?" (Quoted in Hutcheson 1750/1987, 31).

17. Wojcik 1996.

18. Welsch 1974.

19. See Mitchell 1992, 7.

20. Brunvand 2001, 65.

21. Ellis 2002, 13.

22. Ibid., 1.

23. See Choe 2001; Park 2002.

24. http://www.worth1000.com/tutorials.asp.

25. http://www.worth1000.com/faq.asp#C4.

26. Mitchell (1992, 49) notes this phenomenon. The fifty or so images in Snopes.com's "fauxtography" photo gallery include real photos that have "been given false backstories." Similarly, about a third of the twenty "faux photos" on the urbanlegend.miningco.com site are actually "misrepresented" rather than "doctored" photos. In recognition of the mixing

of fake documents and real documents, Snopes does not just debunk false stories but uses a color-coding system to indicate which are false (red), which are true (green), which can neither be verified nor be disproved (white), which are disputed (yellow), and which are part true and part false (multicolored).

I've encountered several items on About.com that prompted me to do a little sleuthing to find out if they were true. One was a photo of President Bush with a bruise on his cheek: real or photoshopped? Real: The bruise was a result of Bush's fall when he fainted while eating a pretzel in January 2002. Another was the graphic "Bush: One of the Worst Disasters to Hit U.S. History" that supposedly appeared on television. Well, it did—not, as it seemed, as a piece of editorializing but as a paraphrase of what the president said about Hurricane Katrina. The graphic was a Sky News (Ireland) Flash.

Others photos that I thought might be fake that turned out to be real caught Bush picking his nose at a Texas Rangers game while he owned the team and flipping the bird while he was governor of Texas. Then there was Bert the Muppet of *Sesame Street* fame appearing on posters carried by supporters of Osama bin Laden in Pakistan in October 2001—surely a photoshopper's handiwork. As Snopes.com reports, with corroboration from stories from the Associated Press, Reuters, and elsewhere, a Pakistani poster manufacturer created a collage from images downloaded from the Internet, one of which, unbeknownst to the collagist, was a photoshop of bin Laden and Bert.

Finally there was the story that cracks in the space shuttle *Columbia*'s wings were visible before it exploded. The photo is a still made from footage supposedly shot by Israeli astronaut Ilan Ramon during a live interview on Israeli television. All true, except the cracks in the wing are actually seams in the shuttle's cargo bay. The image expresses the same doubts about the competence of NASA engineers that were voiced in jokes about the *Challenger* disaster in 1986.

27. Georges 1976, 9.

28. McPhee is quoted in Sims 1984, 15.

29. Rosenberger 1995/1997.

30. See Kibby 2005, 785.

31. http://www.snopes.com/crime/warnings/checktheft.asp.

32. See Snopes, http://www.snopes.com/rumors/upsuniforms.asp.

33. See, for example, Robert Frank 2002.

34. See David Emery's About.com discussion, http://urbanlegends.about.com/od/crime/a/abraham-sands.htm.

35. See Brunvand 2000, 207–8.

36. Holliday 1981.

37. http://urbanlegends.about.com/od/internet/f/chain_letter.htm.

REFERENCES

SCHOLARLY WORKS

Altheide, David. 1996. *Qualitative Media Analysis*. Thousand Oaks, Calif.: Sage.

Apte, Mahadev L. 1985. *Humor and Laughter: An Anthropological Approach*. Ithaca, N.Y.: Cornell University Press.

Baer, Florence E. 1982. "Give Me . . . Your Huddled Masses: Anti-Vietnamese Refugee Lore and the Image of the Limited Good." *Western Folklore* 41:275–91.

Barkin, Steve M. 1984. "The Journalist as Storyteller: An Interdisciplinary Perspective." *American Journalism* 1:27–33.

Baym, Nancy K. 1993. "Interpreting Soap Operas and Creating Communities inside a Computer-Mediated Fan Culture." *Journal of Folklore Research* 30:143–76.

Bell, Allan. 1991. *The Language of News Media*. Oxford: Basil Blackwell.

Ben-Amos, Dan. 1972. "Toward a Definition of Folklore in Context." In *Toward New Perspectives in Folklore*, ed. Richard Bauman and Americo Paredes, 3–15. Austin: University of Texas Press.

Benjamin, Walter. 1935/1969. "The Work of Art in the Age of Mechanical Reproduction." In *Illuminations: Essays and Reflections*. New York: Schocken.

Benton, Gregor. 1988. "The Origins of the Political Joke. In *Humour in Society*, ed. Chris Powell and George E. C. Paton, 33–55. London: Macmillan.

Berger, Arthur Asa. 1976. "Anatomy of the Joke." *Journal of Communication* 26:113–15.

Best, Joel. 2005. "Fashion, Topical Jokes, and Rumor as Short-Term Enthusiasms." In *Rumor Mills*, ed. Gary Alan Fine, Veronique Campion-Vincent, and Chip Heath, 173–87. New Brunswick, N.J.: Transaction.

Bird, S. Elizabeth. 1987. "Folklore and Media as Intertextual Communication Processes: John F. Kennedy and the Supermarket Tabloids." In *Communication Yearbook*, ed. M. L. McLaughlin, vol. 10, 758–72. Newbury Park, Calif.: Sage.

Bird, S. Elizabeth, and Robert W. Dardenne. 1990. "News and Storytelling in American Culture: Reevaluating the Sensational Dimension." *Journal of American Culture* 13:33–37.

———. 1997. "Myth, Chronicle, and Story: Exploring the Narrative Qualities of News." In *Social Meanings of News*, ed. Dan Berkowitz, 333–50. Thousand Oaks, Calif.: Sage.

Boorstin, Daniel. 1962. *The Image: A Guide to Pseudo-events in America*. New York: Atheneum.

Bronner, Simon. 1995. *Piled Higher and Deeper: The Folklore of Student Life*. Little Rock: August House.

Brunvand, Jan Harold. 1981. *The Vanishing Hitchhiker*. New York: Norton.

———. 1984. *The Choking Doberman*. New York: Norton.

———. 1986. *The Mexican Pet*. New York: Norton.

———. 1989. *Curses! Broiled Again!* New York: Norton.

———. 2000. *The Truth Never Stands in the Way of a Good Story*. Urbana: University of Illinois Press.

———. 2001. "Folklore in the News (and on the Net)." *Western Folklore* 60:47–66.

Center for Media and Public Affairs. 2006. "The President as Punchline: Political Humor on Late-Night TV during the Bush Years." *Media Monitor* 20. http://www.cmpa.com/files/media_monitor/06janfeb.pdf.

Davies, Christie. 1996. *Ethnic Humor around the World*. Bloomington: Indiana University Press.

———. 1999. "Jokes on the Death of Diana." In *The Mourning for Diana*, ed. Tony Walker, 253–68. New York: Berg.

Degh, Linda. 1994. *American Folklore and the Mass Media*. Bloomington: Indiana University Press.

Degh, Linda, and Andre Vazsonyi. 1976. "Legend and Belief." In *Folklore Genres*, ed. Dan Ben-Amos, 95–123. Austin: University of Texas Press.

deSousa, Ronald. 1987. "When Is It Wrong to Laugh? In *The Philosophy of Laughter and Humor*, ed. John Morreall, 226–49. Albany: State University of New York Press.

Dorst, John. 1990. "Tags and Burners, Cycles and Networks: Folklore in the Telectronic Age." *Journal of Folklore Research* 27:179–90.

Douglas, Mary. 1991. "Jokes." In *Rethinking Popular Culture*, ed. Chandra Nukerji and Michael Schudson, 291–310. Berkeley: University of California Press.

Drucker, Susan J., and Robert S. Cathcart. 1994. "The Celebrity and the Fan: A Media Relationship." In *American Heroes in a Media Age*, ed. Susan J. Drucker and Robert S. Cathcart, 260–69. Creskill, N.J.: Hampton Press.

Dundes, Alan. 1968. "Folk Ideas as Units of World View." *Journal of American Folklore* 81:143–58.

———. 1980. *Interpreting Folklore*. Bloomington: Indiana University Press.

———. 1987. *Cracking Jokes*. Berkeley: Ten Speed Press.

———. 1989. "Six Inches from the Presidency: The Gary Hart Jokes as Public Opinion." *Western Folklore* 48:43–51.

———. 1997. *From Game to War and Other Psychoanalytic Essays on Folklore*. Lexington: University Press of Kentucky.

Dundes, Alan, and Carl Pagter. 1975/1992. *Work Hard and You Shall Be Rewarded*. Detroit: Wayne State University Press.

———. 1987. *When You're Up to Your Ass in Alligators*. Detroit: Wayne State University Press.

———. 1991a. "The Mobile Scud Missile Launcher and Other Persian Gulf Warlore: An American Folk Image of Saddam Hussein's Iraq." *Western Folklore* 50:303–22.

———. 1991b. *Never Try to Teach a Pig to Sing*. Detroit: Wayne State University Press.

———. 1996. *Sometimes the Dragon Wins*. Syracuse, N.Y.: Syracuse University Press.

———. 2000. *Why Don't Sheep Shrink When It Rains?* Syracuse, N.Y.: Syracuse University Press.

Ellis, Bill. 1991. "The Last Thing. . . . Said: The *Challenger* Disaster Jokes and Closure." *International Folklore Review* 8:110–24.

———. 2001. "A Model for Collecting and Interpreting World Trade Center Disaster Jokes." *New Directions in Folklore* 5. http://www.temple.edu/isllc/newfolk/wtchumor.html.

———. 2002. "Making a Big Apple Crumble: The Role of Humor in Constructing a Global Response to Disaster." *New Directions in Folklore* 6. http://www.temple.edu/isllc/newfolk/bigapple/bigapple1.html.

Fernback, Jan. 2003. "Legends on the Net: An Examination of Computer-Mediated Communication as a Locus of Oral Culture." *New Media and Society* 5:29–46.

Fine, Gary Alan. 1992. *Manufacturing Tales.* Knoxville: University of Tennessee Press.

———. 2004. Review of *Engaging Humor*, by Elliott Oring. *Journal of American Folklore* 117:225.

———. 2005. "An Introductory Essay." In *Rumor Mills*, ed. Gary Alan Fine, Veronique Campion-Vincent, and Chip Heath, 1–7. New Brunswick, N.J.: Transaction.

Fine, Gary Alan, and Irfan Khawaja. 2005. "Celebrating Arabs and Grateful Terrorists." In *Rumor Mills*, ed. Gary Alan Fine, Veronique Campion-Vincent, and Chip Heath, 189–205. New Brunswick, N.J.: Transaction.

Fishman, Mark. 1980. *Manufacturing the News.* Austin: University of Texas Press.

Frank, Robert. 1995/2002. "Men in Brown." In *Floating off the Page*, ed. Ken Wells, 72–75. New York: Wall Street Journal Books.

Frank, Russell. 2003a. " 'These Crowded Circumstances': When Pack Journalists Bash Pack Journalism." *Journalism: Theory, Practice, and Criticism* 4:441–58.

———. 2003b. "Folklore in a Hurry: The Community Experience Narrative in Newspaper Coverage of the Loma Prieta Earthquake." *Journal of American Folklore* 116:159–75.

———. 2004. "When the Going Gets Tough, the Tough Go Photoshopping: September 11 and the Newslore of Vengeance and Victimization." *New Media and Society* 6:633–58.

———. 2006a. "Worth a Thousand Words: The Photographic Urban Legend and the Illustrated Urban Legend." *Contemporary Legend* 6:119–45.

———. 2006b. "Can the News Media Censor Themselves?" *Media Ethics* 18 (1): 8–38.

Freud, Sigmund. 1928/1987. "Humor." In *The Philosophy of Laughter and Humor*, ed. John Morreall, 111–16. Albany: State University of New York Press.

Gamson, Joshua. 1994. *Claims to Fame.* Berkeley: University of California Press.

Gans, Herbert. 1980. *Deciding What's News.* New York: Random House.

Gates, Bill. 1998. "On Spam: Wasting Time on the Internet." 25 March. http://www.microsoft.com/billgates/columns/1998Essay/3%2D25col.asp.

Georges, Robert. 1976. "The General Concept of Legend: Some Assumptions to Be Reexamined and Reassessed." In *American Legend: A Symposium*, ed. Wayland D. Hand, 1–20. Berkeley: University of California Press.

Glassie, Henry. 1982. *Passing the Time in Ballymenone.* Philadelphia: University of Pennsylvania Press.

Goodwin, Joseph. 1995. "If Ignorance Is Bliss, Tis Folly to Be Wise: What We Don't Know Can Hurt Us." *Journal of Folklore Research* 32:155–64.

———. 2001. "Unprintable Reactions to All the News That's Fit to Print: Topical Humor and the Media." *New Directions in Folklore* 5. http://www.temple.edu/isllc/newfolk/reactions1.html.

Green, Archie. 1978. "Industrial Lore: A Bibliographic-Semantic Inquiry." *Western Folklore* 37:213–44.

Grundberg, Andy. 1990. *Crisis of the Real*. New York: Aperture.

Hathaway, Rosemary. 2005. "'Life in the TV': The Visual Nature of 9/11 Lore and Its Impact on Vernacular Response." *Journal of Folklore Research* 42:33–56.

Hine, Christine. 2000. *Virtual Ethnography*. London: Sage.

Holley, Frederick S. 1981. *Los Angeles Times Stylebook*. New York: New American Library.

Holliday, J. S. 1981. *The World Rushed In*. New York: Simon and Schuster.

Horrigan, John B., and Lee Rainie. 2002. *Getting Serious Online*. Pew Internet and American Life Project. http://www.pewinternet.org/pdfs/PIP_Getting_Serious_Online3ng.pdf.

Hutcheson, Francis. 1750/1987. "From *Reflections upon Laughter*." In *The Philosophy of Laughter and Humor*, ed. John Morreall, 26–40. Albany: State University of New York Press.

Irby, Kenny. 2001. "The Photographer behind the Image (and Smoke)." September 21. http://www.poynter.org/Terrorism/kenny7.htm.

———. 2003. "L.A. Times Photographer Fired over Altered Image." April 2. http://www.poynter.org/content/content_view.asp?id=28082.

Jay, Timothy. 1992. *Cursing in America*. Philadelphia: John Benjamins.

Jones, Steve. 1997. "Using the News: An Examination of the Value and Use of News Sources in Computer-Mediated Communication." *Journal of Computer-Mediated Communication* 2. http://jcmc.indiana.edu/vol2/issue4/jones.html.

Kibby, Marjorie. 2005. "Email Forwardables: Folklore in the Age of the Internet." *New Media and Society* 7:770–90.

Knowlton, Steve. 1997. *Moral Reasoning for Journalists*. Westport, Conn.: Praeger.

Kovach, Bill, and Tom Rosenstiel. 2001. *The Elements of Journalism*. New York: Crown.

Kuipers, Giselinde. 2005. "'Where Was King Kong When We Needed Him?' Public Discourse, Digital Disaster Jokes, and the Functions of Laughter after 9/11." *Journal of American Culture* 28:70–84.

Kurtzman, Daniel. 2001. "America Attacked." http://politicalhumor.about.com/library/weekly/aa091301a.htm.

Langellier, Kristin. 1989. "Personal Narratives: Perspectives on Theory and Research." *Text and Performance Quarterly* 9:243–76.

Lasky, Melvin J. 2005. *Profanity, Obscenity, and the Media*. New Brunswick, N.J.: Transaction.

Lévi-Strauss, Claude. 1966. *The Savage Mind*. Chicago: University of Illinois Press.

Lippman, Thomas. 1989. *Washington Post Deskbook on Style.* New York: McGraw Hill.

Lowney, Kathleen S., and Joel Best. 1996. "What Waco Stood For: Jokes as Popular Constructions of Social Problems." *Perspectives on Social Problems* 8:77–97.

Lule, Jack. 2001. *Daily News, Eternal Stories: The Mythological Role of Journalism.* New York: Guilford Press.

Malinowski, Bronislaw. 1948/1954. *Magic, Science, and Religion.* Garden City, N.Y.: Doubleday Anchor.

Mason, Bruce L. 1996. "Moving toward Virtual Ethnography." *American Folklore Society News* 25, no. 2 (April): 4–6. http://www.ucs.mun.ca/~bmason/phd/afsnews.html.

McCarl, Robert. 1984. "An Analysis of Performance in Fire Fighting Culture." *Journal of American Folklore* 97:393–422.

———. 1986. "Occupational Folklore." In *Folk Groups and Folklore Genres: An Introduction,* ed. Elliott Oring, 71–90. Logan: Utah State University Press.

Meyrowitz, Joshua. 1994. "The Life and Death of Media Friends: New Genres of Intimacy and Mourning." In *American Heroes in a Media Age,* ed. Susan J. Drucker and Robert S. Cathcart, 62–81. Creskill, N.J.: Hampton Press.

Mills, Alice, and Jeremy Smith, eds. 2001. *Utter Silence: Voicing the Unspeakable.* New York: Peter Lang.

Miner, Horace. 1956. "Body Ritual among the Nacirema." *American Anthropologist* 58:503–7.

Mintz, Lawrence E. 1983. "Humor and Popular Culture." In *Handbook of Humor Research,* vol. 2, ed. Paul E. McGhee and Jeffrey H. Goldstein, 129–42. New York: Springer.

Mitchell, William J. 1992. *The Reconfigured Eye: Visual Truth in the Post-photographic Era.* Cambridge: MIT Press.

Morreall, John, ed. 1987. *The Philosophy of Laughter and Humor.* Albany: State University of New York Press.

Mullen, Patrick. 1978. *I Heard the Old Fishermen Say.* Austin: University of Texas Press.

Myerhoff, Barbara, and Jay Ruby, eds. 1982. *A Crack in the Mirror: Reflexive Perspectives in Anthropology.* Philadelphia: University of Pennsylvania Press.

Nader, Laura. 1974. "Up the Anthropologist—Perspectives Gained from Studying Up." In *Reinventing Anthropology,* ed. Dell Hymes, 147–56. New York: Vintage Books.

Oring, Elliott. 1987. "Jokes and the Discourse on Disaster." *Journal of American Folklore* 100:276–86.

———. 1992. *Jokes and Their Relations.* Lexington: University Press of Kentucky.

———. 1995. "Arbiters of Taste: An Afterword." *Journal of Folklore Research* 32:165–74.

———. 2003. *Engaging Humor.* Urbana: University of Illinois Press.

Pew Internet and American Life Project. 2008. "Demographics of Internet Users." May. http://pewinternet.org/trends/User_Demo_2.15.08.htm (accessed June 2, 2008).

Pew Research Center for the People and the Press. 2009. "Press Accuracy Rating Hits Two Decade Low." September 13. http://people-press.org/report/543 (accessed September 28, 2009).

Postman, Neil. 1985. *Amusing Ourselves to Death.* New York: Penguin.

Powell, Chris, and George E. C. Paton, eds. 1988. *Humour in Society*. London: Macmillan.

Preston, Michael J. 1994. "Traditional Humor from the Fax Machine: 'All of a Kind.'" *Western Folklore* 53:147–69.

Rainie, Lee, et al. 2002. "One Year Later: September 11 and the Internet." Pew Internet and American Life Project. September 5. http://www.pewinternet.org/pdfs/PIP_9-11_Report.pdf.

Redfield, Robert. 1947. "The Folk Society." *American Journal of Sociology* 52:293–308.

Reuss, Richard. 1974. "That Can't Be Alan Dundes! Alan Dundes Is Taller than That!" *Journal of American Folklore* 87:303–17.

Rheingold, Howard. 2000. *The Virtual Community: Homesteading on the Electronic Frontier*. Cambridge: MIT Press.

Rosenberger, Rob. 1995/1997. "Computer Viruses and 'False Authority Syndrome.'" http://www.vmyths.com/fas/fas.pdf.

Santino, Jack. 1989. *Miles of Smiles, Years of Struggle: Stories of Black Pullman Porters*. Urbana: University of Illinois Press.

Schudson, Michael. 1978. *Discovering the News*. New York: Basic Books.

———. 1989. "The Sociology of News Production." *Media, Culture, and Society* 11:263–82.

Shipley, David, and Will Schwalbe. 2007. *Send: The Essential Guide to Email for Home and Office*. New York: Alfred A. Knopf.

Siegal, Allan M., and William G. Connolly, eds. 1999. *The New York Times Manual of Style and Usage*. New York: Times Books.

Sims, Norman, ed. 1984. *The Literary Journalists*. New York: Ballantine.

Smith, Moira, and Rachelle H. Saltzman, eds. 1995. "Arbiters of Taste: Censuring/Censoring Discourse." Special issue, *Journal of Folklore Research* 32.

Smyth, Willie. 1986. "*Challenger* Jokes and the Humor of Disaster." *Western Folklore* 45:243–60.

Soloski, John. 1999. "News Reporting and Professionalism: Some Constraints on the Reporting of News." In *News: A Reader*, ed. Howard Tumber, 308–19. Oxford, U.K.: Oxford University Press.

Sontag, Susan. 1977. *On Photography*. New York: Farrar, Straus and Giroux.

Stevens, John D. 1985. "Sensationalism in Perspective." *Journalism History* 12:78–79.

Templeton, Brad. n.d. "RHF Submission Guidelines." Rec.Humor.Funny. http://www.netfunny.com/rhf/submit.html.

Thomas, Jeannie B. 1997. "Dumb Blondes, Dan Quayle, and Hillary Clinton: Gender, Sexuality, and Stupidity in Jokes." *Journal of American Folklore* 110:277–313.

Turner, Patricia. 1993. *I Heard It through the Grapevine*. Berkeley: University of California Press.

University of Missouri School of Journalism. 1998. *Can Good Storytelling Sell Newspapers?*

Van Dijk, Teun A. 1991. "The Interdisciplinary Study of News as Discourse." In *A Handbook of Qualitative Methodologies for Mass Communication Research*, ed. Klaus B. Jensen and Nicholas W. Jankowski, 108–20. New York: Routledge.

Vlach, John. 1971. "One Black Eye and Other Horrors: A Case for the Humorous Anti-Legend." *Indiana Folklore* 4:95–140.

Weinberger, David. 2002. *Small Pieces Loosely Joined*. Cambridge, Mass.: Perseus.

Welsch, Roger. 1974. "Bigger'n Life: The Tall Tale Postcard." *Southern Folklore Quarterly* 38:311–23.

Wojcik, Daniel. 1996. "Polaroids from Heaven." *Journal of American Folklore* 109:129–48.

Zelizer, Barbie. 1993. "Journalists as Interpretive Communities." *Critical Studies in Mass Communications* 10:219–37.

NEWSPAPER AND MAGAZINE STORIES

Allbritton, Chris. 1999. "Industry Springs Up around Y2K Bug." *Miami Herald*, 2 January, 14A.

Anderson, Lisa, and Dan Mihalopoulos. 2001. "A Grim Search in a Shattered City." *Chicago Tribune*, 13 September, 1.

Barringer, Felicity. 2001. "A False Challenge to News Photos Takes Root on the Web." *New York Times*, 24 September, C9.

Barry, Dave. 2007. "You've Got Trouble." *New York Times Book Review*, 6 May, 13.

Bearak, Barry. 2001. "Taliban Plead for Mercy to the Miserable in a Land of Nothing." *New York Times*, 13 September, A18.

Beatty, Shannon. 2002. "Back on the Chain Gang." *Columbus Dispatch*, 25 February, 1E.

Benedetti, Winda. 2001. "Are You Being Forward with E-mail? Stop!" *Seattle Post-Intelligencer*, 23 October, 1.

Boule, Margie. 2004. "Check Those Political Tales Before You Spread Dumb Hoaxes." *Oregonian*, 26 August, E1.

Bridges, Tony. 2001. "Urban Legends Ride in Wake of Terrorist Attacks." *Tallahassee Democrat*, 20 October.

Britt, Donna. 2005. "In Katrina's Wake, Inaccurate Rumors Sullied Victims." *Washington Post*, 30 September, B1.

Caldwell, Alicia. 2001. "Whatever It Takes." *St. Petersburg Times*, 18 September, 1B.

Carr, David. 2005. "More Horrible than Truth: News Reports." *New York Times*, 19 September, C1.

Choe, Stan. 2001. "What Is Photoshopping? A New Sport on the Web." Knight Ridder Newspapers, printed in *Centre Daily Times* (State College, Pa.), 10 March, E1.

Christensen, Charles. 2005. "Letter to the Editor." *Newsday*, 1 September, A38.

Connor, Tracy. 2002. "Running Late Saved Them from Trade Center Death." *New York Daily News*, 8 September, Wrap 8.

Cooper, Marc. 2004. "Among the NASCAR Dads." *Nation*, 22 March. Posted March 4 at http://www.thenation.com/doc/20040322/cooper2 (accessed January 17, 2006).

Crary, David. 2007. "Top 2007 Stories." *Evansville Courier Press*, 27 December. http://www.courierpress.com/news/2007/dec/21/top-2007-stories.

Dao, James, Joseph B. Treaster, and Felicity Barringer. 2005. "New Orleans Is Awaiting Deliverance." *New York Times*, 2 September, 15.

DeFao, Janine. 1995. "LSD-Tattoo Story Updated—but Still Nonsense." *Sacramento Bee*, 2 July, 1B.

Duncan, Jeff. 2005. "Superdome Laid Waste by Those Who Sheltered." *Times-Picayune*, 12 September, A5.

Dwyer, Jim, and Christopher Drew. 2005. "Fear Exceeded Crime's Reality in New Orleans." *New York Times*, 29 September, 1.

Fish, Stanley. 2008. "All You Need Is Hate." *New York Times*, 3 February. http://fish.blogs. nytimes.com/2008/02/03/all-you-need-is-hate.

Frank, Russell. 2003c. "Altered Photos Break Public's Trust in Media." *Los Angeles Times*, 7 April, B11.

———. 2007. "Cho the Warrior." *Pittsburgh Post-Gazette*, 29 April, 29.

Gibes, Al. 2001. "Online Wit Turns Hoax to Humor." *Las Vegas Review-Journal*, 15 October. http://www.reviewjournal.com/lvrj_home/2001/Oct-15-Mon- 2001/business/17198704. html.

Gibson, Owen. 2001. "New Media: The Truth about that CNN Email." *Guardian*, 24 September, 3B.

Gibson, William. 2005. "God's Little Toys: Confessions of a Cut and Paste Artist." *Wired* 13 (July). http://www.wired.com/wired/archive/13.07/gibson.html.

Goodman, Ellen. 2004. "Forgetting the 'Dad' in NASCAR Pitch." *Boston Globe*, 19 February. http://www.boston.com/news/globe/editorial_opinion/oped/articles/2004/02/19/ forgetting_the_dad_in_nascar_pitch (accessed January 17, 2006).

Hafner, Katie. 2004. "The Camera Never Lies, but the Software Can." *New York Times*, 11 March, G1.

Harden, Blaine. 2001. "After the Attacks: The Reaction." *New York Times*, 13 September, A15.

Harmon, Amy. 2001. "FBI Debunks E-mail Threat." *New York Times*, 12 October.

Haygood, Wil, and Ann Scott Tyson. 2005. "'It Was As If All of Us Were Already Pronounced Dead.'" *Washington Post*, 15 September, A1.

Heffernan, Virginia. 2006. "Brokeback Spoofs: Tough Guys Unmasked." *New York Times*, 2 March.

———. 2008. "Narrow Minded." *New York Times Magazine*, 25 May.

Hinckley, David. 2001. "Rants in Their Pants." *New York Daily News*, 30 September, Showtime15.

Hinkle, Alice. 1999. "Area Towns Scramble to Cure Y2K Bugs." *Boston Globe*, 3 January, 1.

Horowitz, Jason. 2008. "The Hillary Haters." *GQ*, February. http://men.style.com/gq/ features/landing?id=content_6249.

Indian Express. 1998. "Britan [*sic*] Now Sheds Tears of Laughter over Princess Diana." *Indian Express*, 21 August. http://www.indianexpress.com/res/web/pIe/ie/ daily/19980821/23350024.html.

Ivanovich, David. 2006. "Everybody Knows Enron's Name, for Better or Worse." *San Francisco Chronicle*, 16 March. http://www.chron.com/disp/story.mpl/special/ enron/2655424.html.

Klebnikov, Paul. 2003. "Coke's Sinful World." *Forbes*, 22 December. http://www.forbes.com/ forbes/2003/1222/086.html.

Kornblum, Janet. 2001. "Humor Returns to the Web, but Sites Are Careful in Their Topics." *USA Today*, 26 September, 4D.

Light, Ken. 2004. "Fonda, Kerry, and Photo Fakery." *Washington Post*, 28 February, A21.

Logan, Michael. 1999. "Preparing, for the End of the World as We Know It." *Pittsburgh Post-Gazette*, 3 January, A-1.

LondonNet. n.d. "Death of the Princess." http://www.londonnet.co.uk/ln/talk/news/diheadlines_previous2.html.

Los Angeles Times. 2003. "Editor's Note." *Los Angeles Times*, 2 April, A1.

Maykuth, Andrew. 2006. "Few U.S. Outlets Showing Muhammad Cartoons." *Philadelphia Inquirer*, 4 February, A6.

McClain, Dylan. 2002. "Another Big Fish Story Comes Unraveled." *New York Times*, 7 October, C3.

Morse, Rob. 2001. "Get Out Your Map, This War Won't Be Over by Christmas." *San Francisco Chronicle*, 16 September, A22.

Moss, Mitchell L. 1999. "Has Something Gone Wrong with Suburban Culture?" *Houston Chronicle*, 23 April, A39.

New York Times. 2001. "Wartime Rhetoric." *New York Times*, 19 September, A26.

———. 2005. "Barbara Bush Calls Evacuees Better Off." *New York Times*, 7 September. http://www.nytimes.com/2005/09/07/national/nationalspecial/07barbara.html?scp=1&sq=barbara%20bush%20calls%20evacuees&st=cse.

Nichols, John. 2005. "Barbara Bush: It's Good Enough for the Poor." *Nation*, 6 September. http://www.thenation.com/blogs/thebeat/20080.

Oldenburg, Ann. 2006. "It's Open Season on Dick Cheney." *USA Today*, 14 February, B10.

Park, Michael Y. 2002. "Online Art Form Gains Popularity." FOXNews.com, 18 March. http://www.foxnews.com/story/0,2933,48116,00.html.

Perkins, Joseph. 2001. "We Should Make Perpetrators Pay with Their Blood." *San Diego Union-Tribune*, 12 September, B7.

Peterson, Karen. 2001. "Do We Seek Revenge or Justice?" *USA Today*, 19 September, 1D.

Pitts, Leonard. 2001. "September 12, 2001: We'll Go Forward from This Moment." *Miami Herald*, 12 Sept. http://www.miamiherald.com/living/columnists/leonard-pitts/story/374188.html.

Ramsey, Bruce. 2000. "Y2K Debacle an Embarrassment for the Media." *Seattle Post-Intelligencer*, 12 January, D1.

Rivers, Bryon. 2000. "Believe Every Warning That Comes in Your E-mail?" *Eagle-Tribune* (Mass.), 22 September.

Roeper, Richard. 1997. "Biggest Stories of '97? Have I Got News for You." *Chicago Sun-Times*, 29 December, 11.

———. 2001. "It's All Right to Laugh at Ground Zero Geek." *Chicago Sun-Times*, 17 October, 11.

Rosenberg, Scott. 2000. "Did Gore Invent the Internet?" *Salon*, 5 October. http://archive.salon.com/tech/col/rose/2000/10/05/gore_internet/index.html.

Silva, Mark, and Michael Tackett. 2005. "President Needs to Get, Give Answers." *Chicago Tribune*, 4 September, 1.

Smith, Jerd. 2001. "Worries from the Web: Modern Day Grapevine Speeds Dissemination of False Rumors." *Rocky Mountain News*, 15 October, 1B.

Thevenot, Brian, and Gordon Russell. 2005. "Rape. Murder. Gun Fights." *Times-Picayune*, 26 September, A1.

Tierney, John. 2001. "Fantasies of Vengeance, Fed by Fury." *New York Times*, 18 September. http://www.nytimes.com/2001/09/18/nyregion/the-big-city-fantasies-of-vengeance-fed-by-fury.html?scp=1&sq=fantasies+of+vengeance&st=nyt.

———. 2008. "Living in Fear and Paying a High Cost in Heart Risk." *New York Times*, 15 January. http://www.nytimes.com/2008/01/15/science/15tier.html.

Tomsho, Robert, Barbara Carton, and Jerry Guidera. 2001. "She Got Laid Off, He Missed a Train; Such Lucky Breaks." *Wall Street Journal*, 13 September, A1.

USA Today. 1998. "A Nation Stunned by School Mayhem Searches for Answers." *USA Today*, 26 March, 14A.

Wall Street Journal. 2001. "Fiery Escapes, Surreal Stories at Trade Center." *Wall Street Journal*, 17 September, B1–B4.

Weeks, Linton. 2006. "In the Nawlins Muck, They're Yukking It Up." *Washington Post*, 27 February, C2.

Weingarten, Gene. 2001. "Not Funny: The Rules of Humor Changed on Sept. 11." *Washington Post* (F ed.), 18 September, C1.

INDEX

About.com: humor, 26, 212, 231n; urban legends, 18–19, 68, 74, 96–97, 105, 117, 184, 236–39n, 242–43n

Abramoff, Jack, 27

Abu Ghraib prison photos, 94

Afghanistan: invasion of, 65, 82, 98; news coverage of, 87–88; in newslore of 9/11, 66, 72, 88–89; and Osama bin Laden, 133–34

AIDS: and Magic Johnson, 181–82; in the news, 24; and Republicans, 203–4; urban legends about, 18, 226, 228–30

Al Qaeda, 86, 180, 229

Alabiso, Vin: on World Trade Center/"devil" photo, 22

Albert, Marv, 213

Allbritton, Chris, 240n

Americanhistoryabout.com, 236n

Amoss, Jim, on Hurricane Katrina legends, 104

Anderson, Lisa, 236n

Answerbag.com, 240n

Answerbank.com, and Steve Irwin jokes, 178, 241n

Anvari.org, on Bush reading upside-down photoshop, 109, 239n

AOL, 154, 192, 228–29

Apple Computer, 151, 155

Apte, Mahadev L., 231n

Arafat, Yasir, 127, 213

Arsenio Hall Show, and Bush/Clinton saxophone joke, 111

Arthur Andersen, 3–4, 143, 145–46, 201–2, 231n

Associated Press, 22, 159, 169, 184–85, 222–23, 243n; Top Ten Stories lists, 32, 212–15

Auschwitz jokes, 14, 38–39

Azine (Asian American Movement Ezine), 239n

Baer, Florence, 106, 239n

Baker, Jim, in sex scandal joke, 202

Barney Rubble, in Osama bin Laden joke, 88

Barringer, Felicity, coverage of September 11 photos, 21, 234n, 238n

Barry, Dave: on e-mail spam, 209; and humor in the news, 25

Baym, Nancy, 10, 13, 232–33n

BBC, and September 11 photos, 21

Bearak, Barry, on bombing Afghanistan, 87, 237n

Beatty, Shannon, on e-mail spam, 19, 234n

Benedetti, Winda, on e-mail spam, 19, 234n

Benjamin, Walter, 28, 235n

Bennett, Charles, 65, 68

Benton, Gregor, 12, 232n

Berger, Asa, 235n

Bernstein, Carl, and Deep Throat, 48

Bessette, Carolyn, 171

Bessette, Lauren, 171

Best, Joel, 233n, 242n

Biden, Joe, 193, 212

Big Three automakers, 4–5

Bin Laden, Osama, 63, 75, 80–89, 91–94, 127, 133–34, 147, 153, 212, 214, 236n, 243n. See also Joke texts; Photoshop subjects

Bird, S. Elizabeth, 233n, 238n

Blagojevich, Rod, 190, 192

Blitzer, Wolf, interview with Al Gore, 57

Bobbitt, Lorena, 31; and bin Laden/genie joke, 87

Boese, Alex, and fake news about death of Jon Heder, 187

Bond, Julian, 238n

Bono, Sonny, jokes about, 169–71

Boorstin, Daniel, 233n

Boulder Daily Camera, 238n

Boule, Margie: on Bush IQ legend, 117, 239n; on e-mail spam, 19, 234n

Bradlee, Ben, 24

Branch Davidians, 31, 233n

Brash, Larry, 151, 240n

Bridges, Tony, 234n

Britt, Donna, 239n

Bronner, Simon, 237n

Brown, Divine, in Hugh Grant/Bill Gates joke, 152

Brown, Michael, and Bush/Katrina photoshop, 99

Brunvand, Jan Harold, 13, 18, 232–34n, 239–40n, 242–43n

Bryant, Kobe, in Bush/parachute joke, 117

Buchanan, Pat, and 2000 election, 131

Bud Lite, and *Challenger* disaster jokes, 82

Bumper stickers, 33–34, 101

Bush, Barbara, 121; and "Bush" beer photoshop, 212; and Hurricane Katrina, 97

Bush, George H. W., 3–4, 96–97, 99, 113–14, 203

Bush, George W., 5–6, 15, 21, 27–28, 31, 38, 57, 62, 82, 92, 94–95, 149, 153, 173, 179, 191, 194–95, 198, 200–202, 207, 212, 214, 217, 238–40n, 243n; and Enron, 146–47; and Hurricane Katrina, 95–100, 238n; jokes and photoshops about intelligence of, 108–27; and Mastercard "Priceless" parodies, 130–36

Bush, Jeb, and Terri Schiavo joke, 179

Bush, Jenna, 121; and "Bush" beer photoshop, 212

Bush, Laura: and George W. Bush/gold urinal joke, 112; and Enron stock, 147–49; fake letter from, 115–16

Bush Administration, 28, 63, 65, 94–95, 133–34, 137, 146, 197, 200, 202, 221–22

Byron, George Gordon, Lord, 90

Caldwell, Alicia, 238n

Carr, David, on Hurricane Katrina legends, 103, 238–39n

Carter, Jimmy, 27

Carton, Barbara, 237n

Cathcart, Robert S., 233n

Celebrities: fake news stories about the death of, 180–88; jokes about the death of, 168–80; in the news, 166–68

Center for Media and Public Affairs (CMPA), 120, 214–15, 239n, 242n

Center for Responsive Politics, 147

Centre Daily Times, 33, 36

Chain letters, 154, 226–30

Challenger Disaster jokes, 28, 82, 89, 92, 168, 171–72, 243n

Chavez, Hugo, in Barack Obama rumors, 190

Cheney, Dick: in Bush jokes, 62, 110–11; in fake George W. Bush press conference transcript, 147; in fake Laura Bush letter, 115; and Halliburton, 116; hunting accident, 26–27, 197, 200–202, 207, 211; and Iraq War, 122, 133; role in George W. Bush administration, 95, 108, 112; as target of late-night comedians, 214

Cher, 170

Chertoff, Michael, and Hurricane Katrina, 99

Chinese earthquake (2008), 106

Choe, Stan, 242n

Christensen, Charles, letter to *Newsday*, 238n

Chrysler Corporation, 4

Church's Fried Chicken, Hurricane Katrina joke, 102

Claiborne, Liz, urban legends about, 74, 128, 237n

Clinton, Bill, 24, 28, 31–33, 39, 45, 58, 61, 108, 111–13, 120, 127, 130, 147, 173–74, 204, 212, 215; jokes about, 3–4, 6, 33, 42–43, 46–56, 101, 109, 111–12, 117–20, 127, 153, 179, 189, 200–202, 207, 214. *See also* Joke letters; Joke texts

Clinton, Chelsea, 33, 43, 52, 62, 240n

Clinton, Hillary, 25, 27–28, 31–35, 38–44, 49–55, 57, 59, 61, 87, 112, 117–19, 126, 136, 146, 153, 173–74, 189, 200, 202, 207, 212, 214. *See also* Joke texts; Photoshop subjects

CNN, 21, 57, 181, 187

Coca Cola, 228–29; contamination legends about, 74–75, 128, 237n

Colbert, Stephen, and "truthiness," 220, 242n

Cold War, 16

Columbine High School: and Mastercard "Priceless" commercial parody, 129

Compass, Edwin P., on Hurricane Katrina legends, 102–3

Computer-mediated communication (CMC), 9, 28, 68, 93, 107, 154, 242n

Concorde, in Tourist Guy photoshop, 80

Condit, Gary, jokes about Chandra Levy affair, 3–4, 46

Connolly, William G., 235n

Connor, Tracy, 237n

Cooper, Marc, on George W. Bush's NASCAR campaign stop, 136, 240n

Corddry, Rob, 200

Craig, Larry, 190

Cultural relativism, 16

Cunanan, Andrew, and murder of Gianni Versace, 172, 213

Cruise, Tom, and photoshopping, 216

Cybercartoons, 216. *See also* Photoshops

Cyberspace, 10–11, 15, 26, 68, 107–8, 120, 177, 189, 209, 231–32n

Dahmer, Jeffrey, 31

Daily Kos, 239n

Daily Show, 200

Dalai Lama, in Bill Gates/parachute joke, 118

Dao, James, 237n

Dardenne, Robert, 233n, 238n

Darwin, Charles, in fake Laura Bush letter, 116

Daschle, Tom, photoshop of backwards pledge, 109

Davies, Christie, 93, 233n, 235–36n, 238n, 241n

Dean, Howard, 192

Dear Abby parodies, 54, 140, 146, 219

Deep Throat, in Clinton/Lewinsky joke, 48

DeFao, Janine, 233n

DeGeneres, Ellen, 213

Degh, Linda, 234n

Democratic Party, 28, 31, 34–36, 58, 62, 94, 107, 116, 132, 136, 146, 213

Department of Homeland Security, 99, 225

DeSousa, Ronald, 237n

Digitally altered photographs. *See* Photoshops

Disney movies, in Michael Jackson joke, 174

Disney World, 230; and Dan Quayle/Loma Prieta earthquake joke, 100

Disneyland, 228

Dole, Bob: Depends joke, 46; as target of late-night comedians, 214

Dorst, John, 13, 82, 232–33n, 237n

Douglas, Mary, 11, 29

Drew, Christopher, 238–39n

Drucker, Susan J., 233n

Duke, David, 31

Duncan, Jeff, 238n

Dundes, Alan: on Auschwitz jokes, 14, 38, 233n, 235n; on "the folk," 8, 232n; on folklore of the "paperwork empire," 8–9, 13, 232n, 240n; on function of jokes, 107, 239n; on Gary Hart jokes, 235n; on light bulb jokes, 236n; on meaning of folklore, 11, 232n; on newslore of Operation Desert Storm, 88, 236n; on sexual symbolism in jokes, 84, 237n; on sources of new folklore, 70

Dungy, James, in Mike Vanderjagt fake suicide story, 185–86

Dungy, Tony, in Mike Vanderjagt fake suicide story, 185

Dwyer, Jim, 238–39n

Edwards, John, and sex scandal, 190–91

Ehow.com, and Barack Obama jokes, 190, 241n

Einstein, Albert, in George W. Bush/St. Peter joke, 118–19

Ellis, Bill: on newslore as a "strategy of rebellion," 82, 237n; on newslore of September 11, 69, 85, 88, 236–37n; on photoshops as "cybercartoons," 216, 242n; on researching netlore, 13–14, 231n, 233n

E-mail, 5, 9–10, 12, 14–15, 18–19, 21, 24, 26–28, 34–35, 37, 39, 63–73, 75, 80–82, 90, 92–93, 96, 108, 125, 135, 145, 154, 159, 161, 187, 191–94, 197–201, 204–7, 209–12, 217, 220, 226–30, 233–34n, 236n

Emery, David, 18, 243n

Eminem, fake news story about death of, 184, 187

Ensign, John, 190

Enron, 4, 28, 128, 137–50, 201, 207

Epcot Center, in Dan Quayle/Loma Prieta earthquake joke, 100, 117

Etch-a-Sketch, 161–62

Extreme Makeover, and George W. Bush joke, 124

Fake FAQs, Etch-a-Sketch, 161–62

Fake memoranda: Wal-Mart identity theft warning, 223; Y2K backup systems, 160–61

Fake news stories: Bush library fire, 112; celebrity deaths, 181–87; fellatio study, 222–23; gay marriage study, 221; Microsoft buys federal government, 153; Y1K Crisis, 164

Fake press releases: AIDS/gas pumps, 226; Microsoft/Y2K, 162; UPS uniforms/terrorism, 225

Falwell, Jerry, 6

Family Matters. See White, Jaleel

Fark.com, 93

"Fauxtos." See Photoshops

Fawcett, Farrah, 169, 176

Faxlore, 9, 69, 71, 82, 113, 127, 141, 153, 215, 234n

FBI, 46, 48, 215, 224

Felt, Mark, 48

FEMA, 98–99, 101

Fernback, Jan, 13, 233n

Ferrell, Will, fake news story about death of, 182–84

Fine, Gary Alan, 128, 240n

Fish, Stanley, 44, 189

Fishman, Mark, 238n

Flowers, Gennifer, 45, 50, 56, 61

"Foaflore," 74

Folk, defined, 8

Folklore: in context, 13; defined, 8; faxlore, 8–9; and the Internet, 9; occupational, 8, 231n; "from the paperwork empire," 8; and popular culture, 210–11; variation in, 9

Fonda, Jane, in John Kerry photoshop, 59–61, 236n

Forbes magazine, 32, 75

Ford, Gerald, 153

Ford Motors, 4, 144

Forwards, forwardables. *See* E-mail

Frank, Robert, 243n

Frank, Russell, 33, 36–38, 73, 200, 233–35n, 239n

"Frankly Speaking," 33–44

Fred Flintstone, in Osama bin Laden joke, 88

Freerepublic.com, 240n

Freud, Sigmund, 232n

Gamson, Joshua, 12, 232n

Gans, Herbert, 233n, 238n

Garcia, Jerry, 32

Gartner, Michael, 16

Gates, Bill, 29, 32, 43, 118, 151–56, 158–59, 169, 230, 240n

General Electric, 154

General Motors (GM), 4, 155

Genie jokes, 55–57, 86–87

Georges, Robert, 217, 243n

Ghostbusters, 78, 80

Gibes, Al, 237n

Gibson, Owen, 22, 234n

Gibson, William, 192, 241n

Gingrich, Newt, 31–32, 204, 214

Giuliani, Rudolph, 74, 214

Glassie, Henry, 242n

Godzilla, in Tourist Guy photoshop, 80

Goldman, Ronald, 172, 213

Goldstein, Diane, 239n

Gonzalez, Elian, 130, 136, 215

Goodman, Ellen, 136, 240

Goodman, John, fake stories about death of, 187

Goodwin, Joseph, 69, 235–36, 238

Gore, Al, 28, 45, 131–32; jokes about, 51, 57–59, 62, 111, 153; in Mastercard "Priceless" parody, 131; as target of late-night comedians, 214

Grant, Hugh, 32; in Bill Gates/prostitute joke, 152; in Princess Diana joke, 169

Green, Archie, 231n

Greene, Joe, and elevator legend, 127

Greenspan, Alan, in fake Laura Bush letter, 116

Greenspun, Philip, 239n

Ground Zero Geek. *See* Tourist Guy

Guidera, Jerry, 237n

Gulf War, 82, 84, 113, 133, 236n

Hafner, Katie, 236n

Halliburton, 108, 115–16, 202

Halloween, 18, 46, 72–74, 177, 236n

Harden, Blaine, 238n

Harding, Tonya, 20, 31, 87

Harkness, Timandra, on death of Princess Diana, 180

Harmon, Amy, 236n

Harris, Eric, in Mastercard "Priceless" commercial parody, 129

Hart, Gary, 235n

Hartford Courant, role of, in *Los Angeles Times*'s composite photo of Iraq war, 20

Hathaway, Rosemary, 232n, 237n

Haygood, Wil, 238n

Head and Shoulders shampoo, in *Challenger* disaster jokes, 82

Heder, Jon, fake news story about death of, 187

Heffernan, Virginia, 26, 192, 235n, 241n

Hilfiger, Tommy, legends about, 74, 128, 237n

Hilton, Paris: fake news stories about death of, 187; jokes about, 177; news coverage of, 167

Hinckley, David, 237n

Hindenburg, in Tourist Guy photoshop, 80

Hine, Christine, 232–33n, 242n

Hinkle, Alice, 240n

Hoaxes, 19, 158–59, 216–17, 230; celebrity

death stories as, 180, 187, 241n; computer virus warnings as, 181, 220; Kerry/ Fonda photoshop as, 61; and September 11, 21–22, 74, 77, 80

Holley, Frederick S., 235n

Holliday, J. S., 227, 243n

Holocaust jokes. *See* Auschwitz jokes

Holyfield, Evander, and Mike Tyson joke, 32

Horace, 242n

Horowitz, Jason, 28, 44, 235n

Horrigan, John B., 233n, 241n

Humor: in the news, 25–26; on the Web, 90, 93, 152, 177–78, 190, 192–93, 210–12

Hunter, Rielle, 191

Hurricane Katrina, 27–28, 95–106, 108–9, 215, 238–39n, 243n; French Quarter, 101; Houston Astrodome, 97; New Orleans Convention Center, 27, 98, 102–4; looting, 101, 104–5; Louisiana Superdome, 27, 102–3, 123; Ninth Ward, 104

Hussein, Saddam, 69, 82, 94, 100, 112–13, 124, 127, 133–34, 180, 212, 214

Hutcheson, Francis, 218, 235n, 242n

Hyde, Henry, 204

Iacocca, Lee, 3–4

Idealog, 109, 239n

Indian Express, 180, 241n

I-newswire, 184

INS (Immigration and Naturalization Service), 130

International Society for Contemporary Legend Research, 239n

Iran, 66–67, 83, 114, 133; Iranian hostage crisis, 69, 71, 82, 236n

Iraq War, 6, 82, 84, 88–89, 94–95, 100–101, 108–9, 113–15, 122, 132–34, 136, 179–80, 200, 221–22

Irby, Kenny, 22, 234n

IRS (Internal Revenue Service), 34, 43, 115, 197

Irwin, Steve, 177–78

Ivanovich, David, 240n

Jackson, Jesse, 143, 202

Jackson, Michael, 31, 167–68, 173, 179, 189, 193, 240n; on AP Top Ten stories lists, 213, 215; fake stories about death of, 187; jokes about, 101, 169, 174–76; and photoshops, 123–24

Jackson, Reggie, and elevator legend, 127

Jay, Timothy, 237n

JibJab.com, 47

Jobs, Steve, 151, 158

John, Elton, 170

Johnson, Earlitha "Cookie," in fake news story about death of Magic Johnson, 182

Johnson, Magic: and elevator legend, 127; fake news story about death of, 181–82

Joke letters: from Bill Clinton to FAA, 47; Nigerian scam letter from George W. Bush, 114–15; from Plutonius to Cassius and "Y0K" crisis, 163–64; solicitation of support for Enron executives, 143; from "satisfied taxpayer" to IRS, 197

Joke texts: Afghanistan, 88; Osama bin Laden, 87–88, 236n; Sonny Bono, 171; George W. Bush, 110–12, 117–18, 124–27; George W. Bush and Hurricane Katrina, 100; George W. Bush and Enron, 146–47; Laura Bush and Enron, 148–49; Dick Cheney, 200; Bill and Hillary Clinton, 33, 42–43, 49–51, 54–56; Bill Clinton, 46–50, 52–53, 61, 101, 117, 119–20, 201–2; Bill Clinton and Monica Lewinsky, 52–53; Chelsea Clinton, 33, 43, 52, 62; Hillary Clinton, 42, 126, 189; Bob Dole, 46; Bill Gates, 152–53, 155–57; Al Gore, 51, 57–59; Bernie Madoff, 138; Barack Obama, 190; Branch Davidians (Waco), 219; Bush administration, 202; *Challenger* disaster (Christa McAuliffe), 219; Chinese earthquake, 106; Gary Condit,

46; John Edwards, 191; Enron, 140–42, 146; Farrah Fawcett, 169; Genie, 55–57, 87; Hurricane Katrina, 101; IRS, 197–98; Michael Jackson, 101, 169–76; Michael Jackson and Farrah Fawcett, 176; John F. Kennedy Jr., 171–73; Michael Kennedy, 171; Ted Kennedy, 241n; John Kerry, 59; Ken Lay, 138–39; Monica Lewinsky, 48–49, 55–56; Rush Limbaugh, 219; Microsoft, 157–59; Ministers/sex scandal, 202; Mother Teresa, 170; Newspapers, 141, 202–3; Pope Benedict XVI, 197; Princess Diana, 169–70, 180; Princess Diana and Mother Teresa, 169–70; Dan Quayle, 47, 100, 214; Republicans, 203; Terri Schiavo, 179; September 11 attacks, 89–90; O. J. Simpson, 172, 219; Social Security, 201; St. Peter, 118–19, 170; Taliban, 89; tsunami, 105–6; 2008–9 financial crisis, 145–46, 150; Mike Tyson, 32; Gianni Versace, 172; Tiger Woods, 193–94; World Trade Center, 89–90; Y2K, 160–61

Jokes: as folk media criticism, 92; function of, 107; in the news, 22, 201

Jokesgallery.com, 212, 242n

Jones, Paula, 45, 50, 61; in Al Gore joke, 58; as target of late-night comedians, 214

Jones, Steve, 232n

Jordan, Michael, in Bill Gates/parachute joke, 118

Journal of American Folklore, 13

Journalism: coverage of Hurricane Katrina, 101–4; coverage of September 11, 90–91; and humor, 25; and newslore, 15–18, 21, 26; and newsworthiness, 212–13; and objectivity, 15; and taste, 22–26

Karlin, Ben, on Enron scandal, 137

Kennedy, Jean, 173

Kennedy, John F., 79–80; in Tiger Woods joke, 194

Kennedy, John F., Jr.: on AP Top Ten list, 213, 215; jokes about, 171–73

Kennedy, Michael, jokes about, 169–73

Kennedy, Robert F., 169

Kennedy, Ted, 46–47, 173, 220, 241n; on AP Top Ten list, 213

Kentucky Fried Chicken, and George W. Bush, Hillary Clinton photoshops, 121

Kerrigan, Nancy: and bin Laden/genie joke, 87; and Tonya Harding composite photo, 20; and Tonya Harding jokes, 31

Kerry, John, 28, 212; in fake Laura Bush letter, 115; jokes about, 59, 62, 146; photoshops involving, 59–62, 236n

Kerry, Teresa Heinz, rumors about, 117

Keyes, Alan, 203

Khomeini, Grand Ayatollah Ruhollah, 82–83, 127

Kibby, Marjorie, 240n, 242n

Kilgore, Barney, 29

King, Martin Luther, in Tiger Woods joke, 194

Klebnikov, Paul, 237n

Klebold, Dylan, in Mastercard "Priceless" commercial parody, 129

Knowlton, Steve, 20, 233–34n

Kopechne, Mary Jo, in Ted Kennedy/John F. Kennedy Jr. jokes, 173

Koresh, David, 31

Kovach, Bill, 240n

Ku Klux Klan: and David Duke, 31; and Barack Obama rumors, 190

Kuipers, Giselinde, 90, 236–38n

Kurtzman, Daniel, on September 11 humor, 68, 236n

Langellier, Kristin, 233n

Laughline.com, 179

Lawyer jokes, 146, 190

Lay, Ken, 138–40, 148

Lemay, Curtis, 88

Leno, Jay, 210–11, 242n; and Cheney
hunting joke, 200
Letterman, David, 210, 242n; and Cheney
hunting joke, 200; and Top Ten lists,
211, 219
Levi-Strauss, Claude, and *bricolage*, 123,
239n
Lewinsky, Monica, 4, 6, 24, 45–47, 54, 61,
119, 147, 214–15; jokes about, 3, 48–50,
52–53, 55–57; as target of late-night
comedians, 214. *See also* Joke texts
Lewis, Carl, and fake celebrity death
stories, 187
LexisNexis, 18, 113
Lieberman, Joseph, in Al Gore joke, 51
Light, Ken, and Kerry/Fonda photoshop,
60–61, 236
Limbaugh, Rush, 5–6, 31, 38, 219
Lincoln, Abraham, 3; in Tourist Guy
photoshop, 80; in Tiger Woods joke, 194
Lindahl, Carl, 104
Lippman, Walter, 235n
Literary journalism, 17
Livingston, Bob, 204
Logan, Michael, 240n
Loma Prieta earthquake, 100–101, 106,
237n; in Dan Quayle joke, 100, 117
Longinus, 235n
Los Angeles Times, 234n; Iraq war
composite photo scandal, 20; in
newspaper joke, 141; and taste, 23
Lott, Trent, and Hurricane Katrina, 100
Louisiana Superdome, and Hurricane
Katrina, 27, 102–3, 127
Lowell, James Russell, 232n
Lowney, Kathleen S., 233n, 242n
Lule, Jack, 81, 237n, 240n

Madoff, Bernard, jokes about, 138, 190,
192
Majors, Lee, in Farrah Fawcett joke, 176
Malinowski, Bronislaw, on magic, 69

Marro, Anthony, and Tonya Harding/
Nancy Kerrigan composite photo, 20
Mars *Explorer*, and bin Laden/milk carton
parody, 87
Mason, Bruce, 233n
Mastercard, "Priceless" commercial
parodies, 29, 82, 129–30, 134, 145, 192
Maykuth, Andrew, 235n
McAuliffe, Christa, in *Challenger* jokes,
168, 219
McCain, John, in Bush/Katrina photoshop,
97
McCarl, Robert, 231n
McClain, Dylan Loeb, coverage of shark/
helicopter photoshop, 21, 234n
McClellan, Scott, in fake news story about
Bush library, 112
McDonalds, in Michael Jackson joke, 174
McPhee, John, 217, 243n
McVeigh, Timothy: on AP list of Top Ten
news stories (1997), 213; and UPS truck
warning, 226
Metzenbaum, Howard, 37
Meyer, Eugene, and taste in the
Washington Post, 24
Meyrowitz, Joshua, 236n, 240–41n
Miami Herald, in newspaper joke, 141
Mickey Mouse, Iran hostage crisis folk
cartoon, 68–69, 83
Microsoft, 146, 151–55, 157–59, 162, 198, 215,
228–29
Mihalopoulos, Dan, 236n
Mikkelson, Barbara, urban legends in the
news, 18
Mikkelson, David, urban legends in the
news, 18
Millennium Bug. *See* Y2K
Miller Genuine Draft, on fake George W.
Bush billboard, 121
Mindspring.com, on coverage of death of
Princess Diana, 180, 241n
Miner, Horace, 161, 240n

Mintz, Lawrence E., 233n

Mitchell, William J., 241–42n

Mohammed, 2006 controversy over cartoons in Danish newspaper, 25

Morse, Rob, 88, 237n

Moses, in "promised land" joke, 127

Mossberg, Walter, 151, 155

Mother Teresa: on AP list of Top Ten news stories (1997), 213; in Princess Diana jokes, 169–70

MTV, and Bill Clinton boxers-vs.-briefs joke, 46

Mullen, Patrick, 231n

Museumofhoaxes.com, on fake celebrity death stories, 187, 241n

Myerhoff, Barbara, 17, 233n

Nader, Ralph, 6; and Mastercard "Priceless" commercial parody, 131–32

Nagin, Ray: and Hurricane Katrina, 26, 102

Napoleon Dynamite. See Heder, Jon

NASCAR, and Mastercard "Priceless" commercial parody, 135–36

Nation magazine: on George W. Bush and Hurricane Katrina, 97; on George W. Bush's NASCAR campaign stop, 136

National Geographic, and shark/helicopter photoshop, 21

Neiman-Marcus, 230

Netiquette, 11, 199

Netlore, 9–10, 13–14, 19, 29, 193, 209–10, 217, 232n

Neuman, Alfred E., and George W. Bush photoshop, 117

New Orleans, and Hurricane Katrina, 26–27, 96–98, 100–105, 123

New Orleans Times-Picayune, coverage of Hurricane Katrina, 104

New York Daily News, in newspaper joke, 141

New York Post, in newspaper joke, 141

New York Times: coverage of Afghanistan war, 87; coverage of Cheney hunting accident, 197; coverage of Hurricane Katrina, 103, 238n; coverage of 9/11 attacks, 91–92, 238n; coverage of terrorism, 74, 90; Stanley Fish on Hillary Clinton, 44; and humor, 26; newslore in, 21, 192, 195; in newspaper joke, 141; and taste, 23

New York Times Magazine, 15, 26

New York Times Manual of Style and Usage, 23

New Yorker magazine, on airport security, 47

Newsday: Tonya Harding/Nancy Kerrigan composite photo, 20; letter in about Bush/Katrina, 98

Newslore: defined, 7; as folk media criticism, 92–93, 168; as folklore genre, 9; oppositional function of, 10–11, 92–93; in the news, 14–15, 18–19, 21–22, 93, 99, 117, 201; researching, 13–14

Newspapers: digitally altered photos in, 20–21; and humor, 25; and Mohammed cartoon controversy, 25; newslore in, 15, 18–19, 26, 33–44, 99, 201; and Nigerian scam, 113; and storytelling, 17; and taste, 22–24, 91, 93; urban legends in, 18

Nichols, John, on George W. Bush's handling of Hurricane Katrina, 97, 238n

Nichols, Terry, and UPS truck warning, 226

Nigerian Scam: as letter from George W. Bush, 113, 239n; as letter from Laura Bush, 115

9/11. *See* September 11

Ninjahpirate.com, fake news story about death of, 187

Niva, Steve, 65–66, 68

Numbskull jokes, 117–18, 124, 190

Obama, Barack, 31, 117, 126, 189–90, 212; jokes about, 190, 241n; in photoshop with upside-down phone, 109

Obama, Michelle, 117
O'Brien, Conan, 242n
Ochs, Adolph S., 23
Office copier folklore. *See* faxlore
Oklahoma City bombing, 32, 226
Oldenburg, Ann, 235n
Onion, The, 200, 211
Opensecrets.org, 240n
Operation Desert Storm, 71, 88
Oprah Winfrey Show, 74, 102
Oregonian, coverage of e-mail spam, 19, 117
Oring, Elliott: on *Challenger* jokes, 82, 92,
    237-38n, 240n; on Bill Clinton jokes,
    45, 236n; and fieldwork, 231n; on humor
    Web sites, 211, 242n; on jokes as a
    "strategy of rebellion," 85, 92, 238n; on
    meaning of jokes, 11, 232n
Orwell, George, 11

Packwood, Bob, in Bill Clinton/Dan
    Quayle joke, 46-47
Pakistan, 134, 243n
Palin, Sarah, 126, 190, 212
Park, Michael Y., 242n
Parody, 8, 15, 26, 80, 82, 84-85, 94, 98, 101,
    117, 122-23, 138, 140, 152, 160, 170, 191,
    211-12, 217, 219-20; chain letters, 227-30;
    FAQs, 161-62; "Got Milk?," 27, 97, 120;
    "Have you seen me?," 87; Nigerian
    scam, 113-15; "Priceless," 29, 82, 84,
    128-36, 192
Parody texts: Charity appeal (Enron),
    143-45; "Got milk?," 97, 120-21; "Have
    you seen?" milk carton, 87; *It Takes a
    Village*, 117; Mastercard "Priceless," 82,
    129-37; Nigerian scam, 113-16
Paton, George E. C., 232n
Penn State, 22, 36, 63, 74
Pepsi Cola, contamination legends about,
    74-75
Pepsico, 154
Perkins, Joseph, 87, 237n

Peterson, Karen, 238n
Pew Internet and American Life Project,
    10, 14, 93, 192, 232n, 241n
Pew Research Center for the People and
    the Press, 195
Philadelphia Inquirer, coverage of
    Mohammed cartoons controversy,
    25-26
Photoshop subjects: Abu Ghraib, 94;
    Osama bin Laden, 82-86, 93; Barbara
    and Jenna Bush, 121; George W. Bush,
    109-10, 112-13, 117, 120-25; George W.
    Bush and Hurricane Katrina, 96-99,
    123; Hillary Clinton, 121; Tom Daschle,
    109; John Edwards, 191; John Kerry,
    59-61; Sarah Palin, 190-91; Statue of
    Liberty, 69, 71; Tourist Guy, 76-82;
    World Trade Center, 69-70
Photoshops, 7, 26-27, 59-61, 69-70, 81-82,
    84-86, 93-94, 98-99, 108-10, 112, 117,
    121-22, 135, 138, 191-92, 197-98, 216-18,
    235-36n, 242-43n; in the news, 20-22
Picasso, Pablo, in George W. Bush/St. Peter
    joke, 118-19
Pitts, Leonard, September 11 column, 28,
    65, 235-36n
Pittsburgh Post-Gazette, Y2K coverage, 159
Politicalhumor.com, 97, 231n, 238-39n,
    242n
Pope jokes, 102, 118, 120, 197
Popeye's Fried Chicken, Hurricane Katrina
    joke, 102
Postman, Neil, 232n
Powell, Chris, 232n
Powell, Colin, 5-6
Poynter Institute, 22
Prince Charles, in Princess Diana joke, 169
Princess Diana, 93, 155, 167-71, 180, 189,
    213, 215, 236n, 240-41n
Princess Grace, 171
Procter & Gamble, 128
Pseudo-events, 16

Quayle, Dan, 31, 46–47, 100, 117, 153, 191, 214, 238n

Radcliffe-Brown, A. R., 29
Rainie, Lee, 233n, 238n, 241n
Ramsey, Bruce, 240n
Ramsey, JonBenet, 213
Reagan, Ronald, 203, 213
Rec.funny.net, 210, 212
Redfield, Robert, 13, 37
Reed, Lou, fake stories about death of, 187
Reeve, Christopher, 32
Reno, Janet: role of, in Elian Gonzalez story, 130; as target of late-night comedians, 214–15
Republican Party, 35, 58, 116, 203, 214; Republican National Convention, 120
Reuss, Richard, 231n
Reuters, 21, 243n
Rheingold, Howard, 232n, 242n
Rice, Condoleeza, in fake Bush Nigerian scam letter, 115
Riddle jokes, 5, 33, 42–43, 46–50, 58, 88–89, 100, 105–6, 138, 145–46, 152, 169–74, 176, 179–80, 190–91, 193, 218–19. See also Joke texts
Rivers, Bryon, 234n
Rocky Mountain News, and newslore about Osama bin Laden, 93
Roe v. Wade, in Bush/Katrina joke, 100, 117, 238n
Roeper, Richard, 76–77, 169–70, 213–14, 237n, 242n
Roosevelt, Franklin D., in Bush/"promised land" joke, 127
Rosenberg, Rob, 236n
Rosenstiel, Tom, 240n
Ruby, Jay, 17, 233n
Rumsfeld, Donald, 62, 94, 108
Russell, Gordon, coverage of Hurricane Katrina, 103

Salon.com, 200
San Diego Union-Tribune, coverage of September 11, 87
San Francisco Chronicle, coverage of September 11, 87–88; in newspaper joke, 141
Sanford, Mark, 191
Santino, Jack, 231n
Santorum, Rick, 105
Saudi Arabia, 85, 114
Scambusters.org, 19
Schiavo, Terri, jokes about, 178–80
Schudson, Michael, 233n, 238n
Schwalbe, Will, 242n
Schwarzenegger, Arnold, 212; as target of late-night comedians, 214
Seattle Post-Intelligencer, coverage of urban legends, 19; coverage of Y2K, 160
Secret Service: in Bush/Mastercard parody, 136; in Cheney hunting joke, 200; in Bill/Hillary Clinton joke, 33, 42; in fake Wal-Mart memo, 224–25
September 11, 28, 63–66, 68, 75, 82, 91–95, 98, 133, 197, 225; on AP list of Top Ten stories, 215; hoaxes about, 21–22; jokes about, 28, 82, 86–90, 106; legends about, 70–73; photoshops about, 69–71, 77, 81–86, 236–37n. See also Joke texts; Photoshop subjects
Seung-Hui, Cho, 41
7Up: in *Challenger* jokes, 82
Shipley, David, 242n
Siegal, Allan M., 235n
Silva, Mark, 238n
Simpson, Nicole Brown, 213
Simpson, O. J.: on AP list of Top Ten news stories (1995), 32; and celebrity jokes, 31, 167–68, 189; in Michael Kennedy/Sonny Bono skiing accident joke, 172; news coverage of, 213; as target of late-night comedians, 214
Sims, Norman, 233n

Sinclair, Gordon, 64, 68, 236n
60 Minutes, 24
Skilling, Jeffrey, 138
Sky News, 243n
"Slacktivism," 12
Slumdog Millionaire, 138
Smith, Anna Nicole, 166–68, 177
Smith, Carl, 104
Smith, Jerd, 238n
Smith, Susan, on AP list of Top Ten news
    stories (1995), 32
Smith, Will, in John Kerry joke, 59
Smyth, Willie, 238n, 240n
Snopes.com, 220; Sonny Bono, 171;
    on Bush/binoculars photoshop,
    110, 239n; on Bush reading upside-
    down photoshop, 109; on Church's/
    Popeye's story, 102, 238n; on Hillary
    Clinton/soldier photo, 136–37, 240n;
    on fake UPS press release, 243n; on
    fake Wal-Mart memo, 225, 243n; on
    "fauxtography," 242–43n; on Gordon
    Sinclair column, 236n; on "Got fish?"
    photoshop, 98, 238–39n; on Hilfiger and
    Claiborne legends, 237n; on Hurricane
    Katrina looters, 239n; on Klingerman
    virus, 236n; on legends about Bush's
    lack of intelligence, 112; in the news,
    18–19; on photoshops and rumors,
    93; and "slacktivism," 12, 232n; on Ken
    Starr quote, 235n; on Syrian Mastercard
    "Priceless" commercial parody, 135,
    240n; on Tourist Guy, 76, 237n; on
    tsunami photos, 105, 239n; on Wendy's
    contamination story, 233n
Society of Professional Journalists Code of
    Ethics, 16, 20, 233–34n
Soloski, John, 23, 235n
Solzhenitsyn, Aleksandr, 12
Sotomayor, Sonya, 126
Spam, 10, 14, 135, 199, 230, 239n
Spanier, Graham, 63–64

Spears, Britney, 118, 167, 187, 217
Speed, in Tourist Guy photoshop, 80
Spirit photos, 216
Spitzer, Eliot, 190
Spy magazine, Hillary Clinton photoshop,
    235n
St. Peter jokes, 118–19, 170, 241n
St. Petersburg Times, coverage of
    September 11, 91
Starr, Kenneth, 24–25, 203, 235n
Starr report, 24
Statue of Liberty: and Abu Ghraib
    photoshop, 94; and newslore
    of September 11, 69–70; and
    photoshopping, 217
Stern, Howard, and Afghanistan war, 88
Stevens, John, 234n
Stewart, Jon, 200
Stewart, Martha, as target of late-night
    comedians, 214
Streisand, Barbra, in fake Laura Bush
    letter, 116
Swaggert, Jimmy, joke about, 202

Tackett, Michael, 238n
Taliban, 4, 85, 88–89
Tall-tale photographs, 216
Templeton, Brad (Rec.funny.net), 210
Tenant, George, and Medal of Freedom,
    99–100
Terrorism, 18, 70, 73–76, 84, 90–91, 117, 134,
    146, 180, 200, 218, 225–26, 230, 236n
Theron, Charlize, and photoshopping, 216
Thevenot, Brian, coverage of Hurricane
    Katrina, 103
Thomas, Jeannie B., 235n
Tierney, John, 238n
Timberlake, Justin, fake stories about
    death of, 187
Titanic: in Bill Clinton/Monica Lewinsky
    joke, 52–53; in Tourist Guy photoshop,
    80

Tomsho, Robert, 237n

Top Ten Lists (Letterman show), 152, 158, 200, 211, 219

Tourist Guy, 76–82, 105, 123, 237

Touristofdeath.com, 237n

Toyota, 4

Treaster, Joseph B., 237n

Tsunami (2004): fake photo captions about, 105, 239n; jokes about, 101, 106

Turner, Patricia, 128, 240n

Twin Towers. See World Trade Center

2000 presidential election, 57, 108, 116, 131–32, 215; butterfly ballot, 131

2004 presidential election, 136, 215

2008 presidential election, 107

Tyson, Ann Scott, 238n

Tyson, Mike, joke about biting Evander Holyfield, 32

University of Missouri School of Journalism, 234–35n

UPS, in fake terrorism warning, 225

Urban legend topics: George W. Bush, 112, 116; Halloween terrorism, 72–74; Hurricane Katrina, 102–4; Klingerman virus, 70–72; soft drink terrorism, 74–75

Urban legends, 7, 9, 11–12, 18–19, 22, 27, 29, 70, 72–75, 77, 81, 102–3, 112, 117, 127, 128, 135, 137, 154–55, 158, 160, 181, 184, 190, 209, 215, 217–18, 220, 227–28, 230, 234n, 239n; in the news, 18–19

Urbanlegends.com, 227

Urkel, Steve. See White, Jaleel

USA Today, 91, 93, 141, 197–98

USS Abraham Lincoln, George W. Bush on the deck of, 94, 122

USS Cole, in Tourist Guy photoshop, 80

USS Enterprise, in photoshop depicting war against Taliban, 85

Vanderjagt, Mike, fake news story about suicide of, 185–86

Vazsonyi, Andre, 234n

Versace, Gianni, jokes about murder of, 172

Vietnam War: and George W. Bush, 121; John Kerry in, 59, 61; news coverage of, 16; and newslore of September 11, 69

Virtual ethnography, 13–14

Vlach, John, 239n

Waco. See Branch Davidians

Wal-Mart, in fake memo, 224–25

Walski, Brian, and digitally altered photo of Iraq war, 20

Walters, Barbara, 6

War on Terror, 28

Washington Post: coverage of Watergate, 48; on Hurricane Katrina, 101, 103; and Kerry/Fonda photoshop, 61; in newspaper joke, 141; on September 11 jokes, 236n; as source of Bush "poem," 201

Washington Post Deskbook on Style, 24

Watergate scandal, 23, 48

Weeks, Linton, coverage of Hurricane Katrina, 101–2

Weinberger, David, 14, 232–33n

Weingarten, Gene, on September 11 jokes, 236n

Welsch, Roger, 242n

Wendy's, contamination story about, 18

White, Jaleel, fake news story about death of, 187–88

Whittington, Harry, 197

Who Wants to Marry a Millionaire?, 82

William Tell, in Bill Gates newslore, 158

Williams, Ted, in Al Gore joke, 57

Wills, Mark, in George W. Bush/Hurricane Katrina newslore, 98

Winfrey, Oprah. See Oprah Winfrey Show

Wojcik, Daniel, 242n

Wonder, Stevie, in George W. Bush legend, 112

Wood, Natalie, in John F. Kennedy Jr. joke,
    172
Woods, Tiger, jokes about, 193–94
Woodward, Bob, 48
World Trade Center, 22, 74, 216–17, 236n; in
    the news, 81; in September 11 jokes, 89–
    90; in September 11 newslore, 66–67; in
    September 11 photoshops, 69–70, 76, 78
Worth1000.com, 216–17, 242n

Yednock, Ken, 96, 99
Yeltsin, Boris, as target of late-night
    comedians, 214
Yonchenko, Michael, 99, 197, 211
Yousef, Ramzi, in newslore of 9/11, 66
YouTube, 138, 191–93, 228, 241n
Y2K, 29, 56, 160–62, 215

CPSIA information can be obtained at www.ICGtesting.com
Printed in the USA
BVOW071609190312

285229BV00007B/1/P